LITURGY AS LANGUAGE OF FAITH

A Liturgical Methodology in the Mode of Paul Ricoeur's Textual Hermeneutics

Joyce Ann Zimmerman, C.PP.S.

UNIVERSITY PRESS OF AMERICA

Lanham • New York • London

University Press of America,® Inc.

4720 Boston Way
Lanham, MD 20706

3 Henrietta Street
London WC2E 8LU England

Printed in the United States of America

British Cataloging in Publication Information Available

Library of Congress Cataloging-in-Publication Data

Zimmerman, Joyce Ann, 1945–
Liturgy as language of faith : a liturgical methodology in the
mode of Paul Ricoeur's textual hermeneutics / by Joyce Ann Zimmerman.
p. cm. Bibliography: p. Includes index.
1. Liturgics. 2. Ricoeur, Paul. 3. Hermeneutics. 4. Eucharistic
prayers—Catholic Church—History and criticism. 5. Catholic
Church—Liturgy. I. Title.
BV178.Z55 1988
264'.001—dc 19 88–2797 CIP
ISBN 0–8191–6908–0 (alk. paper)

All University Press of America books are produced on acid-free
paper which exceeds the minimum standards set by the National
Historical Publications and Records Commission.

ACKNOWLEDGEMENT

The English translation of the Order of Mass from *The Roman Missal* © 1973, International Committee on English in the Liturgy, Inc. All rights reserved.

CONTENTS

CONTENTS

INTRODUCTION

As a distinct category of systematics, liturgical theology is a relatively new discipline. Prior to this century, liturgics focused primarily on rubrics. When liturgical theology abandoned this principal concern for rubrics, the approaches to the meaning and purpose of worship and consequent analyses began to take off in various directions. Studies employing historical, theological, and/or pastoral approaches over the last century and a half have helped unfold liturgy in its varied dimensions. Further, these dimensions have all had at least one goal in common: to help the worshipping community actively participate in liturgy so that its celebration becomes a vital, central factor in Christian living.

Two decades after the promulgation of *Sacrosanctum Concilium*, we might ask, To what extent has the proposed liturgical renewal succeeded in revitalizing liturgy as a central aspect of Christian living? Since the changes in liturgy promulgated by Vatican II, there seems to have been a decrease rather than an increase in liturgical participation (at least as far as physical attendance is concerned). While it is true that many factors contribute to decreased church attendance, not least among them sociological and political factors, we still question whether the present form of liturgy allows God to speak to the community and the community to truly speak to God. If liturgy is to be the center of Christian life, then it must speak to and of the lives of the worshipping community about God's dynamic presence.

In this study we are concerned with liturgy as a way of celebrating our relationship to God and we speak of this as a language of faith. Inasmuch as language is a symbolic form whereby we communicate experience and meaning, liturgical language can be the means whereby we communicate in celebration our faith experience. Faith is a gift whereby our deepest, conscious being stands in relationship to the Sacred; it is our "yes-stance" toward God. If we look at faith from a purely intellectual point of view (for example, as assent to *beliefs*), we miss the point: faith involves our whole person, informing the very way we live. As a dynamic, faith always comes to expression in some symbolic form (in our case, liturgical celebration).

When we speak of liturgy as a language of faith, we suggest that liturgy is a paradigmatic (though not the only) communication and celebration of faith experience. Liturgical language makes apparent, reflects, and concretizes a relationship between liturgy and everyday living. Ultimately, to be concerned with liturgy as language of faith is to consider the relationship of liturgy and life.

Two clarifications are in order: what is meant by "life" and what is meant by "liturgy."

Without entering into its more technical meaning, "life" means simply the everyday, actual historical existence of human beings. Our intention is to maintain that liturgy is not coextensive with a particular cultic occasion, but rather (if it is a true liturgical celebration) it implies a shaping of the activities, dreams, hopes, and expectations of everyday Christian living. Our reflections raise questions which Mary Collins stated succinctly as, "How do you study life?"[1] The historical method of liturgical theology which has dominated liturgical research during this century can show that themes pertinent to Christian living have always been embedded in liturgical celebrations.

A problem is raised if we seek to do than historically demonstrate the relationship of liturgy and life themes and try to establish a relationship based on the structure of liturgy itself. Historical liturgical research has contributed much to our understanding of liturgy today. Contemporary liturgists can capitalize on these contributions which have "clarified the fundamental structures of Christian worship and the lines of its structural development."[2] Yet, historical research cannot account for an accommodation of the traditional to contemporary situations nor for contemporary innovation in liturgy. But does a method of research exist which can account for what is factually taking place in contemporary liturgy and at the same time arrive at an understanding of essential link between liturgy and life? We propose that an hermeneutical inquiry is one method which can account for the present shape of liturgy and study the relationship between liturgy and life. To flesh out this proposal a bit more, we move on to our second clarification, that of "liturgy."

Liturgy is first and foremost the celebrative worship of the liturgical assembly before the Lord. This being so, a popular conception of the adjective "celebrative" must not mislead us; liturgical action is not a haphazard, unstructured action. Its

---

[1]M. COLLINS, "Liturgical Methodology and the Cultural Evolution of Worship in the United States," *Worship* 49 (1975), 89.

[2]Ibid., 86.

structure is a pre-given form shaped by the Christian tradition through which it has evolved. The form is fixed by a written text, a term which implies much more than simply a printed page.

Shaped by tradition, the text itself also gives shape to liturgical tradition: it molds the present historical community which, in turn, becomes part of the shaping tradition for subsequent generations. Liturgical texts are not isolated bodies of literature. They have an *arche* and a *telos* derived from their relationship to Christian tradition which is normative[3] for liturgical action. This relationship originates from the fact that liturgical texts are a *fixation* of worshipping communities' liturgical *action*. Thus, liturgical action is primary, but it gives rise through cumulative tradition to fixed texts which, in turn, shape a present liturgical action. The dynamism is action --written text--action. While written text is normative, it is always seen as mediating action from the side of tradition to the side of the present historical situation.

Now if a community gathers to celebrate Eucharist, they use a prescribed text in a sacramentary. If they gather to celebrate a baptism, they use a prescribed text in a ritual book with rites of baptism, and so on for other liturgical celebrations. But to say texts are normative is not to say that texts are unchangeable. Liturgical tradition, indeed, gives evidence to the contrary. It remains significant that from earliest Christian liturgical practice there were fixed texts, though they were numerous and not of invariable form. The case in the *Didache* is particularly interesting. There, in the example of prayers given in Chapters Nine and Ten, the presider[4] is

---

[3]A. GANOCZY, *An Introduction to Catholic Sacramental Theology*, trans. W. Thomas with A. Sherman (New York: Paulist Press, 1984), p. 159. In the early part of Chapter Five we discuss the terms "normative" and "prescriptive."

[4]We use the term "presider" throughout this volume rather than "priest" or "celebrant." See R.W. HOVDA, *Strong, Loving and Wise: Presiding in Liturgy*, Foreword by G. Diekmann, O.S.B. (Washington, D.C.: The Liturgical Conference, 1977), viii. See also T. WELBERS, "What's in a Name?" *Modern Liturgy* 11 (1984), 4; and J. CHALLANCIN, "The Presider as Community," Ibid., 5-7.

instructed to "give thanks *thus*"[5] except for the implication that prophets could speak extemporaneously: "But allow the prophets to give thanks as much as they wish."[6] From this early time there seems to be an established relationship between written text and liturgical celebration. Though the liturgical assembly is not a slave to a written text, the relationship between written text and liturgical celebration is nonetheless evident.

In this light, it is quite understandable that much of current research is a historical critique of liturgical texts, contesting their present order or form and proposing changes. While this work is valuable, it is not essential for understanding the present celebration for it does not allow access to what is factually taking place in a given liturgical assembly. The point is to bracket the question of origins and development, important though this is (without denying the liturgical text has built-in doctrinal biases and celebrative compromises), and instead to address questions such as, How might the *present* shape of the liturgical text in its *present* historical moment be received by the liturgical assembly? Do the various elements belong? Does the present structure flow gracefully and smoothly so that the celebration is a whole instead of disjointed parts? To study text as text is to begin thinking from these and similar questions. Quite possibly this inquiry would, and probably should, lead to historical questions which would allow for a dialogue between methods.

We maintain that the shape of a liturgical text is not a pure accident. Therefore, if a relationship between the text and its celebration can be established, it would be possible to study liturgical action through its textual fixation. This is tantamount to showing the relationship between written text and human cultural existence. Our starting point is to recognize the textual indications or traces of the tradition of liturgical actions which gave rise to the written text within the text itself.

Certain concepts have figured predominately in our remarks thus far: liturgy, language of faith, life, historical research, hermeneutical inquiry, liturgical celebration, liturgical text.

---

[5]*Did* 9:1, 10:1; italics added. Our English translation is from C.C. Richardson, ed. and trans., *Early Christian Fathers*, 4th paperback ed. (New York: Macmillan Publishing Co, Inc., 1978), pp. 171-179.

[6]*Did* 10:7.

We are now in a position to delineate the purpose and task of our study.

Our purpose is to present a methodology that (1) seeks to understand the liturgical celebration by way of its textual form and (2) proposes that a study of liturgy by way of its textual form not only gives an explanation of the sense of meaning of a text but also gives a reference of meaning as an understanding of Christian existence which the text seeks to celebrate. With respect to liturgy, two aims are operative in this purpose: (1) to show an essential relationship between liturgical text and liturgical celebration and (2) to make apparent the relationship of liturgy and life.

Our task is to apply to a select liturgical text a methodology first advanced by the hermeneutics of French philosopher Paul Ricoeur.[7] Ricoeur's hermeneutics is known as a textual or methodical hermeneutics whereby he is able to address the question of text and the relation of written texts to human cultural existence. Ricoeur's textual hermeneutics suggests a framework in which a written text, in our case a liturgical text, can be studied analytically without relinquishing "understanding" which Ricoeur sees as a mode of human existence. Thus his hermeneutic allows the placing of a textual analytic within a framework of a hermeneutics of understanding.

Ricoeur sets the analysis of a written text in a dialectical relationship with understanding. In this way, his method of

---

[7]Paul Ricoeur was born in Valence, France, in 1913. Introduced to existentialism while a graduate student at the Sorbonne in the late 1930s, he was particularly influenced by Gabriel Marcel. However, Ricoeur sought a more rigorous methodology, and found that in the phenomenological writings of Edmund Husserl, which he read while a German prisoner during World War II. Ricoeur assumed a chair in the history of philosophy at the University of Strasbourg in 1948 and began writing his philosophy of the will there. In 1957 he was appointed to a chair in general philosophy at the Sorbonne during a time when psychoanalysis and structuralism had come to challenge the Parisian intellectual milieu. In the second half of the 1960s and during the 1970s Ricoeur held positions at Nanterre and the University of Louvain, and then he returned to Nanterre in combination with a part time professorship at the University of Chicago. Ricoeur has been a prolific writer, with more than a dozen books and several hundred essays. Presently, Ricoeur lives and writes in Paris.

textual hermeneutics situates the explanation of a text within the life experiences of the author(s) who gave rise to it and also within the completion of the hermeneutic enterprise in the engagement of the text and reader. For our purposes, Ricoeur's method allows for a theoretical interpretation of a liturgical text without severing this from the appropriation that takes place at its celebration.

Ricoeur has rarely undertaken an explicit "explanatory" approach to a text. He has indicated its usefulness and which explanatory modes might be appropriate. But Ricoeur is neither a structuralist nor a semiotician. His hermeneutical framework, however, indicates how such an approach might be incorporated in a hermeneutics of understanding. For him, such a complement to understanding is essential. Traditionally, understanding and explanation were held to be incompatible. Understanding is an operation that properly belongs to the human sciences, while explanation is an operation that properly belongs to the physical sciences. By setting understanding and explanation in dialectical relationship, Ricoeur makes both work for him. In this he utilizes a scientific approach to the linguistics of a text which emulates the rigorous methods of the physical sciences without sacrificing the links to human cultural existence to which the understanding of the human sciences attests.

The dialectical relationship of explanation-understanding places certain limitations on our understanding of a liturgical text. These limits are governed by what the linguistics of the liturgical text can deliver; that is, our understanding is limited by our choice of explanatory mode. The explanatory approach we chose for our study is a conflation of Ricoeur's semantics of action with the theory of communication of linguist Roman Jakobson.[8] We chose this approach because it incorporates two important aspects of liturgy: action and communication. Ricoeur himself frequently has focused on these two aspects. He assumes the work of linguistic analysis, especially drawing on A. Kenny's *Action, Emotion and Will* to show

---

[8]Born in Russia in 1896, Roman Jakobson became a member of the Russian formalist school. Between the two World Wars he taught in Czechoslovakia and became a leading member of the Prague circle of linguists. In 1942-1946 he taught in New York where he came in contact with Lévi-Strauss. Since 1950 he has taught at Harvard where he is professor emeritus of Slavic languages and literature and of general linguistics; he is also Institute Professor Emeritus at Massachusettes Institute of Technology.

one way action may be inscribed in a text which he outlines in *Sémantique de l'action*. Ricoeur also takes into account communication aspects of a text, and in this he draws on the theory of Jakobson.

From the outset it must be clear that our analytic only considers these two aspects of liturgical language. Other aspects, for example intentionality or generativity, have not been included. For this reason, the proposed explanatory mode in this method cannot offer a full understanding of liturgy as language of faith. Because of this limitation, our understanding of a liturgical text as outlined in Chapter Six can only be at the level of the semantics of action and communication factors evident in the text's structure. We contend, however, that Ricoeur's method of textual hermeneutics does hold promise as a viable methodology for the interpretation of liturgical texts with its own unique contribution to make. Since it permits a wide range of possible analytical approaches, our hermeneutical methodology can encompass differing aspects of liturgy, depending on the choice of analytic.

We hypothesize that the relationship of liturgy and life can be opened to investigation in terms of Ricoeur's method of textual hermeneutics. We find Ricoeur's method promising for two reasons: (1) he proposes a framework for a hermeneutics of human existence and (2) he incorporates within that hermeneutics room for explanatory approaches. This study is not a work on Ricoeur nor is it concerned with the whole of his philosophy. We are simply using his method as a starting point for our own study which is first and foremost a work in liturgical theology.

Chapter One situates the methodology question by showing that "language" and "text" are not new problematics for liturgical theology. There has always been an attentiveness to language and text with respect to liturgy, but not without significant shifts over the decades in how language and text have been understood. Chapter One explores these shifts and their consequences for the study of liturgy, thus locating the present study within a tradition of sensitivity to liturgical language and text that opens up the space for the methodological contribution of our study.

Chapters Two and Three, respectively, lay out Ricoeur's hermeneutical theory and methodology. Addressing the question of the recovery of meaning, Chapter Two shows why text is the privileged locus for hermeneutics. The key here is that text provides a "distance" from our "participation" in human cultural existence through experience and our "appropriation" of the meaning of that existence as mediated by a text. These three moments (participation, distanciation, and appropriation) are the backbone of Ricoeur's *method* of textual hermeneutics, which we lay out in Chapter Three. Both of these chapters close with broad indications of how Ricoeur's approach is applicable to liturgical studies.

Chapter Four outlines a theoretical analytic[9] that shows how Ricoeur's method of textual hermeneutics functions as a framework in the analysis of text. As we indicated above, several analytical approaches can serve to analyze a text. Our choice of the conflation of Ricoeur's semantics of action and Jakobson's communication theory is guided by the fact that we are sensitive to two key aspects of liturgy: its structure of action and communication.

Chapter Five, a practical analytic,[10] applies the theoretical analytic of Chapter Four to a select liturgical text for the express purpose of interpreting its meaning within our specific parameters. The select text is the Eucharistic text with Eucharistic Prayer II.[11] We take "Eucharistic text" to be the whole Eucharistic rite as it appears in the *Roman Missal*; that is, the "ordinary" of the Mass, which includes both the instructional text and the prayer text. Both kinds of text are included in the analysis for two reasons: (1) obviously, because both are part of the written text; but more importantly, (2) because the instructional text, in its indication of the manner of celebration, offers important clues to the textual traces of the action embedded in the text. Our select text could have included any one of the numerous Eucharistic prayers included in the approved rite. We select Eucharistic Prayer II because it is based on the third-century Anaphora of Hippolytus which is the earliest surviving example of a Eucharistic prayer, because it is short, and because it has all the characteristics of a classical Eucharistic prayer.

---

[9]By "theoretical" I mean an analytic that can be applied to any number of texts; that is, it is not directed to and appropriate for only one particular text.

[10]By "practical" I mean an analytic actually applied to a select text.

[11]We therefore limit our practical analytic to a text reflecting western Roman Catholic liturgical tradition.

Capitalizing on the data of Chapter Five, Chapter Six broadens the interpretation beyond the linguistic analytic comprising the moment of explanation to an understanding which elucidates a text's reference to human cultural existence. Herein lies the most significant consequence of applying Ricoeur's method of textual hermeneutics to liturgical texts: through an explanation of a liturgical text we are in touch with potential ways the text may be received by the liturgical assembly. In this is shown the link between a liturgical text and actual historical existence. The Bibliography is of cited works and is arranged alphabetically by author surname without any divisions so as to enable the reader to quickly recover the full reference of any citation. The Appendix contains an annotated copy of the select liturgical text; underscored words and margin notes designate key applications of the methodology. It is essential that the reader refer to the Appendix while reading Chapters Five and Six. We assume at least a basic familiarity with the select Eucharistic text on the part of the reader. Finally, there is an Index of key words which may be particularly helpful in locating important concepts of Ricoeur.

A volume such as this is usually prepared with the assistance of others. I am especially indebted to Dr. John W. Van Den Hengel, S.C.J., and Dr. James R. Pambrun, professors of the Faculty of Theology of St. Paul University, for their generosity with time and expertise, for their enthusiasm and encouragement; in a spirit of *eucharistia* I laud them for their vivifying creativity and penetrating insight. I also wish to acknowledge the many people--faculty, staff, and students alike--who help mold St. Paul University into the unique academic arena it is. I am grateful to my religious Congregation, the Sisters of the Precious Blood of Dayton, Ohio, for encouraging me in my academic endeavors and for their continued support and care. To my parents, family, and friends I wish to express gratitude for helping me grow in an atmosphere of curiosity and challenge, of love and wholesomeness. I thank Dr. Kenneth Russell for reading and correcting the manuscript; his invaluable suggestions greatly improved the text.

In drawing this Introduction to a close, we note that it is impossible to exhaust the meaning of liturgy because the nature of liturgy as mystery militates against such an endeavor. It is enough to hope that our study contributes in some small way to the ongoing unfolding of this great mystery we call Christian liturgy.

CHAPTER ONE

LANGUAGE, TEXT, AND METHODOLOGY

From its inception in France in the second half of the last century to the present, the liturgical movement has grappled with liturgical renewal from a variety of perspectives.[1] No movement is without its many facets and ramifications, and the liturgical movement is no exception to this. A comprehensive appreciation of the accomplishments of the liturgical movement would not only have to consider the theological and ceremonial aspects of liturgy with their pastoral and social praxis, but would also have to consider these in terms of the various Christian denominations. Our intent in this chapter is a more modest one. We wish to show how the renewal initiated by the liturgical movement encompasses issues bearing directly on our own interest in language and text. By uncovering the liturgical issues involved in the notions of language and text, we are led to a methodology question: What methodology (if any) is adequate to address the many and complex questions involved in language and text? We wager that sensitivity to liturgical language and text demands a variety of methodologies to plumb the variety of questions. We want to show how our present study proposes one particular methodology in order to address a particular set of questions.

In this chapter we speak to the major terms of reference for our study. Our remarks necessarily only point us in certain directions, as the later chapters address more extensively the concerns we raise here. Our purpose in this chapter is threefold. First, we wish to uncover with respect to liturgy some of the questions and issues that arise from a contemporary focus on linguistics. Second, we wish to show that at least the seeds of linguistic concerns have been addressed in liturgical studies, though often these seeds have grown more thorns than roses. Our own critique of these efforts leads to our third intent which is to suggest methodological implications when we

---

[1] For a critique and expanded comments on the strengths and weaknesses of the early liturgical movement, see L. SHEPPARD (ed.), *The People Worship: A History of the Liturgical Movement* (New York: Hawthorn Books, Inc., 1967), pp. 20, 23-25; also, L. BOUYER, *La vie de la liturgie: une critique constructive du mouvement liturgique* (Paris: Editions du Cerf, 1956).

delve deeper into the question of language with respect to liturgy.

To these ends, we divide Chapter One into four parts. The first part deals with issues at the basis of prayer and liturgical language use and how those issues point to a broader context implicating the worshipping community. The second part of the chapter looks specifically at the notion of text, considering what liturgical scholars have been doing with liturgical texts and examining recent post-Vatican II documents and their contributions to an initial query into the notion of liturgical text. Thirdly, this chapter addresses the question of methodology, showing how the usual methodologies employed by liturgists address certain questions related to liturgical language and text, while other questions seem to demand different methodologies. Finally, a summary section draws the chapter toward a clear focus on the scope of this present study.

A. Language

Whatever else liturgy is, part of it is certainly words or language. For a long time, the words of the text could be ignored. This was especially true when the liturgical language was Latin as a language of unity. With only a few versed in the language, liturgy conveyed meaning through the nonverbal aura of a sense of the Sacred which its mysteries could engender rather than through the words themselves. The words in themselves were unimportant for the general populace.

When permission was granted for liturgy to be celebrated in the vernacular, initial efforts were directed to the problems of translation. Only in the aftermath of this reform could the deeper questions of words in particular and language in general emerge as vital issues. The timeliness of research in the area of language and text also reflects contemporary concerns: just consider the proliferation of vocabulary in modern times. The age of the computer has ushered in a whole new language which, to uninitiates, is tantamount to a foreign tongue. Other examples abound in other specialized fields. As society develops, language naturally changes and develops. As such, language may be a barometer of what is happening in society. If worship tenaciously retains language that reflects a past society, then someone is bound to challenge whether worship is related to life as it is being presently lived. On the other hand, if worship becomes simply a wholesale take-over of present-day language, then "someone is certain to ask, 'If we are to worship, is this the way it should sound?'"[2] The language of worship has a double-cutting edge: it is a language that speaks of the Sacred, but within the idiomatic genius of peoples. The liturgical articulation of experience implicated in this is more than pastoral issues to be addressed. Indeed, the articulation forms the very substance out of which larger questions of the nature and structure of liturgy can be brought into focus. These larger questions in our study emerge from a linguistic perspective.

1. Linguistic Issues

We begin by asking two questions which enable us to expose deeper issues involved in the prayer of worship and liturgical language: How is language used in prayer? How is language used in liturgy? The salient points at the end of these sections list and critique issues that are particularly important for our methodological concern. Here we begin to show how the linguistic issue does not go far enough in addressing the current liturgical malaise. A fuller dimension of the meaning of language can only be addressed within a holistic context of meaning in use. We are interested, then, in composites of language which bear a particular structure. We will see later in this study how these composites of language (which we call "text" as generated by genre) contribute significantly to a richness of meaning.

a. How is Language Used in Prayer? At issue in this question is the nature of religious experience and how that is expressed in religious language. This presupposes a resonance between the language used to express religious experience and our basic understanding of and faith relationship to God.

Two types of articulation are possible for expressing religious experience. One, which may be termed "second-order reflection," is theological. It "derives from reflection, from discursive statement of meaning."[3] Though prayer and liturgy may have an instructive, didactic element that liturgical scholarship ought not ignore,[4] this is another question which cannot be

---

[2]See D.B. STEVICK, *Language in Worship: Reflections on a Crisis* (New York: Seabury Press, 1970), p. 3.

[3]D.B. STEVICK, "Language of Prayer," *Worship* 52 (1978), 557.

[4]See *Sacrosanctum Concilium*, Document #1 in *Documents on the Liturgy 1963-1979: Conciliar, Papal, and Curial Texts* (Collegeville: The Liturgical Press, 1983), #33, 34, 35; hereafter cited as "SC."

addressed here without going too far afield. Suffice it to recognize that while this is a proper, necessary, and fruitful endeavor, it is not necessary for prayer encounter and can sometimes even preclude it. For example, in a liturgy where explanations and commentaries so abound that liturgy is really a catechism lesson, we sense its disintegration as community prayer. Here language would articulate a *reflection* on who God is rather than an *expression* of an experience of God or an openness to encounter. Reflection may be an antecedent or consequence of prayer, but it is not prayer. Although liturgists have long accepted the principle *lex orandi, lex credendi*,[5] at least in Roman Catholic circles the *lex orandi* has priority over the *lex credendi*.[6] This suggests that another type of articulation should perhaps be operatively prior.

A second type of articulation of religious experience is "the language of prayer, doxology, worship [which] is first-order discourse [reflection]. It is formed in encounter, confrontation, recognition, and it is full of the awed sense of the other: the 'you.'"[7] Religious language as expressed in prayer is vocative. It addresses itself to the God who "discloses" Godself to both individual and community. Prayer language has within itself the power to articulate our (community's) experience of who God is, where we "should catch the moment of recognition, illumination, insight--what someone called 'the Aha! factor.'"[8] The nature of prayer allows for the expression of what (who) is really the inexpressible. "Expression" here must be understood in terms of the symbols which capture the *recognition* and the *acknowledgement* of a

---

[5]See, for example, G. WAINWRIGHT, *Doxology: The Praise of God in Worship, Doctrine and Life* (New York: Oxford University Press, 1980), pp. 218-283. The usual way of putting this phrase (*lex orandi, lex credendi*) is really a shorthand version of *legem credendi statuat lex supplicandi*, the law of worship establishes the law of belief. R. Taft points out that the maxim was often turned around so that the theology determined the prayer. See R. TAFT, "The Structural Analysis of Liturgical Units: An Essay in Methodology," *Worship* 52 (1978), 316 and especially Note 5.

[6]See G. WAINWRIGHT, *Doxology*, p. 251.

[7]D.B. STEVICK, "Language of Prayer," 557.

[8]Ibid., 558.

religious experience rather than in terms of *cognitions* which seek to understand it. This presence of God is the *sine qua non* of religious language which is conveyed principally in symbols.[9] Let us look more closely at how the notion of symbol is used in this context.

The presence of God in encounter can only be disclosed by prayer that is truly expressive of our experience of God. This is not to imply that prayer is simply a matter of finding the right words to say the right thing. On the contrary, a true encounter with God may well leave us "speechless." It is precisely here that religious language can best be expressed through symbol, which by its very nature functions on different levels. What may very well *seem* like an inadequate articulation of a religious experience, may in fact still capture the reality of the experience. Christian prayer forms have a tradition of symbolic expression precisely because what we are attempting to express cannot be total nor adequate.

Symbol is "the code that makes it possible ... for sender and receiver to understand each other and to speak a common idiom."[10] Further, this code "not only formally but as well in substance ... can be defined as communication, as *events of saving exchange between God and the faithful*."[11] A symbol does not act like didactic nor propositional speech, where the denotation is clear and explicit. Rather, a symbol suggests and evokes a reality that is present yet hidden.[12] Further,

---

[9]Though paramount, the liturgy is not the only occasion for the disclosure of God's presence; the Council Fathers also underscored the importance of paraliturgical prayer, devotions, sacramentals, and private prayer. See SC #12, 13, 35, 60.

[10]A. GANOCZY, *An Introduction to Catholic Sacramental Theology*, trans. W. Thomas and A. Sherman (New York: Paulist Press, 1984), p. 178.

[11]Ibid., p. 174; italics his.

[12]See A.R. DULLES, *A Church to Believe In: Discipleship and the Dynamics of Freedom* (New York: Crossroads, 1982), pp. 46-47. See D. POWER, *Unsearchable Riches: The Symbolic Nature of the Liturgy* (New York: Pueblo Publishing Company, 1984), p. 65 for a brief discussion of what happens when one attempts to "tie down the meaning" in liturgical symbols. See also p. 67. Also, see P. TILLICH, "The Religious Symbol," in F.W. DILLISTONE, ed., *Myth and Symbol* (London: S.P.C.K., 1966), p. 15.

> working on the imagination, emotions, and will, and through them upon the intelligence, the symbol changes the point of view, the perspectives, the outlook of the addressee. They grasp what is meant by sharing in the world indicated by the symbol. Symbolic knowledge is in the first instance participatory and implicit; only through a subsequent process of reflection does it become, in some measure, objective and explicit. ... To accept a symbol is to take the risk that in following out the line of action and consideration suggested by the symbol one will achieve a richer and more authentic penetration of the real.[13]

The primary import of a symbol is an immediate encounter with it which allows the symbol-seeker to share in the experience which gave rise to it. Without denying the value of the possibility of a second-order reflection directed to cognitive behavior, or that the language of prayer calls for interpretation and understanding, the real aim of a symbol is a first-order encounter which is then directed to emotive behavior.

Prayer mediates an apprehension of reality. On the one hand, prayer is personal. In this, the symbols of prayer may be personal symbols. On the other hand, when that prayer is community prayer the experience that is mediated is a common vision of God and life which arises from the religious tradition of the community. Here, the language of prayer is both corporate and historical, shared by a community. This leads to the second question, How is language used in liturgy?

b. How is Language Used in Liturgy? When considering the language of prayer, certain key factors emerge: faith, symbol, experience. These have their parallels with language use in liturgy that shape the very identity of the worshipping community.

The faith, symbol, and experience specified by liturgical language are rooted in the corporateness of the worshipping

---

[13] A.R. DULLES, *A Church to Believe In*, p. 47. See also D. POWER, "Theological Trends: Symbolism in Worship IV," *The Way* 15 (1975), 138-139.

assembly.[14] Liturgical language is plural:[15] Let *us* pray, *we* offer, *we* give thanks. This plurality in language indicates that the worshipping community is a concretization and extension[16] of the faith experience captured by language. Without denying the formative factor, liturgical language presupposes a faith to which it witnesses.[17]

The Christian experience which the worshipping community shares is a historical vision. It is based on past historical events which are at once singular as events, but in liturgy they are also repeatable. Central to these historical events is the life, death, and resurrection of Jesus which is memorialized in the liturgical celebration:

> By a tradition handed down from the apostles which took its origin from the very day of Christ's resurrection, the Church celebrates the paschal mystery every eighth day ... so that ... they may call to mind the passion, the resurrection, and the glorification of the Lord Jesus.[18]

While the originary experience of liturgy is of the salvific events being celebrated, the specific modality of the expression of those events is the liturgical symbol.[19] Hence, the lacuna between originary event which is memorialized and the faith-assent by the worshipping community can be filled by symbol. How is this envisioned?

---

[14]See SC #10, 14, 21, 27, 42, 106, 112.

[15]See D.B. STEVICK, *Language in Worship*, p. 165. G. ELLARD in *Men at Work at Worship: America Joins the Liturgical Movement*, Preface by Most Rev. J.G. Murray (New York: Longmans, Green, 1940), pp. 123-126 also makes the point that the Mass text is based on corporate consciousness.

[16]See A.R. DULLES, *A Church to Believe In*, p. 44.

[17]See SC #9, 59.

[18]Ibid., #106; see also #2, 5, 6, 16, 107, 108.

[19]See Ibid., #7, 21, 23. At this point, "liturgical symbol" is yet an ambiguous expression. The notion of symbol in liturgical writings usually points to water, oil, bread, wine, etc. While these are, indeed, symbols, we seek a broader, linguistic connotation.

D.B. Stevick makes two suggestions that operate primarily at the affective level:

> Is this not what we are looking for in liturgy: speech that is alive because in its very rhetorical patterns the community of faith can recognize the marks of flawed human life touched by divine grace?
>
> ... My guess would be that the real lift and joy in worship, when it has been there, has come more from what was sung by the congregation than what was said by the celebrant.[20]

The suggestion here is that liturgical language is first-order discourse which witnesses to language's ability to express the nonverbal through a certain kind of verbal expression. Liturgical language, then, does not have as its purpose "to explain or hold discourse about what is happening, but to carry the participants along and absorb them in the mystery."[21]

There is a danger that either the liturgical language or the faith experience it expresses will be overemphasized. If there is emphasis on the verbal at the expense of the nonverbal, then the mystery being expressed comes under suspicion.[22] If, on the other hand, there is preference for the nonverbal, then a doubt about language ensues and language can no longer be expressive of mystery.[23] What is called for is a dynamic relationship between language and experience, between verbal and nonverbal.[24] Then

---

[20]D.B. STEVICK, "Language in Prayer," 557 and 559, respectively.

[21]D. POWER, "Theological Trends. Symbolism in Worship: A Survey, I," *The Way* 13 (1973), 310.

[22]Cf. D. POWER, *Unsearchable Riches*, p. 76: "Where word has first place in the expression of the holy, the nonverbal comes under suspicion."

[23]See Ibid. See also C. VAGGAGINI, *Theological Dimensions of the Liturgy: A General Treatise On the Theology of the Liturgy*, trans. L.J. Doyle and W.A. Jurgens, 4th ed. (Collegeville: The Liturgical Press, 1976), p. 49.

[24]See A. GANOCZY, *An Introduction to Catholic Sacramental Theology*, p. 158: "It is necessary to strive for a *reciprocity* and a *balance* between the two"; italics his.

language can be expressive of mystery and mystery can be exposed in language.[25]

As indicated above, a symbol operates on two levels: both encounter and reflection. Liturgical language calls for a reflection born of a thematic awareness of liturgy that leads to greater self-understanding rooted in the community experience, in addition to an encounter with the mystery being celebrated:

> To gain access to Jesus as the Christ, we must accept both facts and interpretation, and neither of these can be grasped apart from the testimony of the Christian community and its acknowledged leaders. To make an act of Christian faith, therefore, is to submit (not blindly but with open eyes) to the testimony of the Church ...[26]

By implication, liturgical language is not only communication, but it is, even more, a language which expresses the experience linking the community to the Sacred as symbolic mediation.

c. **Salient Points.** If language were simply denotative and only second-level discourse, then interpretation of liturgical texts would be fairly straightforward and its methodology would emulate any scientific, analytical approach. However, our previous remarks indicate that this is anything but the case.

Several key points stand out. First, prayer language is essentially first-level discourse. It is disclosure and, as such, the language can never totally express the experience which gives rise to it. Language in use is a rich, meaning-laden symbolic mediation of an experience and its communication. This approach to symbol has the distinct advantage of recognizing that symbols carry a freight of meaning that, really, is inexhaustible. But a word of caution is in order. It would be easy to identify symbol as an independent entity (be it word or object) and by so doing lose the fundamental difficulty of the relationship between language and experience. If we posit that language is a *derived* form, and we do, then the "saying" is

---

[25]For a concise historical discussion of language as symbol in the context of a religious experience, see F.W. DILLISTONE, *Traditional Symbols and the Contemporary World* (London: Epworth Press, 1973), Chapter 9: "Symbolic Forms of Language," pp. 143-161.

[26]A.R. DULLES, *A Church to Believe In*, p. 45.

intrinsically related to the "said." In this approach "symbolic mediation" carries more freight than layers of meaning, even though this is not a moot point. We wish to say more about a symbol: the layers of meaning uncovered enable a deeper penetration into experience itself.

The second key point: we use "symbolic" here in a wide, holistic sense. We are not concerned with symbol as individual words or objects, but with symbol in terms of larger linguistic units that cooperate in a single communication process. We search for the experience which gave rise to a symbol not within specifics but within a larger context of a whole communication process.

A third key point is that the originary event of liturgical language is none other than the Christ event. The experience that gives rise to liturgical language is the life, death, resurrection, and promised coming of the Lord as it is memorialized. As expression of that Christ event, liturgical language renders it symbolically present to the Christian community. Liturgical language, then, is the articulation of the link between the present historical community and the originary event they celebrate.

These points have important ramifications for a methodological approach interpreting liturgical language. A method must know its limits, and not claim to deliver more than it is able within given parameters. A method must respect the deeper layers of meaning which liturgical language embodies. The method of interpretation must be able to take into account the originary experience which the language discloses yet cannot capture completely. A method of interpreting liturgical language would seek to uncover the richness of experience articulated by that language. Such a method of interpreting liturgical language would ultimately reveal the community issues raised by this approach. We now turn to the community issues which this method of interpreting liturgical language would ultimately reveal.

2. Community Issues

We do not have to look very far to discover certain issues implicating the worshipping community. With respect to liturgical language, some of these issues hit at the very heart of problems that have been with us for a long time: Whose domain is liturgy? What kind of experience gives rise to liturgical language? These questions are addressed in the next two paragraphs, Active Participation and Faith, and are once again followed by a reflection on methodology fleshed out by salient points.

a. Active Participation. Supposedly gone are the days when the very celebrating of liturgy witnessed to a cleavage between clergy and laity because liturgy was the private domain of the clergy and the laity "attended" by praying their own private devotions. With a renewal in liturgy came a fresh look at the community's involvement in the liturgical celebration. Pastoral-minded leaders of the liturgical movement based much of their work on their desire to foster more active lay participation in liturgical celebrations.[27] One way lay participation was concretized was to focus on promoting the Dialogue Mass,[28] though at that time "Dialogue Mass" was understood simply to mean the people's joining their responses to those of the server in Latin.[29] The intent was to draw the community into the

---

[27] *Questions Liturgiques et Paroissiales* has thirty-six articles or notes addressing participation in the volumes from 1927 to 1958. *Bulletin Paroissial Liturgique* (Volume 1, 1919) first addresses liturgical language in 1927 in an article expounding the Church's attitude favoring greater, more interior, and community participation. Articles on liturgical language and participation appear fairly regularly in this latter periodical.

[28] Though the first experiments with dialogue Mass were in Belgium (see M.H. SHEPHERD, Jr., ed., *The Liturgical Renewal of the Church: Addresses by Theodore Otto Wedel [and Others]* [New York: Oxford University Press, 1960], p. 31) the dialogue Mass became a major issue in the liturgical movement in the United States. No periodical has devoted so much attention to the dialogue Mass and related issues as has *Orate Fratres* (*Worship*). In the first thirty volumes (1926-1956) no fewer than seventy-three articles or notes are directed toward promoting the dialogue Mass. Even more significant, 156 articles or notes are concerned with various aspects of liturgical language, including such diverse topics as translation, style, and catechetical and missionary effectiveness. By and large, though, the discussion focused on the question of vernacular in the liturgy. See G. ELLARD, *Men at Work at Worship*, especially p. 131 and Chapter 14, pp. 237-254.

[29] This precipitates such articles as those concerned with correct pronunciation of the Latin. See, for example, *Revue liturgique et bénédictine*, Volume 2 (1911-1912) and Volume 4 (1913-1914).

liturgical celebration itself as active participants in the mysteries being celebrated by making texts available to people and encouraging them to follow the presider's words and actions. No doubt, these early efforts made great strides in helping the community understand liturgy better, and even more dramatically by showing that a positive response by the community feeds their life.[30]

Solving one problem often leads to another, and the encouragement of lay participation opened a can of vernacular worms. Until this century, vernacular translations of liturgical texts were not available to people. Liturgical reformers took another step forward when they proposed translations and explanations of the liturgical texts.[31] Thus, in both the early and later phases of the liturgical movement the focus on active participation revolved largely around the question of the vernacular.[32] If the community was to be encouraged toward

---

[30]See G. ELLARD, *Men at Work at Worship*, p. 125 for people's positive reactions to greater participation in liturgy.

[31]See L. BOUYER, *La vie de la liturgie*, pp. 71, 83, 87. It is well to note that these developments were the concern of the liturgical movement of the twentieth century. Dom Prosper Guéranger, the father of the modern Liturgical Movement (see O. ROUSSEAU, *Histoire du mouvement liturgique: esquisse historique depuis le début du xix*[e] *siècle jusqu'au pontificat de Pie X* [Paris: Editions du Cerf, 1945], p. 1) was "only moderately interested in making the Liturgy available in the vernacular" (M.H. SHEPHERD, Jr., *The Liturgical Renewal of the Church*, p. 25) and was reluctant to translate liturgical texts (see O. ROUSSEAU, *Histoire du mouvement liturgique*, pp. 37f). Primarily an ecclesiastic and historian (see D. TUCKER, "The Council of Trent, Guéranger and Pius X," *Orate Fratres* X [1935-1936], 541-542), Dom Prosper saw liturgy as the principal instrument of Church tradition (see O. ROUSSEAU, *Histoire du mouvement liturgique*, pp. 25-26), and advocated a return to the theology and spirit of the Middle Ages. It is no wonder, then, that one does not find in Dom Prosper's agenda any great sympathy for the vernacular.

[32]This is more or less reflected in the periodical literature up to the first half of this century. *Revista Liturgica* (Volume 1, 1914) only has one reference to the vernacular, an article on translating the Roman Breviary in Volume 19, 1932; likewise, *Jahrbuch für Liturgiewissenschaft*

active participation in the liturgical celebration, certainly it would be helpful if they could use their own language. Though the principle seems sound enough to our contemporary ears, in the earlier phases of the liturgical movement it met with serious opposition. Pius X, in #7 of his November 22, 1903, instruction on sacred music, *Inter Plurimus Pastoralis*, asserted that Latin is the language of the Church and categorically forbade anything in the vernacular to be sung during liturgy.[33] Pius XII, in his November 9, 1947, encyclical *Mediator Dei*, cited the use of vernacular as an instance of abuse that was creeping into liturgy (#59). He lauded the Latin language as the sign of unity within the Church and as an antidote for any corruption of doctrinal truth (#60).

Nevertheless, even in the early part of his papacy Pius XII recognized that the use of the vernacular might be helpful for

---

(Volume 1, 1921) has one article, appearing in Volume 10, 1930. *Questions Liturgiques et Paroissiales* (Volume 1, 1910) has five articles dealing with the vernacular (in 1928, 1933, 1946, 1950, 1958). The earliest mention of the vernacular in *Ephemerides Liturgical* (Volume 1, 1887) appears in 1894, with a half dozen articles in all. However, the vernacular here is discussed in relation to Benediction, solemn exposition, hymns, Baptism; no article addresses the question of vernacular and the eucharistic text. An interesting exception to this early limited scope of language and liturgy appears in G. ELLARD's *Men at Work at Worship* where, on pp. 118-123, he analyzes the Mass text and focuses on pronominal person and number, though he does not develop the ramifications of his observations.

[33]In spite of this, though, Pius X had a great interest in the liturgy and did much to bring about reforms. See his decree on the necessary dispositions for frequent and daily reception of Holy Communion, *Sacra Tridentina Synodus* (December 20, 1905); decree on the age of children who are to be admitted to first Holy Communion, *Auam Singulari* (August 8, 1910); and the apostolic constitution on the new arrangement of the psalter in the Roman Breviary, *Divino Afflatu* (November 1, 1911). The above are available in English translation in V.A. YZERMANS (ed.), *All Things in Christ: Encyclicals and Selected Documents of Saint Pius X* (Westminster, MD: The Newman Press, 1954). For a summary of Pius X's liturgical contributions, see G. ELLARD, "Gregory and Pius, Fathers of Liturgy," *Orate Fratres* 1 (1926-1927), 12-16; also, O. ROUSSEAU, *Histoire du mouvement liturgique*, pp. 201-215.

the laity in several liturgical rites other than the Eucharist (#60). Further, a large section of *Mediator Dei* is devoted to promoting the fuller participation of the laity in liturgy (#80-112). Though participation was seen in this document primarily as the laity's uniting themselves to the presider's offering by virtue of the shared baptismal priesthood, the encyclical does suggest concrete steps toward fuller participation that have linguistic implications: the laity were to become more familiar with the *Roman Missal*, to answer the presider in an orderly and fitting way, to sing hymns during low Mass, and to sing the responses and chants at high Mass (#105).[34] Later in his papacy, in the September 3, 1958, instruction *De Musica Sacra*, Pius XII suggested that the epistle and Gospel could be read in the vernacular to be more useful for the laity, but after being read in Latin (#14c and #16c). In the years immediately preceding Vatican II, the discussion on vernacular in the liturgy increased in intensity with many books and articles being written both pro and con.[35]

In *Sacrosanctum Concilium*, the first schema promulgated by the Council Fathers, Vatican II opened wide the door to the vernacular in liturgy. However, even at this time certain hesitation remained for it was a matter of vernacular *in* liturgy, not of a vernacular liturgy. Granting permission that "a suitable place may be allotted to their mother tongue," #54), initially this included the use of the vernacular only for the readings, the common prayers, and other parts of the Mass where the local culture would indicate the vernacular to be beneficial (#54; cf. #36, § 2). At the same time, *Sacrosanctum Concilium* intended Latin to remain (#36, §1) and called for the instruction of people in saying or singing in Latin the parts that pertain to them (#36, §1). With the final determination of extent and regulation of vernacular in liturgy being left to the competent territorial ecclesiastical authority (#36, § 3,4; #39), the question remained open and discussions continued.[36]

---

[34]Note, though, that #107 cautions that the value of the people's participation is not to be exaggerated.

[35]See A.A. DE MARCO, *Rome and the Vernacular* (Westminster, MD: Newman Press, 1961) for a good bibliography on the works on the vernacular to that time.

[36]See, for example, favoring the change, C. HOWELL, "The Use of English in the Liturgy" in *The Liturgy and the Future*, ed. J.D. Crichton (Tenburgy Wells, Worcestershire: Fowler Wright

In accord with the Vatican II call for a revision of rites (SC #25), the first English versions of the Eucharistic liturgy (1964) were a combination of Latin and English. English was permitted for the Lord, Have Mercy, the Gloria, the readings, Profession of Faith, Preface Dialogue, the Holy, Holy, Holy, the Lord's Prayer, the Prayer for Peace and its greeting, Lamb of God, and concluding dialogue; all else remained in Latin. All-English missals did not appear until the early 1970s.[37] Practical problems concerning such aspects as singing[38] and the theological and cultural problems relating to translation[39] continued to plague scholars.

While even today vernacular in liturgy, the proper translation of liturgical texts, and the concern for a common language continue to be discussed,[40] this discussion has

---

Books, 1966), pp. 88-104. For a more negative assessment see A. LO BELLO, "The Mass in Latin and in English," *Downside Review* 101-344 (1983), 194-215.

[37]The bound United States volume appeared in 1974 after confirmation by the Congregation for Divine Worship on February 4, 1974. The first editions available in Canada were loose-leaf bound so later revisions could inexpensively be made; the bound volume appeared in 1973.

[38]See, for example, P. JONES, *English in the Liturgy: Some Aesthetic and Practical Problems* (London: G. Chapman, 1966).

[39]See, for example, A. GIGNAC, "Prière liturgique et 'langue vivante,'" *Liturgie et vie chrétienne* 75 (1971), 22-30. See also J.H.J. WESTLAKE, "Problems of Modern Vernacular Liturgy," *Studia Liturgica* 6 (1969), 147-157; P.D. GARRETT, "Problem of Liturgical Translation: A Preliminary Study," *St. Vladimir's Theological Quarterly* 22 (1978), 83-113 and "The Problem of Liturgical Translation: An Addendum [Φῶς ἱλαρόν]," *St. Vladimir's Theological Quarterly* 24 (1980), 37-50.

[40]See F.R. ANDERSON, "Liturgy in the Vernacular," *Reformed Liturgy and Music* 17 (1983), 185; A.A. DE MARCO, *Rome and the Vernacular* (Westminster, MD: Newman Press, 1961); G. AVERY, "Dvornick on National Churches," *Eastern Churches Review* 10 (1978), 17-25; P.D. GARRETT, "Problems of Liturgical Translation: A Preliminary Study," *St. Vladimir's Theological Quarterly* 22 (1978), 83-113; P.D. GARRETT, "The Problem of Liturgical Translation: An Addendum [Φῶς ἱλαρόν]," *St. Vladimir's*

broadened to include important linguistic considerations such as matters of literary form and style,[41] various aspects related to tonal performance,[42] and the aesthetics of the language used.[43] As the work of translation continues, scholars recognize more and more their responsibility to choose language conveying the

---

Theological Quarterly 24 (1980), 37-50; N. GOTTERI, "Tradition and Translation," *Sobornost* 2 (1980), 41-49; F.M. ISHAK, "Celebration of Eucharist in Appropriate Language," *Coptic Church Review* 1 (1980), 27-29; C. KOROLEVSKY, *Living Languages in Catholic Worship: An Historical Inquiry*, trans. D. Attwater (London: Longmans, Green, 1957); A. LO BELLO, "From East to West: On Certain ICEL Translations," *Communio* 8 (1981), 392-399; A. LO BELLO, "The Mass in Latin and in English," *Downside Review* 101-344 (1983), 194-215; R. POWER, "The Liturgy in Translation," *Orate Fratres* 1 (1926-1927), 203-207; A. TEGELS, "The Demand for Latin in the Liturgy," *Worship* 56 (1982), 63-65; J.H.J. WESTLAKE, "Problems of Modern Vernacular Liturgy," *Studia Liturgica* 6 (1969), 147-157; P. WINNINGER, *Langues vivantes et liturgie*, pref. Mgr. J.-J. Weber (Paris: Editions du Cerf, 1961).

[41]See, for example, D.G. BUTTRICK, "On Liturgical Language," *Reformed Liturgy and Music* 15 (1981), 74-82; H.P.R. FINBERG, "The Problem of Style," in *English in the Liturgy: A Symposium* (London: Burns and Oates, 1956), pp. 109-122; R. TOPOROSKI, "Language of Worship," *Communio* 4 (1977), 226-260; R. TOPOROSKI, "The Language of Worship," *Worship* 52 (1978), 489-508.

[42]See, for example, J.B. FOLEY, "An Aural Basis for Oral Liturgical Prayer," *Worship* 56 (1982), 132-152; G. GRINDAL, "The Language of Worship and Hymnody: Tone," *Worship* 52 (1978), 509-516; G. GRINDAL, "Stopping by the Pit Stop: Liturgies Call for the Prose of Speech Rather than the Prose of Print," *Christian Century* 94 (1977), 453-457; M. GODGETTS, "Sense and Sound in Liturgical Translation," *Worship* 57 (1983), 496-513; K.J. LARSEN, "Language as Aural," *Worship* 54 (1980), 18-35.

[43]See, for example, D.L. FROST, "Dying Church, or a Living World?" *Theology* 74 (1971), 499-512; R. HARRIES, "Alternative Services: The Test of Practice," *Theology* 79 (1976), 221-226; P. JONES, *English in the Liturgy: Some Aesthetic and Practical Problems* (London: G. Chapman, 1966); R. SPEAIGHT, "Liturgy and Language," *Theology* 74 (1971), 444-456.

presence of the Sacred,[44] to attend to the theological and cultural problems tied to the language question,[45] and to pay close attention to the fact that words convey meaning.[46] Thus the problem of the vernacular and translating liturgical texts really embraces a whole gamut of linguistic concerns. However, a direct focus on language is still lacking.

More recently, a different slant on the vernacular and translations which focus on the question of "inclusive" language[47] for liturgical texts has come a bit closer to recognizing more of the problems involved in the language issue. A difficulty arises not when inclusivity/exclusivity takes shape with respect to those who share the same Gospel vision vis-à-vis those who do not, but rather when it arises within the Christian community itself among those who supposedly share the same vision. The central issue of how liturgical language both reflects and effects the unity of that local worshipping community is purportedly what is at stake in this concern. To be sure, liturgy does, in one sense, have both inclusive and exclusive aspects. On the one hand, liturgical language is inclusive in as much as it articulates the tradition and human concerns common to the Christian community; on the other hand, it expresses the exclusive interests and experiences of the particular worshipping community.[48] Liturgy is inclusive in that

---

[44]See E.S. BROWN, "Whose Liturgical Language?" *Dialogue* 20 (1981), 107-111; also, K.G. SCHMUDE, "Redeeming the Word: The Future of Christian Language," *Communio* 7 (1980), 157-169.

[45]See A. GIGNAC, "Prière liturgique et 'langue vivante,'" *Liturgie et vie chrétienne* 75 (1971), 22-30.

[46]See C. HOWELL, "The Use of English in the Liturgy," in *The Liturgy and the Future*, ed. J.D. Crichton (Tenburgy Wells, Worcestershire: Fowler Wright Books, 1966), p. 96; also, K.J. LARSEN, "Some Observations about Symbols and Metaphors," *Worship* 54 (1980), 221-245.

[47]For an evaluation of a proposed inclusive language lectionary, see G. RANSHAW-SCHMIDT, "An Inclusive Language Lectionary," *Worship* 58 (1984), 29-37; also, J.C. LYLES, "The NCC's Nonsexist Lectionary," *Christian Century* 100 (1983), 1148-1150.

[48]See D. COCKERELL, "The Language of Initiation: A Critique of Series 3 Baptism," *The Modern Churchman* 23 (1980), 21-29.

the community embodies a common vision transcending time and space. It is exclusive in that the community, by proclamation of the vision, declares itself unique. But there is more to say than this.

Changes in culture and society are reflected in language use.[49] Consequently, the challenge to inclusive language in liturgy has focused largely on sexist language,[50] with the appeal that the language of liturgy reflect the cultural changes in contemporary western society with respect to the status, role, and equality of women. This applies as well to other categories of worshippers: to the aged, handicapped, and people of different ethnic backgrounds.[51] Not just a peripheral quibble, this discussion has significant theological ramifications. For example, what symbols, metaphors, and pronouns should we use in referring to God,[52] in the propositions which are used to express the essential content of faith and morality, and in relating the language of Scripture to diverse sociocultural milieu.

---

[49]See H.T. KERR, "Wash Your Language," *Theology Today* 30 (1973), 211.

[50]See, for example, M. BLACKLOCK, "Popularizing Non-sexist Liturgies," *Witness* 64 (1981), 10-11; I.C.E.L., "The Problem of Exclusive Language with Regard to Women," *Afer* 23 (1981), 312-317; J.M. MAXWELL, "Inclusive Language in Theology and Worship," *Austin Seminary Bulletin* 97 (1981); "NCC's Bisexual Lectionary Brings More Problems," *Christianity Today* 27 (1983), 40; J.H. PENFIELD, "COCU Consultation on Language and Liturgy," *Journal of Ecumenical Studies* 19 (1982), 668-669; E. ROUTLEY, "Sexist Language: A View From a Distance," *Worship* 53 (1979), 2-11; G.R. SCHMIDT, "A Dream of the Rood," *Dialogue* 18 (1979), 103-107.

[51]See J.C. LYLES, "New Language for Liturgy," *Christian Century* 98 (1981), 1358-1359); T. McANALLY, "Language and Liturgy in the COCU Context," *Mid-Stream* 21 (1982), 422-423.

[52]See J.W.H. BOS, "To Whom Then Will You Liken Me," *Reformed Liturgy and Music* 17 (1983), 169-171; M. BOUCHER, "Scriptural Readings: God-language and Nonsexist Translation," *Reformed Liturgy and Music* 17 (1983), 156-159; W.E. MARCH, "Language About God: What Shall We Say?" *Reformed Liturgy and Music* 17 (1983), 152-155; P. MURRAY, "The Holy Spirit and God Language," *Witness* 66 (1983), 7-9; E. ROUTLEY, "The Gender of God: A Contribution to the Conversation," *Worship* 56 (1982), 231-239.

Over and above these necessary and worthwhile endeavors, some scholars recognize that the problematic of liturgical language runs deeper than the issues of vernacular, translations, and inclusivity to more radical questions that implicate life issues. As early as 1970, D.E. Saliers wrote on the crisis of liturgical language in a brief article by that title.[53] Saliers made the point that language involves more than vocabulary; it involves *meaning* which points to a deeper dimension of investigation. He sees the task as "not so much to change the language as it is to understand how the language is to be taken and how it is to be used."[54] Saliers' interest in the more profound issues of liturgical language was further underscored when he edited Volume 52 (1978) of *Worship* which was devoted to the special theme of liturgy and language. In his editorial remarks he wrote that "problems concerning language in the liturgy are intrinsic to the renewal of worship."[55] He sets out the agenda as searching for a worthy vernacular, forging new forms of liturgical utterance, and shaping more relevant styles of public prayer.

Other authors have specified particular dimensions of these deeper linguistic issues in the direction indicated by Saliers. G. Ramshaw-Schmidt outlines the scope of this broader task: words, images, syntax, tone, and structure.[56] Cognizant of the ramifications of language, D. Cockerell relates language to human self-understanding and asserts that language "has a constitutive, not merely a reportative function."[57]

---

[53]D.E. SALIERS, "On the 'Crisis' of Liturgical Language," *Worship* 44 (1970), 399-411.

[54]Ibid., 408.

[55]D.E. SALIERS, "Language in the Liturgy: Where Angels Fear to Tread," *Worship* 52 (1978), 482.

[56]See G. RAMSHAW-SCHMIDT, "The Language of Eucharistic Praying," *Worship* 57 (1983), 419-437.

[57]See D. COCKERELL, "Liturgical Language, Dead and Alive," *Theology* 80 (1977), 112. An important application of this is the relationship of liturgy and morality. See, for example, the fall, 1979 issue of *The Journal of Religious Ethics* (Volume 7, Number 2) with the title "Focus on Liturgy and Ethics"; contains articles by Ramsey, Saliers, Farley, Everett, Yaffe, Green, and Rossi.

Two related areas extensively addressed as a result of this more profound concern for language in liturgy are the relationship of liturgical language to communication theory[58] and speech-act theory.[59] The former involves an analysis of the actual effects the symbols of communication have on the worshipping community. G.V. Lardner makes a pointed observation:

---

[58]See, for example, G.V. LARDNER, "Communication Theory and Liturgical Research," *Worship* 51 (1972), 299-306; M. SEARLE, "Liturgy as Metaphor," *Worship* 55 (1981), 98-120; G.V. LARDNER, "Liturgy as Communication: A Pragmatics Perspective" *Religious Education* 77 (1982), 438 [dissertation abstract]; A. GANOCZY, *An Introduction to Catholic Sacramental Theology*, Chapter 4: "Toward a Communications Theory of Sacraments," pp. 142-182.

[59]See, for example, H.K. HUGHES, *The Opening Prayers of the Sacramentary: A Structural Study of the Prayers of the Easter Cycle*, Doctoral Dissertation, University of Notre Dame, 1981; D. BREWER, "Liturgy: Need and Frustration," *Theology* 80 (1977), 173-177; B. BRINKMAN, "Sacramental Man and Speech Acts Again," *The Heythrop Journal* 16 (1975), 416-420; R. CHAPMAN, "Linguistics and Liturgy," *Theology* 76 (1973), 594-599; D. CRYSTAL, "Linguistics and Liturgy," *Christian Quarterly* 2 (1969), 23-30; P. DONOVAN, *Religious Language* (New York: Hawthorn Books, 1976); P.E. FINK, "Three Languages of Christian Sacraments," *Worship* 52 (1978), 561-575); S.D. GILL, "Prayer as Person: The Performative Force in Navaho Prayer Acts," *History of Religions* 17 (1977), 143-157; A. JEFFNER, *The Study of Religious Language* (London: SCM Press, 1972), Chapter 4: "Religious Performatives," pp. 88-104; J. LADRIERE, "The Performativity of Liturgical Language," *Concilium* 9-1 (1973), 50-62; P. LUCIER, "Le statut épistémologique de la situation liturgique," *Liturgie et vie chrétienne* 82 (1972), 256-278; A. MARTINICH, "Reply to B. Brinkman, 'Sacramental Man and Speech Acts Again,'" *The Heythrop Journal* 17 (1976), 188-189; A. MARTINICH, "Sacraments and Speech Acts," *The Heythrop Journal* 16 (1975), 289-305; H. SCHMIDT, "Language and Its Function in Christian Worship," *Studia Liturgica* 8 (1970-1972), 1-25; W.H. SWATOS, "Liturgy and *Lebensform*: The Personal God as a Social Being," *Perspectives in Religious Studies* 7 (1980), 38-49; R. VOLPE, "La liturgie en tant que comportement social: Réflexions en vue de l'élaboration de méthodes empiriques de recherches," *Social Compass* 22 (1975), 157-174; J.H. WARE, Jr., *Not With Words of Wisdom* (Washington: University Press of America, 1981); W.T. WHEELOCK, "The Problem of Ritual Language: From Information to Situation," *Journal of the American Academy of Religion* 50 (1982), 49-71.

methodologies for a pragmatic evaluation of the liturgy do not yet exist, though such methodologies do exist in the fields of sociology, social psychology, and communication.[60] M. Searle also sees liturgy as a communication event, but cautions against understanding this in the contemporary vein of simply conveying information. This is too much of a propositional approach to communication in liturgy. It must rather be understood within the wider scope of engagement in a relationship, disclosure, and orientation[61] which takes more seriously language's disclosure of experience.

The second and related area concerns liturgical language with respect to speech-act theory. Though there is a variety of ways this theory has been applied to liturgy,[62] at issue is the fact that the saying is related to the performing. For example, when we make such statements as "I believe," "I bless," "I thank," "I promise," we imply that the belief, blessing, gratitude, promise are already present in the very saying. Saying is bound up with sentiments and desired results. A seminal article in this regard is the one by J. Ladrière.[63] After a brief exposition of speech-act theory, Ladrière applies this theory to liturgy in terms of its bringing about an affective disposition which opens the worshipping community to a specific reality, institutes that group of people as community, and presents the reality about which it speaks.[64] Liturgy employs language as more than words or sentences. It also

---

[60]See G.V. LARDNER, "Communication Theory and Liturgical Research, 303.

[61]See M. SEARLE, "Liturgy as Metaphor," 102ff.

[62]See G. RAMSHAW-SCHMIDT, "The Language of Eucharistic Praying," 421.

[63]See J. LADRIERE, "The Performativity of Liturgical Language," passim. For a brief overview of both speech-act theory and Ladrière's article, see F. ISAMBERT, *Rite et efficacité symbolique: Essai d'anthropologie sociologique,* Rite et Symboles #8 (Paris: Les Editions du Cerf, 1979), Chapter 3: "Langage performatif et action rituelle," pp. 87-113.

[64]See J. LADRIERE, "The Performativity of Liturgical Language," 56-62.

includes ritual and actions[65] carrying it beyond information to the *realization of a situation* which both recalls and anticipates. The positive contribution of speech-act theory is that it recognizes that language is far more than information conveyance. In its use language both affects and effects. While the contribution of speech-act theory in widening the scope of language is significant, what is lacking yet is a comprehensive framework in which linguistic studies are undertaken within a context of self-understanding. We seek a methodic framework which accounts for the fundamental relationship between language and experience. Our next community issue brings us closer to this problem.

b. Faith. For Ladrière and others, faith constitutes both the starting point which grounds liturgical language and the goal toward which the experience moves.[66] Faith is "a resumption of the mystery of Christ, the acceptance of salvation and hope of benefits yet to come."[67] Beginning with this notion of faith, C. Raschke sees ritual language as "belief realized through expressive activity."[68] For him, this language cannot be

---

[65]See H. SCHMIDT, "Language and Its Function in Christian Worship," *Studia Liturgica* 8 (1970-1972), 1-25; and W.T. WHEELOCK, "The Problem of Ritual Language: From Information to Situation," *Journal of the American Academy of Religion* 50 (1982), 49-71.

[66]See, for example, R.F. ADLWINCKLE, "Worship and Prayer: Principles and Problems: Liturgy and Language," *Canadian Journal of Theology* 15 (1969), 157-165; K.B. CULLY, *Sacraments: A Language of Faith* (Philadelphia: Christian Education Press, 1961); I.-H. DALMAIS, "The Expression of the Faith in Eastern Liturgies," *Concilium* 9-1 (1973), 77-85, trans. F. McDonagh; L. GILKEY, "Addressing God in Faith," *Concilium* 9-1 (1973), 62-76; J. LADRIERE, *Language and Belief*, trans. G. Barden (Notre Dame: University of Notre Dame Press, 1972); G. LUKKEN, "The Unique Expression of Faith in the Liturgy," *Concilium* 9-1 (1973), 11-21; J.-P. MANIGNE, "The Poetics of Faith in the Liturgy," trans. F. McDonagh, *Concilium* 9-1 (1973), 40-50; D. POWER, "Two Expressions of Faith: Worship and Theology," *Concilium* 9-1 (1973), 95-103.

[67]J. LADRIERE, "The Performativity of Liturgical Language," 62.

[68]C. RASCHKE, "Meaning and Saying in Religion: Beyond Language Games," *Harvard Theological Review* 67 (1974), 99.

analyzed according to analytic models,[69] but a more comprehensive model is to be sought. The desired model ought to take into consideration, first, the awareness of God which is at the basis of liturgical language, and, second, the body of images which conveys this awareness.[70] Similar reflections are offered by A. Vergote. For Vergote, a more comprehensive model is an anthropological model whereby the language, gestures, and actions of the liturgical rite unite the worshipping community both with the space-world in which they live and with the God they worship. The function of liturgical gesture is to express inner sentiment. As such it is the medium between the language used and what the ritual action achieves. It is in this context as medium that Vergote asserts liturgical gesture to be faith in action. For him,

> Faith ... is a disposition towards God which is actualized only in expression. To express it is thus to effectuate it. So no faith exists that is not actualized in a rite that is indissolubly efficacious gesture and word.[71]

Vergote continues: as a sentiment, faith is also expressed in the gestures that accompany language; language and gesture complement each other. Language without gesture is not expressive of the existential situation of the worshipping community; gesture without language has no significance.

The power of liturgy as a language of faith is that of the liturgical celebration definitively revealing Mystery in such a way as to draw the worshipping community into that Mystery. The only response on the part of the worshipping community in face of this dynamic is a response in faith. We admit here to a circular movement. Mystery is revealed to the worshipping community in liturgical language as the Triune God who is there before the community acting through the originary events that root the Christian experience of the community. The worshipping community orients itself to the Triune God in a faith response. Faith in turn expresses itself in liturgical language, which is a medium of encounter with God. Liturgical language is co-original with

---

[69]Ibid., 105.

[70]D.B. STEVICK, "Language of Prayer," *Worship* 52 (1978), 546.

[71]A. VERGOTE, "Symbolic Gestures and Actions in the Liturgy," trans. B. Wall, *Concilium* 7-2 (1971), 43.

faith-event: it is the dynamic mediary between God who is both *alpha* and *omega* of the liturgical celebration and the faith response of the community who thereby comes to understand themselves in a new way.

The self-understanding that liturgical celebration can effect is first and foremost a community self-understanding. There is a universality about this self-understanding which marks the Christian community as one throughout its tradition. This implies that there is more at stake in the liturgical text than the question of liturgical language, symbol, and their relevance or their power to evoke an encounter.[72] The formation and totality of the liturgical text suggest that its structure is neither accidental nor peripheral. An inquiry into liturgical language leads inevitably to an inquiry into liturgical text. But before moving on to the next part of the chapter which addresses liturgical text, we pause to summarize the salient points.

c. **Salient Points**. These reflections on community issues all point to one conclusion: the aim of liturgical language is to engage the community in a celebration rather than to produce an esoteric text that only the "select" can appreciate. Liturgical language does not belong to the private domain of the clergy, but necessarily derives from the faith experiences of a tradition of community celebrations. Through their active participation, the assembled community continues in this tradition of celebration. Through this participation, too, the community is able to concretely express their faith response to the mystery being celebrated.

With a more engaging approach to liturgy comes a need for methodological models which can account for the disposition toward God which faith-filled participation bespeaks. We are looking for a method, then, which can address this engaging aspect of liturgy.

---

[72]For a discussion of four approaches to dealing with inherited Christian symbols, see D.B. STEVICK, *Language in Worship*, Chapter 4: "Evaluating Inherited Images," pp. 54-70.

B. Text

We begin by proposing an analogy: though the word of God is contained in the written text of Scripture, we recognize that the word is not the printed page but that which is proclaimed and lived. So, too, we insist that the fullness of liturgy is only evident in its celebration. Nevertheless, the written liturgical text does provide a certain access to the meaning of liturgical celebration. This part of the chapter looks at the notion of text by considering what liturgical scholars have been doing with text and by examining documents reflecting the liturgical renewal of Vatican II. There is a summary section of salient points.

1. Liturgical Scholars' Use of Text

No doubt, in the last century scholars have been doing good things with liturgical texts. In addition to providing vernacular translations, as mentioned above, we have benefitted from other scholarly pursuits which have taken liturgical texts seriously.

Work has been done in searching out Jewish origins to Christian liturgy.[73] Other work has searched both early and contemporary liturgical texts to uncover structures, themes, and historical precedents for elements of liturgy.[74] Still other

---

[73]See, for example, W.O.E. OESTERLEY, *The Jewish Background of the Christian Liturgy* (New York: Oxford University Press, 1925); L. BOUYER, *Eucharist: Theology and Spirituality of the Eucharistic Prayer*, trans. C. Underhill Quinn (Notre Dame: University of Notre Dame Press, 1968).

[74]See, for example, A. BAUMSTARK, *Comparative Liturgy*, revised by B. Botte, O.S.B., English edition by F.L. Cross (Westminster, Maryland: Newman, 1958); G. DIX, *The Shape of the Liturgy*, 2nd ed. (Westminster: Dacree Press, 1945); J. JUNGMANN, *The Mass of the Roman Rite*, 2 vol., trans. F.A. Brunner (New York: Benzinger Brothers, Inc., 1951, 1955); L. BOUYER, *Eucharist*; R. TAFT, "Structural Analysis of Liturgical Units: An Essay in Methodology," *Worship* 52 (1978): 314-329; A. KAVANAGH, "Confirmation: A Suggestion from Structure," *Worship* 58 (1984): 386-394; T.J. TALLEY, "The Literary Structure of Eucharistic Prayer," *Worship* 58 (1984): 404-419; C. JONES, G. WAINWRIGHT, and E. YARNOLD, S.J., eds., *The Study of Liturgy* (New York: Oxford University Press, 1978); H.A.J. WEGMAN, *Christian Worship: A Study Guide to Liturgical History*, trans. G.W. Lathrop (New

work has been done in examining the elements of current rites.[75] From another direction, the present interest in culture has posed challenges for contemporary liturgical scholars and is not without its demands on those working with liturgical texts.[76] Other important areas of research would also have direct or indirect bearing on the shape and use of liturgical texts, including spirituality, pastoral ministry, and paraliturgical practices. While all this research has undoubtedly contributed much to a wealth of liturgical knowledge, one conclusion still stands: liturgical scholars have not as yet looked at text *qua* text within the parameters of a text theory.[77] Our own study is an effort to begin filling this lacuna.

2. Post-Vatican II Liturgical Documents

At first sight, the notion of text in post-Vatican II documents is limited to its written forms and how they are used. Yet, a perusal of liturgical documents suggests a deeper penetration of the notion of liturgical text that, at least implicitly, the Council Fathers addressed. Fleshing out these implications not only underscores the fact that there is more at

---

York: Pueblo Publishing Company, 1985); G. KRETSCHMAR, "Recent Research on Christian Initiation," *Studia Liturgica* 12 (1977): 87-106; G. WINKLER, "Confirmation or Chrismation? A Study in Comparative Liturgy," *Worship* 58 (1984): 2-16.

[75]See, for example, G. HUCK, *Liturgy with Style and Grace* (Chicago: Liturgy Training Publications, 1984); A. KAVANAGH, *Elements of Rite: A Handbook of Liturgical Style* (New York: Pueblo Publishing Company, 1982); J.H. EMMINGHAUS, *The Eucharist: Essence, Form, Celebration*, trans. M.J. O'Connell (Collegeville: The Liturgical Press, 1978); *The Mystery of Faith: A Study of the Structural Elements of the Order of Mass* (Washington, D.C.: Federation of Diocesan Liturgical Commissions, 1981).

[76]See, for example, A.J. CHUPUNGCO, O.S.B., *Cultural Adaptation of the Liturgy* (New York: Paulish Press, 1982); F.C. SENN, *Christian Worship and its Cultural Setting* (Philadelphia: Fortress Press, 1983).

[77]One exception to this is the article by W.T. Wheelock, "The Mass and Other Ritual Texts: Computer Assisted Approach" (*History of Religions* 24 [1984]: 49-72) where he examines the eucharistic rite in terms of content analysis theory.

stake than written forms and how they are used, but it also indicates an agenda for further pursuit.

a. *Sacrosanctum Concilium.* *Sacrosanctum Concilium* addresses the question of how the Sacred Mysteries can best *express*, best communicate, their deepest reality: "In this reform both texts and rites should be drawn up so that they express more clearly the holy things they signify ... " (#21; see also #11, 14, 59). Further,

> The Order of Mass is to be revised in a way that will bring out more clearly the intrinsic nature and purpose of its several parts, as also the connection between them, and will more readily achieve the devout, active participation of the faithful (#50).

These references indicate a sensitivity to the communicative value of the liturgical text, to the value of the different parts of the rite, to how those parts cooperate in shaping a whole, and to the purpose of promoting participation by the people. Implied is a complex relationship between the text of the liturgy and its potential effectiveness. The work of renewal is largely directed to this.

Even though the ensuing paragraphs in *Sacrosanctum Concilium* spell out some of the practical implications of the Council Fathers' proposed revisions,[78] these concrete reforms primarily involve peripheral aspects with respect to the question of liturgical language and text. More to the heart of the matter are aspects concerning linguistic structures, meaning, and uses.

While they are few in number, the references to text in *Sacrosanctum Concilium* pretty well summarize the notion of text as it is generally understood in the Christian tradition: a text has a wholly pragmatic *raison d'être* focusing on how liturgical texts are to be used. Consequently, the document addresses the purpose, form, and regulation of texts. There is no concern about text *qua* text.

---

[78]In brief, SC #50, eliminate duplicate and out-moded elements; #51, use a more representative portion of Scripture in the lessons; #52, promote more care and esteem for the homily; #53, restore the prayer of the faithful; #54, restore the vernacular in suitable places; #55, receive communion bread from the same Mass attended and restore communion under both kinds; #56, take part in the entire Mass; #57 and 58, draw up a new rite and restore concelebration.

The purpose of the revised text is succinctly stated: to "express more clearly the holy things they signify" (#21). When this expressive purpose is transposed into practical consequences for celebration by the Christian community, it suggests a specific form: the texts (rites) should be

> marked by a noble simplicity; they should be short, clear, and unencumbered by useless repetitions; they should be within the people's powers of comprehension and as a rule not require much explanation (#34).

This is so that the community may understand and participate in the liturgy fully and actively (#21). That liturgical texts are normative is established through the paradigmatic Latin texts and through regulation of their authorized translations only by "competent, territorial ecclesiastical authority" (#36, § 4; #22, §2). In short, what this pragmatic approach says about liturgical texts is that they remain a means to an end. Nothing is said about their production or meaning as texts.

b. *General Instruction of the Roman Missal.* As an aid for the use of the new *Roman Missal*,[79] it is not surprising that the *General Instruction* has a greater number of references to text than does *Sacrosanctum Concilium.* But what is surprising is the ambiguity of the implications of those remarks. To be sure, comments on use are present; for example, there is still a reference to adapting texts to foster active and full participation (Introduction #5). Yet this is complemented by a varied approach to text.

In the Introduction, three ideas about liturgical text come through. First, the *General Instruction* insists that the texts ("formularies") witness to an unchanged faith (Introduction #2-5): "In this new Missal, then, the Church's rule of prayer (*lex orandi*) corresponds to its constant rule of faith (*lex*

---

[79]The apostolic constitution *Missale Romanum*, issued by Pope Paul VI on April 3, 1969, approved the new *Roman Missal* which went into effect on the first Sunday of Advent, November 30, 1969. The *General Instruction of the Roman Missal* (hereafter cited as "GIRM") accompanied *Missale Romanum* and was first issued on April 6, 1969. It has been through several revisions, the fourth and latest revision issued March 27, 1975. The text here is this revision and is taken from *Documents on the Liturgy 1963-1979*, Document #208, pp. 465-534.

credendi)."[80] Second, text as a witness to an unbroken tradition "shows us how the Holy Spirit endows the people of God with a marvelous fidelity in preserving the deposit of faith unchanged, even though prayers and rites differ so greatly" (Introduction #9). In both of these ideas, it would seem that the *General Instruction* is laboring under the reversal of the *lex orandi, lex credendi* principle and sees text as that which preserves through tradition a "deposit" of faith. There is implied here a chasm between "faith" (understood more as a body of truths to which we assent rather than as an assent of our being and as a turning toward the Sacred) and its expression, which is tantamount to saying that linguistic expression is separate from (and secondary to) faith experience.

Third, the liturgical text (the *General Instruction* is referring specifically to the *Roman Missal*) witnesses to an adaptation of text to modern conditions (Introduction #10-15). The *General Instruction* suggests a catechetical and pastoral perspective for this adaptation in order that the text present more clearly "the mystery that is part of the celebration itself" (Introduction #13). This language of the document carries an ambiguity about the status of a text. "Adaptation" by a "catechetical and pastoral perspective" seems to suggest that the language of a text is peripheral to the originary experience which gave rise to the language although the desire is to present the mystery more clearly. This suggests an awareness that there is definitely a relationship between mystery and the language used to express it.

Over and above these ideas of text emerging from the Introduction, we perceive that the *General Instruction* hints at a broad extension of the notion "text." Though there is a recognition that there are several parts to the Mass--the *General Instruction* specifically mentions the Liturgy of the Word, the Liturgy of the Eucharist, and the Introductory and Concluding rites--there is nonetheless a sense that there is a configuration toward a whole, the parts being connected in such a way that they "form but one single act of worship."[81] The *General Instruction* does not go so far as to seem to consider the whole as a text.

---

[80]GIRM, Introduction #2. See also Note 5, p. 4, above; the *General Instruction*'s use of the principle seems to be an example of a turn-around of the principle, where the belief determines the prayer.

[81]GIRM #8; see SC #48, 51, 56.

On the contrary, there is also a recognition of different "texts" within the one Eucharistic rite (#14-17). These "texts" include the various dialogues between presider and community and the acclamations (#14), the professions and intercessions (#16), and other "texts" in which the community shares (#17). These different "texts" require various tones of voice, depending on whether they are a reading, a prayer, an acclamation, an instruction, a song (#18). By relating various tonal modalities to diverse literary genre (#18), the *General Instruction* highlights that different "texts" and presentations carry different meanings and values.

Actions and postures are mentioned as not only as a sign of the unity of the worshipping community (#20-22), but also as expressing and fostering "the spiritual attitude of those taking part" (#20). Though not specifically referred to as "text," actions and postures are still seen as integral parts of the celebration intimately connected with its very spirit and purpose.[82] A recognition of different "texts" suggests that there may also be alternate ways the liturgical text could be enacted in the actual celebration. In general, it is seen as a dialogue, as communication.[83] As such, the various contexts of the text determine how it is to be spoken (#12, 13, 18) and in this, too, "the idiom of different languages and the genius of peoples" (#18) should be considered.

While no implication is intended here that the *General Instruction* in any way presents a text theory, the above remarks do indicate that serious attention is paid to the notion

---

[82]Paragraphs on movements and postures (#20-22) and one on silence (#23) conclude the second section, "Different Elements of the Mass," of Chapter II of the *General Instruction*. Other paragraphs include guidelines on reading and explaining Scripture (#9), prayers and other parts assigned to the presider (#10-13), other texts in which the community shares (#14-17), vocal expression of different texts (#18), and the importance of singing (#19). By implication it would seem that movements postures, and silence have a certain textuality about them since they are included in a section that deals with more common denotations of text. See C. VAGGAGINI, *Theological Dimensions of the Liturgy*, pp. 49-50.

[83]See GIRM #14; also, #9; also, the January 25, 1969 instruction *Comme le prévoit*, *Documents on the Liturgy 1963-1979*, pp. 284-291, #5.

of "text" because the work is more than simply a book of prayer and liturgical instructions. Text is seen as a bearer of faith and tradition, as varied, as including more than printed word, as calling for various tonal modalities, as communicative. In this the text has a sort of life of its own that cannot be ignored when ferreting out the life of the liturgical celebration, though the *General Instruction* has not addressed the question of the status of a text as text and the relationship of language and experience.

c. **Other Post-Vatican II Liturgical Documents**. References to text in other post-Vatican II liturgical documents add nothing essentially new to the above remarks, but they do nuance and specify them. We shall complete this survey with a brief consideration of these references.

A 1974 report of the Sacred Congregation for Divine Worship raises the problem of private persons creating and using their own liturgical texts.[84] Dangers of this practice focus on the purity and integrity of faith and the unity of the Church. The report, echoing the *General Instruction*, asks that the essential elements preserving the deposit of faith through tradition and the secondary elements rendering the text in an acceptably contemporary idiom be distinguished. The implication here seems to be that the content of liturgical texts is invariable, and all that remains is to translate that content into more palpable, contemporary expression. This attitude neglects the essential relationship between language and experience which we pointed out above.

The January 25, 1969, instruction *Comme le prévoit* addresses essential and secondary elements of a text, using the Roman prayers as a concrete example. The instruction says the *structure* of the Roman prayers can be retained. This includes the divine title, motive of petition, the petition itself, and the conclusion. Other elements which cannot be retained are the Latin oratorical movement or flow of style and the rhetorical

---

[84]Report *Sacra Congregatio* of Cardinal J.R. Knox, Prefect, to the September 27 to October 26, 1974 Synod of Bishops, Document #100, pp. 247-252 in *Documents on the Liturgy 1963-1979*. See parallel sentiments in a November 10, 1965 address of Pope Paul VI to translators of liturgical texts (*Documents on the Liturgy 1963-1979*, Document #113, pp. 272-274.

prose cadence.[85] Related to this is the whole question of literary genre.

Comme le prévoit asserts that "a liturgical text is a 'linguistic fact' designed for celebration" (#27). As a written form, it poses stylistic problems[86] and the task is to "discover the significant elements proper to the genre" (#27). Using literary genre in a broad sense as "spoken or rhetorical style" (#25), the literary genre "depends first of all on the nature of the ritual act signified in the words" (#26); that is, on whether the text is acclamation or supplication, proclamation or praying, reading or singing, spoken by one person or by many, whether it is prose or poetry or song (#26). In identifying literary genre with tonal modality, the intent is not only to indicate the manner of speaking or singing the text, but also to indicate that the very words used in the text[87] are bound up in the manner of the performance.[88]

3. Salient Points

Organizing the language of a liturgical celebration into a written liturgical text paves the way for an ongoing witness to "unchanged faith" which we call tradition. This remains available for examination and interpretation because it is a concrete form. These remarks raise a question about the status of a text in terms of static meaning or dynamic experience. The remarks on text in post-Vatican II documents also raise certain questions about written liturgical texts. What is the relationship of language and experience, and the written text and its actual celebration? What is essential in a written text and how might that be recovered? What is tied to a cultural ethos and must be changed to respect the inculturation process so important today? How does a written text embody actions, postures, attitudes that are fundamental to human expression?

---

[85]*Comme le prévoit* #28; see also #27 in *Documents on the Liturgy 1963-1979*, Document #123, pp. 282-291.

[86]The Instruction is directed to translators, which must be kept in mind as the context for its remarks.

[87]Here, the words chosen for translation. By extension and implication, the same principle would apply when composing new texts; that is, the words chosen must fit the tonal performance.

[88]See also GIRM #18.

These questions point to broad implications when we take seriously the textual moment. We seek a methodology that at least begins to address some of these questions.

C. Methodology

Since Vatican II the scope of liturgical studies has broadened in such a way that research areas of liturgical scholars have also broadened considerably.[89] Reflecting this burgeoning of scope, a significant amount of liturgical research has been pursued in the more specific area of language and liturgy, certainly enough to warrant the claim that it is an important aspect of the ongoing liturgical research initiated in the aftermath of Vatican II. Liturgical language has been addressed by scholars in relation to such diverse special factors as time, social groups, glossolalia, hope, mysticism, culture, ritual, peace, and justice.[90] Further, the previous questions precipitated by our reflections on text point to a number of significant issues we can raise with respect to text. In the three sections on salient points we have already given indicators

---

[89] A cursory perusal of the topic headings in a periodical index is informative. In the first six volumes of *Religious Index One: Periodicals* (1949-1964, Chicago: American Theological Library Association), only five topic headings are listed with respect to liturgy: liturgical movement, liturgical year, liturgies, liturgies--early Christian, and liturgy. One interesting exception to this is Volume 2 (1953-1954) which lists "liturgies--vernacular." After 1964, the year *Sacrosanctum Concilium* appeared, the topic headings are more numerous, varied, and much wider in scope. At this time we find such diverse headings under "liturgy" as history, theology, language, culture, reform, and the arts, liturgical movement, vestments, liturgical year, renewal, drama, dancing, terminology, experimental liturgies, architecture, liturgy of the hours, Jewish liturgies, and liturgical planning. Most interesting to note, and giving weight to the present work, is the fact that only two headings, liturgical language and liturgy and culture, appear in all volumes after 1966, the year the Council closed.

[90] See B.P. DAUENHAUER, "Some Aspects of Language and Time in Ritual Worship," *International Journal for the Philosophy of Religion* 6 (1975), 54-62; D. DAVIES, "Social Groups, Liturgy and Glossolalia," *The Churchman* 90 (1976), 193-205); J.M. DUFORT, "Le langage de l'esperance dans la prière liturgique," *Science et Esprit* 26 (1974), 233-250; J. FITZER, "Liturgy, Language and

as to what liturgical methodology must take into consideration in view of our questions. In this third part of the chapter we seek to more specifically address the methodological priorities that arise out of the broader perspective.

While liturgists have always been aware that different methods are important for a more comprehensive analysis of liturgical data,[91] by and large the focus has been on an historical method[92] with a special interest in early liturgical manuscripts. The benefits of this research have been immense, not least among them being a clarification of the fundamental structures of liturgical rites and the meaning those structures can deliver.[93] Yet, we can find in these very studies the limitations of historical research and its theological conceptualization. Historical method can do very little to

> endorse the addition to a rite of something new, to approve the revival of what had long been dormant, to frame proposals that would accommodate the traditional to new times and places and/or to advocate organic development of possibilities latent in the tradition, even experimenting

---

Mysticism," *Worship* 47 (1973), 66-79; A. KAVANAGH, "Cultural Diversity and Liturgical Language," *Una Sancta* 24 (1967), 69-71; E.T. LAWSON, "Ritual as Language," *Religion* 6 (1976), 123-139; E. MVENG, "Christ, liturgie et culture," *Bulletin de théologie africaine* 2 (1980), 247-255; L.P. TRUDINGER, "Onward Christian Peacemakers," *Frontier* 18 (1975-1976), 235-238; J.F. WHITE, "Justice and the Work of Liturgical Renewal," *Christianity and Crisis* 40 (1980), 173-177.

[91]See, for example, R. GUARDINI, "Über die systematische Methode in der Liturgiewissenschaft," *Jahrbuch für Liturgiewissenschaft* 1 (1921): 97-108; A. BAUMSTARK, *Comparative Liturgy*; A. HAÜSLING, "Die kritische Funktion der Liturgiewissenschaft," in *Liturgie und Gessellschaft*, ed. H.-B. Meyer (Innsbruck: Tyrolia, 1970), pp. 103-130.

[92]See A. SCHMEMANN, *Introduction to Liturgical Theology*, trans. A.E. Moorhouse (New York: St. Vladimir's Press, 1966), p. 17; M. COLLINS, "Liturgical Methodology and the Cultural Evolution of Worship in the United States," *Worship* 49 (1975), 86-87.

[93]See M. COLLINS, "Liturgical Methodology," 86; and A. SCHMEMANN, *Introduction to Liturgical Theology*, p. 18.

> with transforming liturgy, so that things as yet unknown might appear.[94]

Other limitations of the historical method include its inability to account for the relationship between verbal and nonverbal expression or discursive/nondiscursive uses of language[95] or to account for cultural differences and a preoccupation with human life and relationships that social sciences methods address.[96]

Another problem which faces the contemporary liturgical interpreter is that of meaning itself. As D. Power claims, there are three kinds of meaning implicated by liturgical celebration: that which derives from the ritual as text, from the contribution of the participants, and from the official Church interpretations.[97] This suggests that meaning is dynamic, not reached by any one source or approach but by taking into consideration a wide range of participants and sources. This also suggests that the code (language) of a text cannot deliver a full measure of its own meaning either, but encompasses extra-textual modalities that must be investigated.

We suggest that any one method that can address all these heuristic problems and possibilities does not presently exist, nor could we probably discover one. Closer to the truth is the fact that different methods address different exigencies and an interpretation approaching a comprehensive one would have to allow for a dialogue among these methods and their respective discoveries. Seeking a new method, then, would first of all involve identifying the particular set of questions or problems to be addressed.

We have already identified three major areas of our own concern in the sections above on salient points. These are respect for the relationship of language and experience and for the layers of symbolic meanings embedded in language use, the

---

[94]M. COLLINS, "Liturgical Methodology," 86-87.

[95]See Ibid., 90 and 94.

[96]See K. SEASOLTZ, "Anthropology and Liturgical Theology: Searching for a Compatible Methodology," in *Concilium* 112 (New York: Seabury Press, 1979), p. 5.

[97]See D. POWER, "People at Liturgy," in *Concilium* 170 (New York: The Seabury Press, 1983), pp. 9-11.

need to be cognizant of engagement aspects of a text, and the extra-textual indicators of language which push a hermeneut beyond a text. In actuality, all three of these indices show how a text through its linguistic structures points to the relationship of text and human cultural existence, whether the latter be defined as the originary event which gave rise to the language or to the actual lives of the participants presently occupied by the text. Most importantly, these indices refine the notion of "symbol" to include linguistic use.

In addition to these larger "life" issues, our attention is also directed by a search for an analytic that studies a text *qua* text. Our interest is to seek a methodology that uncovers the intelligibility structure of a text without sacrificing access to textual features that point to extra-linguistic implications. We concur with R. Taft that "structure outlives meaning."[98] We wager, then, that identifying the "deep structure" of a text gains access to a certain meaning, albeit not the whole of its meaning.

D. Summary

Certain claims which are warranted by liturgical scholars' growing recognition of the importance of language, text, and methodology have been made in this chapter. The contemporary realization of the broad scope of the linguistic problematic and greater awareness of the implications of these areas of liturgical research point to a step forward in liturgical studies. What is at stake in this? And what is the ensuing agenda?

At stake is a possible new avenue for approaching liturgy as a language of faith. To make this approach more accessible, an ensuing agenda calls for an approach which pares liturgy to its structural core. Using the Roman prayers as an example, one possibility is that the essential elements of liturgy can be discovered in structure. This indicates a methodology directed to structure where the importance of the text in all its parts and aspects including its extratextual, life-implicating dimensions is underscored.

Though speaking to the formation of the biblical canon, W. Brueggemann provides some insight into a liturgical agenda that recognizes the structural import of a text. Both the *process* of

---

[98]R. TAFT, "Structural Analysis of Liturgical Units," 315.

the formation of a text as well as the final *shape* of the text are significant.[99] Here the community's self-understanding and its legacy for the generations after them are discovered. Brueggemann shows that there is an interplay between tradition as stable, normative expression of the originary community's faith experience and fresh articulations of that tradition which are derived from the contemporary community's response to the tradition (pp. 4 and 6). He believes that "a method must be found to respect the judgment of the community" (p. 4) with respect to texts that are "normative and enduring, true and reliable" (p. 4) and "engaging the text in subtle ways as the live Word of God which can give vitality to the community" (p. 6). He sees this as essentially a hermeneutical enterprise (p. 6).

If we understand liturgy as a *language* of faith, then the door to hermeneutics opens since language is connotative as well as denotative, a fact which is particularly true when language is approached as symbol. But further, if *structure* is seen as an essential element of the text, then the hermeneutical task is extended to include not only the various layers of meaning of the symbol, but also underlying experience in which every text is rooted. In the case of liturgy, the task is to elucidate the meaning of symbols as well as point to the originary event to which the text is linked by tradition. Rather than simply a hermeneutics of symbols, a methodology showing promise for analysis of liturgical texts may be termed a *textual* hermeneutics. It takes into account both the normative tradition the text embodies as an originary event as well as a contemporary reading of that text.

One such textual hermeneutics exposing a methodology is that outlined by French philosopher Paul Ricoeur. The next chapter sets forth aspects of Ricoeur's textual hermeneutics to show that a fuller recovery of meaning is through text.

---

[99]See W. BRUEGGEMANN, *The Creative Word: Canon as a Model for Biblical Education* (Philadelphia: Fortress Press, 1982), p. 3.

CHAPTER TWO

THE RECOVERY OF MEANING

The recovery of meaning is essentially a hermeneutical process. And hermeneutics, as the art of interpretation, is certainly not a new enterprise. Each time anyone asks "What do *you* mean?" the interlocutors enter into a hermeneutical process, straightforward though it may be in a dialogical situation. But change the question to "What does *that* mean?" as asked no longer of a hearer to a speaker but of a reader to what is read, and the hermeneutical process is not so straightforward. This change from speaking-hearing to writing-reading is crucial because it radically affects the process of recovering meaning.

Paul Ricoeur is a contemporary French philosopher who has been sensitive to vicissitudes in the recovery of meaning, particularly when the object of interpretation is the unique writing he calls "text." It is not the purpose of this chapter to lay out Ricoeur's text theory per se, much less his philosophical journey. Others have done this already.[1] The work here begins from these syntheses. This chapter is concerned with

---

[1]For brief accounts of Ricoeur's movement in thought from the earlier philosophical anthropology centered in a phenomenology of the will to his present phenomenological hermeneutics, see P. RICOEUR, *The Rule of Metaphor: Multi-disciplinary Studies of the Creation of Meaning in Language*, trans. R. Czerny with K. McLaughlin and J. Costello, S.J. (Toronto: University of Toronto Press, 1977), Appendix, "From Existentialism to the Philosophy of Language," pp. 315-322. See also P. RICOEUR, *Hermeneutics and the Human Sciences: Essays on Language, Action and Interpretation*, ed. and trans. J.B. Thompson (Cambridge: Cambridge University Press, 1981), "Editor's Introduction," pp. 1-26 and "A Response by Paul Ricoeur," pp. 32-40. For a brief presentation of the development of Ricoeur's hermeneutical theory, see D. PELLAUER, "The Significance of the Text in Paul Ricoeur's Hermeneutical Theory," pp. 98-114 in *Studies in the Philosophy of Paul Ricoeur*, ed. C.E. Reagan (Athens: Ohio University Press, 1979). For an extensive presentation of Ricoeur's textual hermeneutics, see J.W. VAN DEN HENGEL, *The Home of Meaning: The Hermeneutics of the Subject of Paul Ricoeur* (Washington, D.C.: University Press of America, 1982). The latter work has a complete bibliography of Ricoeur's corpus to 1981.

why Ricoeur's hermeneutics is a *textual* hermeneutics. It lays out salient points of his textual hermeneutics in order to point to a methodological procedure outlined in the next chapter which promises rich rewards for uncovering the meaning of liturgical texts.

Ricoeur's textual hermeneutics is inviting for one seeking to uncover the meaning of a liturgical text precisely because the latter is a *text*. That a written text shapes liturgical celebrations can hardly be denied. Questions arise, however, in qualifying the exact relationship of liturgical text to celebration. On the one hand, is the liturgical text only *peripherally* related to its celebration as, for example, a ritual guide for the presider? Or, on the other hand, is the liturgical text *essentially* related to its celebration as, for example, a concretization of cumulative community celebrations with a wealth of stored meaning? Ricoeur's textual hermeneutics supports the second description of liturgical text as essentially related to its celebration since, for Ricoeur, text is a dynamic document of life embodying human action.

As might be expected, hermeneutics concedes no single approach to the recovery of meaning. Some approaches, structuralism and linguistic analysis for example, give access to meaning solely within the confines of language as a code system. While these approaches gain objectivity by focusing on language as an object of science, in Ricoeur's estimation they lose a dimension that extends beyond language. Without sacrificing some degree of objectivity in the hermeneutical process, Ricoeur's approach moves to salvage this other dimension in language.

For Ricoeur, language is not primarily a vehicle of communication (though it is also that). Language is primarily a showing, a disclosure.[2] Language communicates *something*, and to this extent language is a *derived* form.[3] The dimension of language beyond linguistic code which Ricoeur wishes to expose is "the *as such* (*als*) which adheres to the articulations of

---

[2]See P. RICOEUR, "The Task of Hermeneutics" in *Hermeneutics and the Human Sciences*, p. 58.

[3]See P. RICOEUR, "Phenomenology and Ontology" in *Main Trends in Philosophy*, ed. P. Ricoeur (New York: Holmes & Meier Publishers, Inc., 1979), p. 130.

experience."[4] With roots in a given, interpretation "is not something absolute, resulting from the existence of texts, but stems from the possibility of explicating in a number of ways our understanding of the relationship between our situation and our possibilities."[5] The hermeneutical process is a process of making the human mode of existence one's own.[6] As Ricoeur puts it,

> The very work of interpretation reveals a profound intention, that of overcoming distance and cultural differences and that of matching the reader to the text which has become foreign, thereby incorporating its meaning into the present comprehension [understanding] a man is able to have of himself.[7]

If interpretation is directed simply toward linguistic signs, e.g. as in structuralism, then meaning lies only within those signs; here, language is closed in upon itself because linguistic signs are defined in terms of the opposition of one sign to another within the language system. But for Ricoeur language must be a relationship of a subject to the real. With a subject as an active agent in the recovery of meaning, interpretation can lead to something new.

Ricoeur's textual hermeneutics goes beyond a theory of signs in which language is objectively closed in upon itself and opens "up the philosophy of language to the concerns of phenomenology regarding the human subject."[8] Yet we ought not consider these two approaches as mutually exclusive in Ricoeur's textual

---

[4]P. RICOEUR, "The Task of Hermeneutics" in *Hermeneutics and the Human Sciences*, p. 57.

[5]See P. RICOEUR, "Phenomenology and Ontology" in *Main Trends in Philosophy*, p. 130.

[6]Cf. J.W. VAN DEN HENGEL, *The Home of Meaning*, p. 189.

[7]P. RICOEUR, "Existence and Hermeneutics" in *The Conflict of Interpretations: Essays in Hermeneutics*, ed. D. Ihde (Evanston: Northwestern University Press, 1974), p. 4. Ricoeur's French term "*compréhension*" is usually translated "understanding" and this will be retained throughout this volume, except when in a direct quotation the translator employed "comprehension."

[8]J.W. VAN DEN HENGEL, *The Home of Meaning*, p. 22.

hermeneutics. Ricoeur respects the autonomy of the object by taking seriously the preoccupation of language philosophy with linguistic code. He respects the creativity of the subject by taking seriously phenomenology's preoccupation with the subject. Ricoeur's textual hermeneutics is a grafting[9] of hermeneutics onto phenomenology which bridges language philosophy's objectivity and phenomenology's subjectivity.

These varied approaches, one focusing on the objectivity of the code and the other focusing on language as derived from the subject's relation to what is, are not mutually exclusive for Ricoeur. He capitalizes on the positive gains of both approaches by being attentive to the various uses of language.

Language in itself is ambiguous; it can mean more than one thing.[10] Differing uses of language (as code, as discourse, as text, as written text) are more or less affected by this inherent ambiguity of language. When language is taken strictly as a linguistic code, ambiguity is relatively non-existent and we only need check the meaning of one sign as opposed to the others within the language system. Each time we look up the meaning of a word in a dictionary, we use language in this way. The procedure is more complex when language is a spoken event between interlocutors. Here too, however, ambiguity can be minimized through a "checking-up" process possible because of the shared context typical of a dialogical situation. The conversation's context limits the meaning of the discourse; when we as hearers are unsure of meaning, we simply need to question the speaker about her/his intent. When communication takes place in other

---

[9]See P. RICOEUR, "Existence and Hermeneutics" in *The Conflict of Interpretations*, 1974), pp. 3-24. In grafting hermeneutics onto phenomenology, Ricoeur passes from a specific to a general hermeneutics. Hermeneutics has traditionally been practiced within regions (for example, exegesis and psychoanalysis) and so specific rules of hermeneutics paralleled the rules and parameters of the discipline. Explanatory methods reigned. Deregionalization of hermeneutics can take place only when the explanatory moment is subordinated to an ontological moment in which understanding is a *way of existing* and a way of relating (see P. RICOEUR, "The Task of Hermeneutics" in *Hermeneutics and the Human Sciences*, pp. 43-53).

[10]This is why, for Ricoeur, hermeneutics has a privileged relation to language. See P. RICOEUR, "The Task of Hermeneutics" in *Hermeneutics and the Human Sciences*, p. 44.

than a dialogical situation, then the shared context is lost for the interpreter. Also lost is the possiblity for checking-up on an intended meaning. Now, the procedure for overcoming the ambiguity of language is maximized. A key circumstance for hermeneutics is the realization of discourse as written text where the context of the dialogical situation is no longer definitive. The ambiguity of the language of a text calls for an interpretation that cannot be clarified within a shared context with speaker or author. The autonomy of a written text from the author's intention as well as from the original audience and context suggests that the ambiguity of the language of a written text must be overcome within the text itself, not behind it in terms of recovering a dialogical event or the intention of an author. Meaning is recovered from a text in a different way from how meaning is disclosed in a shared dialogical situation.

The recovery of meaning relies on differing methods, depending on the use of language to which it is directed. Ricoeur is cognizant of different methods of recovering meaning for various uses of language. Since text is the paradigmatic object of interpretation according to Ricoeur, his own method of recovering meaning focuses on a textual use of language. The next four major parts of the chapter unfold different layers in the recovering of meaning by addressing the question, Wherein lies meaning? Beginning with (A) Language in general, the discussion delves deeper into uses of language encompassing fuller dimensions of meaning: (B) Discourse, (C) Text, and (D) Written Text.

A. Language

The simplest level for the recovery of meaning is that of words as oppositions of signs. As we indicated above, the distinct advantage of this level is the objectivity that can be gained from looking at language very broadly as a code system. Two considerations shape our remaining remarks on language. First, we briefly describe the basic tenets of structuralism in order to give an example of an objective approach to meaning as well as to show how even the very terms of the method already strain its limits. Second, we show how a consideration of linguistic code leads inevitably to a consideration of larger units built out of the code, explored here as the distinction between *langue* (language) and *parole* (discourse).

1. Structuralism

Structuralism brackets (sets aside, suspends) language as message for the sake of approaching language as a code, as an object of science. Certain theoretical postulates "that govern semiology in general and structural linguistics in particular"[11] determine structuralism to be a model for a method of interpretation:

(1) Language is to be treated as a synchronic system.

(2) This system may be treated as a finite set of discrete elements.

(3) The significance of the elements of this system depends on the oppositions between them and not on any element taken by itself.

(4) The system is closed. It does not refer beyond itself.[12]

This structural model gives an approach to language as an object of science that provides rules for how the discrete elements of the system may be combined to ensure univocal sense. An objectivity with respect to explanation can be achieved because the sense is the immanent content of the language code. Structuralism's contribution to clarification of the question of meaning is precisely the possibility of objectivity with respect to explanation.

But we must pay a price for this objectivity. Structuralism is limited in that it posits no relationship between language and reality, for in this structural model language "constitutes a world of its own."[13] Though language in itself may say something, it cannot say something *about something*. For Ricoeur, however, language is not a closed system but a mediation of reality. Meaning is not only lodged in words which form a closed

---

[11]P. RICOEUR, "Language as Discourse" in *Interpretation Theory: Discourse and the Surplus of Meaning* (Ft. Worth: The Texas Christian University Press, 1979), p. 4.

[12]D. PELLAUER, "The Significance of the Text" in *Studies in the Philosophy of Paul Ricoeur*, p. 102.

[13]P. RICOEUR, "Language as Discourse" in *Interpretation Theory*, p. 6.

system; meaning must be sought in larger entities than words. This leads Ricoeur to highlight the distinction between language and its uses, which we take up next.

2. *Langue* vs. *Parole*

Swiss linguist Ferdinand de Saussure in his *Cours de linguistique général* made an important distinction between *langue* (linguistic code) and *parole* (message). *Langue* is collective, set in time as contemporaneous elements, anonymous (not intended), and systematic and compulsory for a given linguistic community. As such it has an independent, universal quality about it with respect to its linguistic community. In this sense, language is always ideal. On the other hand, *parole* is individual, a temporal event, intentional, and arbitrary and contingent. *Parole* is directed toward communication, getting a message across. While *langue* implies linguistic unity, *parole* is concerned with how those linguistic units are combined in a larger act of speech or communication.

Ricoeur takes seriously the fact that meaning is richer than defining the signs and words which make up a linguistic code.[14] As we indicated above in the basic postulates of structuralism, the structuralist model involves a specific notion of time at the expense of historicity: synchrony takes precedence over diachrony.[15] But without a historical component, the recovery of the fullness of meaning is diminished. For Ricoeur, hermeneutics implies historicity (i.e., is diachronic) since "interpretation does not spring from nowhere; rather, one interprets in order to make explicit, to extend, and so to keep alive the tradition itself, inside which one always remains."[16] In reversing the structuralists' synchronic approach, the interpreter respects the

---

[14]de Saussure saw the sign as a word *par excellence* (see P. RICOEUR, "Metaphor and the Semantics of the Word" in *The Rule of Metaphor*, p. 103). Ricoeur, however, makes a distinction: the sign is wholly within the language system while the word correlates with an idea (see Ibid., p. 102).

[15]See P. RICOEUR, "Structure and Hermeneutics" in *The Conflict of Interpretations*, p. 33. "Synchrony" means a-temporal and ignores historical antecedents; "diachrony" implies change extending through time.

[16]Ibid., p. 27.

precedence of historicity over structure, and so "understanding is finding the genesis, the previous form, the sources, and the sense of the evolution."[17] Because of the inherent historicity of hermeneutics, there is a "surplus of meaning" in language which the structuralists can neither exhaust nor for which they can account. Ricoeur does not link the surplus of meaning to the polysemy of words, but rather to the polysemy of a larger unit, the sentence.

Even though the structural model may be applied beyond linguistics properly speaking in larger works such as myths, it can give no linear progression from linguistic sign to sentence. Its concern is only the association and dissociation of its constitutive parts.[18] Structuralism is limited in terms of the meaning it can recover. It cannot account for the dynamism that is captured by a sentence. The sentence "is not a larger or more complex word, it is a new entity."[19] The meaning of a sentence is not recoverable in the various components out of which it is composed. A study of the sentence is immediately concerned with the concept of sense in its recovery of meaning. For this reason Ricoeur favors the use of the term "discourse" over the term *parole* since the latter "expresses only the residual aspect of a science of *langue*."[20] "Discourse" points to the recovery of meaning as primary.

Discourse emphasizes "the synthetic structure of the sentence itself as distinct from any analytic combination of discreet entities."[21] Thus is introduced a creative element that

---

[17]Ibid., p. 31.

[18]See P. RICOUER, "Language as Discourse" in *Interpretation Theory*, pp. 4-8.

[19]Ibid., p. 7. See also P. RICOEUR, "Metaphor and the Semantics of Discourse" in *The Rule of Metaphor*, p. 67.

[20]P. RICOEUR, "Language as Discourse" in *Interpretation Theory*, p. 4. Translations for "*parole*" include "word," "utterance," "remark."

[21]Ibid. "Discourse" legitimates "the distinction between semiotics and semantics as the two sciences which correspond to the two kinds of units characteristic of language, the sign [the basic unit of linguistics] and the sentence [the basic unit of discourse]" (Ibid.). Semiotics is concerned with achieving

is lacking in structuralism's presupposition that larger units are structurally analogous to the smaller units out of which they have been constructed. The sentence is determined by the predicative characteristic of the verb. The words of a sentence can be combined in endless variations and creativity; the key to this is the predicate, a universal which can be applied to a limitless number of nouns.[22] An analytic of the sign is based on the oppositions of meanings within the closed linguistic system. However, the meaning of a sentence cannot be determined by combining the meanings of the words which make it up. While a sentence is a combination of words, it is more than just the sum of the oppositions of meanings of a closed language system. A sentence is more than just the sum of its parts because its predicate introduces a dynamic that cannot be accounted for within a closed system of language.

The recovery of meaning begins to break open in the shift from word to sentence as basic unit. As a new entity, the sentence requires a different analytic methodology from the sign. A methodology that serves to analyze words alone cannot serve to analyze sentences because sentences do not form a closed system; they rather "constitute a class of distinctive units."[23] Ricoeur's hermeneutical enterprise is directed toward combinations of sentences. The first such combination upon which we reflect in the recovery of meaning is discourse itself.

B. Discourse

The shift in focus from word to sentence is crucial for the process of the recovery of meaning. This shift implies that recovering meaning from a system of signs capitalizes on only one aspect of language. In actuality, language does not begin with signs. We do not begin saying words by consulting a dictionary. We begin to use language because we have something to say, something to communicate. In other words, language begins with its use: "It is in discourse, realized in sentences, that

---

univocal meanings for signs; semantics is concerned with uncovering an excess of meaning in the sentence.

[22]See below, p. 68.

[23]P. RICOEUR, "Metaphor and the Semantics of Discourse" in *The Rule of Metaphor*, p. 67.

language is formed and takes shape. There language begins."[24] The recovery of meaning must consider the dynamics of discourse in addition to gleaning the objective fruits of an analysis of linguistic signs.

Ricoeur rests his hermeneutical method on certain operative dialectics.[25] Three sections follow, which probe key dialectics. The first section addresses the dialectic of event and meaning in which meaning emerges as a recoverable residue of the passing situation of the event and is identified as the "message" of the communication act. Since this meaning can be identified and re-identified, the dialectics of the second section demonstrate that meaning is dynamic. The third section shows how meaning can also be extralinguistic; it operates in a dialectic of sense and reference.

1. Event and Meaning

So long as language remains within a code or closed system, it is only virtual. Language is actualized when it is used in discourse. Language takes on a temporal dimension in use, characterizing it as event.[26] Though singular, the event is nonetheless actual in a speaking-hearing relationship between interlocutors.

---

[24]Ibid., p. 69. Ricoeur is quoting E. Benveniste's *Problems in General Linguistics*, trans. M.E. Meek (Coral Gables, Florida: University of Miami Press, 1971), p. 111.

[25]Cf. P. RICOEUR, "Metaphor and the Semantics of Discourse" in *The Rule of Metaphor*, p. 69. According to Ricoeur, "dialectic" means relative moments of concrete polarity between two abstract poles (cf. P. RICOEUR, "Language as Discourse" in *Interpretation Theory*, p. 8). Both abstract poles are operative in any given dialectical moment; neither pole is obliterated by the force of the other, but the concrete polarity need not be the same in various dialectical moments involving the same abstract poles.

[26]See P. RICOEUR, "Language as Discourse" in *Interpretation Theory*, p. 9; also, P. RICOEUR, "The Hermeneutical Function of Distanciation" in *Hermeneutics and the Human Sciences*, p. 133 and "Metaphor and the Semantics of Discourse" in *The Rule of Metaphor*, p. 70.

This speaking-hearing pair "constitutes language as communication."[27] An event is "the temporal phenomenon of exchange, the establishment of a dialogue which can be started, continued or interrupted."[28] An event consists of someone speaking something to someone else and in this it is relational. Event links discourse first of all to a speaker and, therefore, discourse is self-referential. Event also links discourse to the interlocutor to whom the discourse is addressed. Intersubjectivity is constitutive of the event pole of discourse.

Event cannot describe the fullness of discourse precisely because it is an "instance of discourse," fleeting and vanishing.[29] There is as well something about the event of discourse that can "be identified and reidentified as the same so that we may say it again or in other words."[30] Ricoeur identifies this as "meaning," which permits "repeatability of an event."[31] It is not the event but the "meaning which endures."[32] While the event is passing, there is a residue (meaning) which survives that passing event: "the suppressing and the surpassing of the event in the meaning is characteristic of discourse itself."[33] Repeatability is constitutive of the meaning pole of discourse.

The repeatability of meaning ensures that it objectively endures. At the same time, intersubjectivity remains as a

---

[27]P. RICOEUR, "Language as Discourse" in *Interpretation Theory*, p. 14.

[28]P. RICOEUR, "The Hermeneutical Function of Distanciation" in *Hermeneutics and the Human Sciences*, pp. 133-134.

[29]See P. RICOEUR, "Metaphor and the Semantics of Discourse" in *The Rule of Metaphor*, p. 70.

[30]P. RICOEUR, "Language as Discourse" in *Interpretation Theory*, p. 9.

[31]P. RICOEUR, "Metaphor and the Semantics of Discourse" in *The Rule of Metaphor*, p. 70.

[32]P. RICOEUR, "The Hermeneutical Function of Distanciation" in *Hermeneutics and the Human Sciences*, p. 134.

[33]See P. RICOEUR, "Language as Discourse" in *Interpretation Theory*, p. 12.

dynamic within meaning with the result that the event is never totally eclipsed in the recovery of meaning. Ricoeur calls the interplay of subjectivity and objectivity in meaning the noetic and noematic poles, respectively. For Ricoeur, meaning is both noetic and noematic. Meaning is noetic because it is linked to what is intended in terms of the self-reference of discourse. This is so because "the inner structure of the sentence refers back to its speaker through grammatical procedures, which linguists call 'shifters.'"[34] For example, the pronoun "I" has no objective meaning by itself. The function of "I" in a sentence "is to refer the whole sentence to the subject of the speech event."[35] "I" has a new meaning each time it appears in a sentence. Verb tenses are also shifters in that they refer to the present tense of the speech event and its speaker. Adverbs of time and space and demonstratives perform the same function. It is not difficult for us to see how the event side of the speech act is emphasized in the noetic aspect of reference. On the other side, meaning is noematic because it refers to something. Ricoeur locates reference in the sentence itself, since sentences are about *something*; they are propositional.

The noematic side of the balance keeps the self-reference of discourse from being reduced to mere psychological intention. The noetic side of the balance keeps the propositional side of discourse from being merely virtual rather than originating from an actual event. In either case, the very grammar of the sentence shows the fullness of meaning that can be recovered. Noetic meaning retains an interlocutionary, communicative aspect recovered with the aid of shifters. Noematic meaning retains an enduring aspect recovered through the propositional content of the sentence. Thus the hearer enters into a kind of "dialogue" with the speaker through the grammar of the sentence. The adage of phenomenology "meaning lies in its use" is more richly significant in terms of this dialogue, testifying to more happening in discourse than what can be uncovered on a purely propositional level. The next section shows how the very grammar of the language captures the dynamic of discourse.

2. Dynamic of Meaning

Since repeatability allows meaning to endure, we might conjecture that meaning is static because, after all, meaning

---

[34] Ibid.

[35] Ibid.

remains the same, it endures. Yet, we propose that meaning is dynamic. This seeming contradiction is resolved when we consider the creativity and force of language use. These are addressed in the next two paragraphs.

a. Identification and Predication. The most obvious place for us to turn for the recovery of meaning is in the basic unit of discourse, the sentence itself. Since sentences purport to convey *something*, they are propositional. Two functions constitute propositions: the identifying and predicative functions. These two functions parallel but extend the entities of noun (subject) and verb (predicate) which make up the sentence.

The identifying function aims at particulars; the "subject [of the sentence] is the bearer of singular identification."[36] As such, Ricoeur adopts the position that the identifying function involves the question of existence.[37] As a linguistic sign, the noun points to something beyond itself otherwise it could not be a sign. But we say more: the identifying function as a sign must point to something that exists. Whether "something that exists" has a previous actual existence (for example, the man Jesus), is something actually present to the interlocutors in the particular instance of discourse (for example, bread), or is even something existing only in the imaginations of the interlocutors (for example, the unification of Christians) makes no difference. Certain grammatical devices such as proper names, pronouns, demonstratives, and definite descriptions[38] help make clear the "existence" to which the discourse refers. Our point is the identifying function enables interlocutors to recognize the subject to whom or to which the communication refers.

The predicative function aims at universals since the verb ascribes a quality, class, action, or relation to *any* logical

---

[36] Ibid., p. 10.

[37] Cf. P. RICOEUR, "Language and Ontology" in *Main Trends in Philosophy*, p. 125.

[38] See P. RICOEUR, "Language as Discourse" in *Interpretation Theory*, p. 10.

subject.[39] The predicate, as a classifying function, "can always be treated as a 'universal' feature of the subject."[40] With the predicative function we break out of the "signifier-signified" relationship constitutive of signs and introduce a unique, *creative* element. At the propositional level, meaning is not static but it is a dynamic relation between an existing, singular subject and a universal predicative function creatively ascribed to it.

This relationship between identification and predication already indicates that meaning cannot be totally captured merely at the propositional level. The dynamism and creativity introduced by the predicative function open up deeper dimensions of meaning. One such dimension is that the "saying" of a proposition also involves the *force* of what the speaker *does* in the saying. The next paragraph focuses on the dynamism characteristic of meaning which implicates human action, folding back on the intersubjectivity of the event pole of meaning.

b. Performativity. A dynamism of meaning is indicated by certain linguistic clues pointing to human action incorporated at a semantic level. Ricoeur draws on the proponents of speech-act theory in distributing meaning over three distinct but interrelated levels: the locutionary, illocutionary, and perlocutionary.[41] These are "performative" predicates because they imply an agent *performing* an *act*. The recovery of meaning in discourse includes examining the semantic clues to action.

The locutionary act (the act of saying something) is exteriorized at the propositional level. This is the level where the identifying and predicative functions are combined, as we discussed above. But the saying of a proposition also involves what the speaker *does* in the saying. This is the illocutionary

---

[39]See P. RICOEUR, "Metaphor and the Semantics of Discourse" in *The Rule of Metaphor*, p. 71.

[40]P. RICOEUR, "Language as Discourse" in *Interpretation Theory*, p. 12.

[41]In "Metaphor and the Semantics of Discourse" in *The Rule of Metaphor* (pp. 72-73), Ricoeur only discusses locution and illocution since perlocution "is not relevant in the context of the present discussion" (Ibid.). However, for our purposes, the perlocutionary level *is* relevant, and so it is included here.

level.[42] For example, if someone says "I promise to do such and such," the utterance is much more than a declarative statement. The latter is measured by "true" or "false." This is not the case for illocutionary utterances where the speaker binds her/himself to some action. We can speak of fulfilling or not fulfilling a promise, but not of the truth or falsity of a promise. Grammatical paradigms such as indicative or subjunctive moods as well as gestures and gesticulations indicate discourse with illocutionary force.[43] Moreover, in addition to saying something with force, effects are also produced; this is the perlocutionary level.[44] This level is difficult to detect in grammatical inscriptions but we can identify it through, for example, certain verb forms such as the imperative. For example, "I command you to do such and such" not only implies an attitude on the part of the speaker ("you" is to do such and such), but also that the force of the command actually moves the hearer to perform the action.

These three levels identify the full force of a speech act. The phrase "speech *act*" is a felicitous one. More than just propositional content, discourse is the performing of an action in its very saying. Thus, by the meaning of discourse it is not enough to understand merely the propositional content of the utterance, but also the illocutionary force and the perlocutionary effects. The force of discourse which is the human act points to discourse as really more than simple inscription. Discourse also points to extralinguistic reality. Meaning, in terms of illocutionary force and perlocutionary

---

[42]For J.L. Austin, in addition to saying something, a proposition (utterance) also carries *force*: it is the performance of an action in the very saying. See J.L. AUSTIN, *How to Do Things With Words*, The William James Lectures Delivered at Harvard University in 1955 (Oxford: At the Clarendon Press, 1963), p. 1.

[43]See P. RICOEUR, "The Hermeneutical Function of Distanciation" in *Hermeneutics and the Human Sciences*, p. 135. Austin puts it thus: "questions and exclamations, and sentences expressing commands or wishes or concessions" (J.L. AUSTIN, *How to Do Things With Words*, p. 1).

[44]Austin determines that an utterance can also "produce certain consequential effects upon the feelings, thoughts, or actions of the audience, or of the speaker, or of other persons" (J.L. AUSTIN, *How to Do Things With Words*, p. 101).

effects, now has a fuller extension than linguistic content. The next section deals with the relationship between linguistic content and extralinguistic reality; Ricoeur explicates this by the sense-reference dialectic.

3. Sense and Reference

For Ricoeur, meaning is essentially defined as a dialectic of sense and reference. In this dialectic the basic difference between language and the uses of language is most striking. Only in use (for example, as discourse) "can what is said be distinguished from that of which one speaks."[45] The sense of meaning is the "what is said." It can be linguistically identified as the internal structure or organization of discourse.[46] Sense is an ideal meaning wholly immanent to the discourse.

Language does not refer to anything outside the linguistic system: "there is no reference problem in language: signs refer to other signs *within* the same system."[47] However, when we go beyond the linguistic system to linguistic use, then "language passes outside itself; reference is the mark of the self-transcendence of language." Only the use of language as an organized whole reveals the "about which," the reference.

The event of discourse witnesses to its actuality as well as to the immediacy of the situation of discourse. The event of discourse is an experience of being in the world which is the condition for its expression in language: "it is because there is first something to say, because we have an experience to bring to language, that conversely, language is not only directed towards ideal meanings [the sense] but also refers to what is."[48] Reference relates language to the world. True, the subject as bearer of the identification function does involve the question of existence because a subject is a specific object which must

---

[45]See P. RICOEUR, "Metaphor and the Semantics of Discourse" in *The Rule of Metaphor*, p. 74.

[46]P. RICOEUR, "Introduction" in *The Rule of Metaphor*, p. 6.

[47]P. RICOEUR, "Metaphor and the Semantics of Discourse" in *The Rule of Metaphor*, p. 74; italics Ricoeur's.

[48]Ibid.

have existence in order to be identified. However, the subject's realization of existence in language remains "a questionable leap beyond language"[49] because the subject in itself is merely a linguistic unit. Language is rescued from the suspicion about its relationship to existence when reference is considered.

Ricoeur identifies reference as the "world" of discourse, that "about which" and "before which" the discourse speaks. While analysis of the structure of discourse (its sense) uncovers one level of meaning, deeper layers of meaning are also available in terms of the world of discourse. Reference is uncovered in the depth-meaning of language in use and it points to extralinguistic reality. The reference of meaning is that logically prior existence in which the speaker first participates, then articulates, then participates again in a new way. This adds an extralinguistic dimension to meaning which relates the "what is said" to the "real." While something of the reference of meaning can be extracted from the manifest structure of the discourse itself, something more is needed to actually expose this reference. Ricoeur shows the progression from language to reality in the interaction of various modes of discourse. In turn, this interaction demands a return to the subject.[50] We cover these two interrelated thoughts in the next two paragraphs.

a. **From Language to Reality**. An analytical approach resting on semantics "can only allege the relation of language to reality but cannot *think* this relation as such."[51] A different mode of discourse is necessary if we are able to *think* the relation of language to reality. This mode is speculative discourse. It is not a linguistic, but a philosophical undertaking. Ricoeur's basic presupposition is that there is "a collective unity of modes of discourse as modes of use, such as poetic discourse, scientific discourse, religious discourse, and

---

[49]P. RICOEUR, "Language as Discourse" in *Interpretation Theory*, p. 21. This "experience of being in the world" is explained as "participation" in Chapter Three below, pp. 77-80.

[50]Ibid.

[51]Here, "discourse" is used in an equivocal sense of a particular manner for formally discussing a topic and "subject" is used in the phenomenological sense of an intuitively conscious self rather than the grammatical sense of a part of speech.

so on."[52] This unity allows for diverse applications of a select analytic. But within this unity of modes of use, there is in addition a radical *discontinuity* that assures the autonomy of one mode of discourse from another. The discontinuity provides the key in going from language to reality:

> It is only on the basis of this difference in discourse, established by the philosophical act as such, that we can elaborate the modalities of interaction, or more precisely, of interanimation between modes of discourse required for the task of making explicit the ontology that underlies our investigation.[53]

This discontinuity allows for an innovative element to enter into language.

Ricoeur illustrates the discontinuity by drawing on a specific example of poetic discourse, the metaphor. A metaphor has a semantic "twist" about it that results in two interpretations: a literal interpretation that takes the words at face value, and a metaphorical interpretation that results from the innovation produced by the statement as a whole. For Ricoeur, the gain in meaning is not a *conceptual* gain because it is a reading only between two conflicting interpretations. Rather, "the semantic shock produces a conceptual *need*."[54] In

---

[52]P. RICOEUR, "Metaphor and Philosophical Discourse" in *The Rule of Metaphor*, p. 303.

[53]Ibid., p. 257.

[54]Ibid., p. 258. Ricoeur proceeds by first arguing for the *discontinuity* among the modes of discourse. Drawing specifically on a comparison of poetic and speculative discourses, he seeks to refute three ways that poetic discourse (which Ricoeur specifies as metaphor in his discussions on this point) and speculative discourse are bound together: by Aristotle's doctrine of the analogical unity of the multiple meanings of being, by the onto-theology of the Thomists, and by the problematic of the dead metaphor which places metaphor *outside* metaphysics. To outline Ricoeur's arguments in even the sketchiest of forms would take us too far afield; for these discussions, see Ibid., pp. 259-272, 272-280, and 280-295, respectively. At least noting his refutations shows the "need to abandon the naive thesis that the semantics of metaphorical utterance contains ready-made an immediate ontology, which philosophy would then have only to

saying something *is like* something else, the predicative assimilation is not that of identity but implies both sameness and difference. The gain in meaning of a metaphor is caught in a conflict of this sameness and difference. This describes a "split" sense which results in a "split" reference. To lodge the split sense of a metaphorical statement within the copula "is" says that the Being of the split reference is both being and not being. Thus, "the dynamism of meaning allowed access to the dynamic vision of reality which is the implicit ontology of the metaphorical utterance."[55] The movement from language to reality occurs in the response to the need for conceptualization demanded by the structure of meaning which determines the metaphorical utterance. It is necessary to pursue further this structure of meaning.

Ricoeur asserts that a dynamism of meaning occurs in the dialectic of sense and reference. In the case of poetic discourse, Ricoeur identifies meaning in terms of a "split" sense and reference. As we saw above in the section on dynamism of meaning, sense is determined by the interaction of the identification and predicative functions. While the identification function in its signifying aims at singular identification, the predicative function is a universalizing function. So the dynamism of meaning is relegated to the crossing of two functions, the predicative (universalizing) and the identification (signifying). This opens up two fields of reference with two fields of meaning. The first field of meaning relates to a field of reference which embodies those entities to which the predicate, in its established meaning, can be applied. This is tantamount to the literal interpretation or constituted meaning. The second field of meaning relates to a field of reference which embodies those entities for which there is no direct characterization, hence no constituted meaning. The universalizing function of the predicate demonstrates that this second field of meaning is hidden and must be made apparent.[56]

---

elicit and to formulate" (Ibid., p. 295). While arguing for a radical discontinuity among the modes of discourse, Ricoeur's presupposition must be recalled: that through discourses' *modes of use* they share a collective unity, the second pole of the interaction.

[55]Ibid., p. 296; italics added.

[56]Ibid., p. 297.

It is this duality of referential fields that "explains how two levels of meaning are linked together"[57] in poetic discourse.

Every metaphorical utterance has an "ontological vehemence"[58] set in motion by the second referential field which is not constituted but is an unknown. This unknown cannot be reached by any explanation based on perception or images; it requires the resources of a conceptual field. These resources "belong to the mind itself, ... are the mind itself reflecting upon itself."[59] At this point, Ricoeur can define "speculative discourse" as the "discourse that establishes the primary notions, the principles, that articulate primordially the space of the concept."[60] The "speculative is the condition of the possibility of the conceptual. It expresses the systematic character of the conceptual in a second-order discourse."[61]

Interpretation guarantees that speculative discourse does not preclude poetic discourse. This, because interpretation itself is a composite discourse that straddles the metaphorical and the speculative. On the one hand, "interpretation seeks the clarity of the concept; on the other, it hopes to preserve the dynamism of meaning that the concept holds and pins down."[62] While speculative discourse shows how language reaches reality, poetic discourse preserves the surplus of meaning inherent in the dynamism of discourse.

Language brings experience to its articulation in discourse. In this, language begins in reality and mediates reality, yet requires interpretation. For Ricoeur, the interpretation of experience itself is dialectical. The poles of the dialectic are cognition and the object of cognition: conception turns outward toward an object; consciousness returns the object to the self.[63] In the last analysis, then, the movement from language to reality only happens through a return to the self as subject.

b. Return to the Subject. Ricoeur's thesis is that language is the "being-said" of reality. Language designates both itself and its other. Its reflective capacity "allows

---

57 Ibid., p. 299.

58 Ibid.

59 Ibid.

60 Ibid., p. 296.

61 Ibid., p. 300.

62 Ibid.

63 Ibid., p. 303.

language to know that it is installed in being."[64] To put it another way, "the *I am* is more fundamental that the *I speak*."[65] Language is clearly secondary. With a return to the subject, the reign of objects is shattered in favor of a "primordial belonging to a world which we inhabit, that is to say, which at once precedes us and receives the imprint of our works."[66] For Ricoeur, "first there is being-in-the-world, then understanding, then interpreting, then saying."[67]

Ricoeur notes that "something must be for something to be said."[68] While the former implicates an object or experience, the latter implicates a subject. Only a subject can speak. Further, while it is theoretically conceivable to have language without a subject, it is impossible to have discourse without a subject.[69] In effect, Ricoeur's insistence on a return to the subject allows for the dialectic of discourses whereby poetic discourse gives rise to speculative discourse in a moment of self-understanding.

---

[64]See P. RICOEUR, "Le 'lieu' de la dialectic" in *Dialectics/Dialectiques*, International Institute of Philosophy, ed. C. Perelman (The Hague: Nijhoff, 1973), pp. 105-106.

[65]P. RICOEUR, "Metaphor and Philosophical Discourse" in *The Rule of Metaphor*, p. 304.

[66]P. RICOEUR, "The Question of the Subject: The Challenge of Semiology" in *The Conflict of Interpretations*, p. 265.

[67]P. RICOEUR, "Metaphor and Philosophical Discourse" in *The Rule of Metaphor*, p. 306. Ricoeur's priority of experience over language opposes the presupposition of linguistic analysis that experience is not prior to language but experience itself is linguistic. Even thought, which may not be externalized in concretizations such as sounds or jottings, remains an interiorization of language. Indeed, "linguistic form is the condition of the possibility of thought" (L. DEWART, *Religion, Language and Truth* [New York: Herder and Herder, 1970], p. 44).

[68]P. RICOEUR, "The Question of the Subject" in *The Conflict of Interpretations*, p. 266.

[69]P. RICOEUR, "Metaphor and Philosophical Discourse" in *The Rule of Metaphor*, p. 304.

For Ricoeur, there are three stages of understanding that stake out the movement which advances from *living in* a surplus of meaning toward thought that *thinks from* a surplus of meaning.[70] The first stage of understanding is a matter of connecting the language of poetic discourse within its total domain, within a system. This understanding involves uncovering the multiple layers of meaning within the language, understanding one meaning by another, by a ritual or myth, or by unifying several levels of experience. This stage leads to questions which characterize the second stage of understanding, such as, Do I myself believe that? What do I personally make of these meanings?[71]

At the second stage, we enter into a relationship with language characterized by a *living in* it. Calling for a critical stance that requires interpretation, this stage overcomes the forgetfulness of being because it posits the fullness of being. These first two stages of understanding derive from poetic discourse. The semantic aim is a living in language which is a grasping of the fullness of meaning. If we remain at the first stage of understanding, we can never grasp the fullness of being. If we remain at the second stage of understanding, we can never enter into a dialectic of poetic and speculative discourses. It is only at the third stage of understanding that a properly philosophical stage is reached.[72]

The third stage of understanding is a reflective stage characterized by thought *starting from* language. Through reflection, this stage permits a positing of self "within all the density of its works."[73] At this final stage, all understanding

---

[70]As belonging to the semiological order, language as a system needs no subject which raises language to the *semantic* order; see P. RICOEUR, "The Question of the Subject" in *The Conflict of Interpretations*, p. 260.

[71]See P. RICOEUR, "The Hermeneutics of Symbols and Philosophical Reflection: I" in *The Conflict of Interpretations*, p. 297. Here, Ricoeur's development is within the context of symbol, which has a surplus of meaning similar to a metaphor, discussed above.

[72]See Ibid., pp. 297-298.

[73]P. RICOEUR, "The Hermeneutics of Symbols and Philosophical Reflection: II" in *The Conflict of Interpretations*, p. 328.

is self-understanding because of the relationship of self to works. The relationship of language to reality is finally made explicit in terms of the self-understanding which is a task: "that of equating my concrete experience with the affirmation: *I am.*"[74] In other words, self-understanding is the realization of a new "I am." Ultimately, the relationship of language and reality demands a reflective process which views human action beyond a linguistic level. Now, human action is viewed as "a good referent"[75] for discourse as well as a way of living that results from discourse.

The recovery of the fullness of meaning is only possible when the richness of discourse is plumbed. It is largely the grammar of the sentence that carries the freight of meaning. Yet, our operative concept has been "discourse." Composed of sentences, discourse necessarily has an inherent logical flow about it if the communicative act is to make any sense at all to the interlocutors. However, there is another kind of discourse that has a more purposeful structure about it suggesting that the recovery of meaning through that structure is even more fruitful. With the notion of text, another dimension is added to the recovery of meaning: the importance of discourse configured as a whole.[76]

C. Text

For Ricoeur, a text has an intended configuration that is lacking in discourse. It is true, in a discourse such as a conversation there is a logical flow because most conversations are not "streams of consciousness." But in spite of a logical

---

[74]Ibid., p. 329; italics Ricoeur's.

[75]P. RICOEUR, "Explanation and Understanding: On Some Remarkable Connections Among the Theory of the Text, Theory of Action, and Theory of History" in *The Philosophy of Paul Ricoeur: An Anthology of His Work*, ed. C.E. Reagan and D. Stewart (Boston: Beacon Press, 1978), p. 160.

[76]J.B. Thompson's critique of Ricoeur's use of reference is more favorable to the notion of text: "The core of Ricoeur's contribution to the problem of reference is to be found at the level of text" (J.B. THOMPSON, *Critical Hermeneutics: A Study in the Thought of Paul Ricoeur and Jürgen Habermas* [Cambridge: Cambridge University Press, 1981], p. 192).

flow, the shaping of a conversation is usually not predetermined. A conversation unfolds according to the give-and-take of the interlocutors.

The purposeful creation of a text implies the purposeful creation of meaning.[77] With the advent of text, the recovery of meaning must necessarily take into consideration how the text is structured. Because it is a structured whole, any analysis of texts must proceed from a consideration of the whole.

Ricoeur uses the "term 'work' to describe the closed sequence of discourse which can be considered as a text."[78] He implies by this that the creation of a text demands effort; the *process* by which a text comes into existence is so important as to actually precipitate the components by which a text is identified and through which meaning can be determined. Meaning, then, is radically affected by these components; they are three: composition, literary genre, and style.

1. Composition

A text does not just happen, but a true text is a production, a "form applied to some matter in order to shape it."[79] Through the work of production, text is integral: "A text is more than a linear succession of sentences. It is a

---

[77]The word "text" conjures up the notion of "writing" for most people: newspapers, magazines, term papers, are "texts." Ricoeur, however, does not necessarily limit the notion of text to written text. Thus ballads, narrative poems, myths are all texts because they have the characteristic of configured structure, even though all derive basically from oral traditions. The special case of the written text is examined in the next section. For a broad overview of the notion of text in Ricoeur's earlier as well as later writings, see D. PELLAUER, "The Significance of the Text" in *Studies in the Philosophy of Paul Ricoeur*, pp. 108-109,

[78]P. RICOEUR, "Metaphor and the Problem of Hermeneutics" in *Hermeneutics and the Human Sciences*, p. 166.

[79]P. RICOEUR, "Speaking and Writing" in *Interpretation Theory*, p. 32.

cumulative, holistic process."[80] Between a "once upon a time" and a "they lived happily ever after" there is an intentional organization which characterizes a particular text and requires effort to produce as a *structured* work. In other words, text is *composed*. It is not a haphazard combining of propositions, but it "is a particular sequence of sentences which in their configuration form a totality that is irreducible to the individual sentences."[81]

The configured nature of a text suggests it does not arise out of thin air, nor does it lead to some nether land. As Ricoeur explains, "What is at stake, therefore, is the concrete process by which the textual configuration mediates between the prefiguration of the practical field and its refiguration through the reception of the work."[82] Text is a mediator between the human living which roots the production of the text and the motivation to action (praxis) which dialoguing with a text precipitates in the recipient.[83] From its inception to conclusion, therefore, a text is rooted in human action. No wonder Ricoeur insists that text formation is a *process*. It is not an arbitrary process, however; the configuring of sentences to form a text is accomplished according to certain rules, pointing us to the second component of a text.

2. Literary Genre

The composition of a text follows rules of linguistic codification which make the text a particular kind of configuration, identified as a *literary genre*. Literary genres are the generative devices which determine that text is a

---

[80]P. RICOEUR, "The Model of the Text" in *Hermeneutics and the Human Sciences*, p. 212. See also P. RICOEUR, "Metaphor and Reference" in *The Rule of Metaphor*, p. 219.

[81]J.W. VAN DEN HENGEL, *The Home of Meaning*, p. 41.

[82]P. RICOEUR, *Time and Narrative*, Volume 1, trans. K. McLaughlin and D. Pellauer (Chicago: University of Chicago Press, 1984), p. 53.

[83]This insight is so important as to actually characterize Ricoeur's method of textual hermeneutics, discussed in Chapter Three below.

narrative or poem (or whatever).[84] They are derived from examining existing literary works in a comparative procedure which explicates the rules involved for each specific genre. Literary genres belong to the general domain of tools available for generating literary works. Genres are not limited to specific fields (such as what we usually think of as "literature") but cut across all fields that employ texts. For example, narrative as a genre is found in a literary work such as a novel, but it may also be found in other diverse works such as biography, historical reporting, scientific field study reports, and scriptural and liturgical texts.

Without literary genres serving as generative devices, new entities larger than the sentence lasting longer than an instance of discourse could not be produced. Because it is a generative device, the choice of which literary genre to draw upon enters into the intended meaning of the text. Interpreting the meaning of a text necessarily involves addressing the choice and use of the literary genre which generated the text. Yet, this is still not all that enters into the question of recovering meaning in a text. Two individuals might begin with the same topic using the same literary genre in generating two texts, but those texts may end up very different. A good example of this is the three synoptic Gospels; all three use the gospel genre, all three address the life, death, and resurrection of the same historical Jesus, yet all three Gospels are very different. Another good example is liturgical texts where the celebration of a local worshipping community makes *their* celebration different from all others. In addition to composition and literary genre, a third component enters into the production of a text: style.

3. Style

Texts exhibit elements of *style* which particularize them in certain ways. Style links a text to a particular speaker or

---

[84]See P. RICOEUR, "Speaking and Writing" in *Interpretation Theory*, p. 32. As with text, literary genres are usually thought of in terms of written material. In applying the notion of literary genre to discourse, Ricoeur remarks that there is a "specific affinity that reigns between writing and specific codes which generate the works of discourse. This affinity is so close that we might be tempted to say that even oral expressions of poetic or narrative compositions rely on the processes equivalent to writing ... memory appears as the support of an inscription similar to that provided by external marks" (Ibid., p. 33).

author. As we mentioned above, while there may be many narratives (to use just one example of a literary genre) about the same topic, style stamps *this* particular narrative as different from *that* particular narrative. By means of style, structure is particular; style lends to a text a kind of singular identification.

The style component of text accents the noetic dimension of meaning. A speaker/author's individuality remains so that the recovery of meaning is never totally severed from the person or situation at the source of the text. A note of caution is in order, however: this individuality does not relegate the recovery of meaning to a matter of "climbing inside" a speaker/author's psyche. Precisely because style is inscribed in text the latter is released from its singularity "in much the same way that a predicate in a sentence releases the individuality of the subject."[85] Style is a matter of contributing to the fullness of meaning within the parameters of composition and genre. It is not a matter of reverting meaning back to a speaker/author. Here again, we encounter the event-meaning pair in the relationship between the particularity of style and the universality of genre.

These three components of composition, literary genre, and style bring text from a macro-structure (composition) level to a micro-structure (stylistic) level. The literary genre mediates these general and particular levels. There is an organization and purposefulness about text that distinguishes it from simple discourse. As a work of production a text displays a structure that is constitutive of its meaning. This is a critical juncture for hermeneutics. To change that structure is to change the meaning. To uncover that structure is to uncover the meaning.

In spoken discourse, meaning is largely determined by the dialogical situation. Meaning is tied into the intentionality of the speaker and the message s/he wishes to convey to the interlocutor(s). How the interlocutor understands the message is aided by the gestures, voice tone, contact, etc. of the speaker and by the shared context of the dialogical situation. In spoken discourse, the meaning almost coincides with the speech event. Even when spoken discourse takes on the formal components constituent of text, meaning is largely determined by the dialogical situation. Thus, myths shared by a people generally need no "explanation," but are "understood." Something else

---

[85] J.W. VAN DEN HENGEL, *The Home of Meaning*, p. 43.

quite different happens when that text is written. An examination of the recovery of meaning from a written text is the final step in our inquiry into the fullness of meaning.

D. Written Text

Writing explodes the singularity of the discourse event into a universal residue that can be recognized over and over again. In other words, the "what is said" is recorded so that it can be repeated in many situations at different times. Hence, a whole new relationship ensues. The writing-reading pair replaces the dialogical relationship of the speaking-hearing pair. In this there is an upheaval of the shared world of the situation of the dialogical relationship of discourse. The reader is not confined to the situation of the author as the hearer is confined to the situation of the speaker. Through the freeing effect of going from discourse to writing, the writing-reading pair takes on a life of its own. Ricoeur insists that "the relation between writing and reading is no longer a particular case of the relation between speaking and hearing."[86] The "freeing of the written material with respect to the dialogical condition of discourse is the most significant effect of writing."[87] A whole range of consequences opens when writing is freed from a dialogical situation; these changes radically affect the recovery of meaning.

The most obvious consequence in going from speaking to writing concerns the medium of exchange: in speaking, that medium is the human voice and/or gestures; in writing, the medium is the external marks on stone or paper (or whatever). What is fixed is the "said" of speaking. The implication here is that meaning can be detached from the dialogical situation. Certain other consequences follow from this.

First, the self-reference of communication is affected. In discourse, self-reference is immediate since there is a shared situation between the interlocutors. Consequently, the intention of the speaker and the meaning of the discourse intersect. In the case of writing, however, there is no longer a shared situation between the writer and reader, and so the intention of

---

[86] P. RICOEUR, "The Hermeneutical Function of Distanciation" in *Hermeneutics and the Human Sciences*, p. 139.

[87] Ibid.

the writer does not identify the verbal meaning of what is written. This semantic autonomy of writing makes the recovery of meaning more complex. The authorial meaning is refined to a dimension of the writing and is recovered only in the writing.

Second, the audience toward whom communication is directed is affected. In discourse, the hearer is "someone who is determined in advance by the dialogical situation."[88] On the contrary, writing is addressed to a universal audience who could conceivably be anyone who reads. Since the semantic autonomy of the text allows for a universal range of readers. Yet, a text creates its own audience which also makes a text contingent. Since a text addresses a certain segment of the public, reading is a social phenomenon subject to limitations of exclusion and admission. Thus, "the recognition of the work by the audience created by the work is an unpredictable event"[89] which makes a text significant and enduring and open to multiple interpretations by a larger audience, or makes a text insignificant, passing, and limited in interpretation.

Third, the reference is affected. In oral discourse, reference is ostensive; that is, it is a known, shared reference arising from the shared dialogical situation of the interlocutors. An ostensive reference can be further detected through indicators such as demonstratives, adverbs of time and place, verb tenses, and definite descriptions.[90] All these point to singular identifications which make the reference the speaker intends clear to the hearer. But "the functioning of reference is profoundly altered when it is no longer possible to identify the thing spoken about as part of the common situation of the interlocutors."[91] The alteration of the reference that takes place when passing from speaking to writing consists in its removal from the shared situation of the interlocutors where reference is ostensive. While some ostensive indicators may remain in writing through certain grammatical devices inscription may employ, writing nevertheless opens up a gap "between

---

[88]P. RICOEUR, "Speaking and Writing" in *Interpretation Theory*, p. 31.

[89]Ibid.

[90]See Ibid., pp. 34-35.

[91]P. RICOEUR, "The Hermeneutical Function of Distanciation" in *Hermeneutics and the Human Sciences*, p. 140.

identification and monstration."[92] In writing, reference is freed "from the limits of situational reference."[93] Reference is a possible "world" addressed to the reader. It is an "unostensive" reference in that it is no longer a manifested reference arising out of the shared situation of the interlocutors, but rather now the reference is part of the meaning uncovered within the writing.[94] Reference carries writing to the level of possibility as opposed to the ready-at-hand reference of discourse.

The process of the recovery of meaning has its reward on each level through which it passes. In this process, it does not have to be a matter of opting for one level of meaning (with its particular reward) over another. For example, while the shared dialogical situation of discourse allows for a shared reference to enter into the meaning of a discourse, this does not necessarily have to happen at the expense of the inherent objectivity of language and the meaning that can be uncovered through a purely linguistic analysis. The important point is, of course, that the recovery of meaning from a written text has the decided advantage of incorporating the rewards plumbed from analyses at other levels. Ricoeur maintains that the written text proffers the fullness of meaning; he directs his unique method for recovering that meaning to this kind of text. A few preliminary remarks on hermeneutics and liturgical text are in order before turning to the next chapter and Ricoeur's method of textual hermeneutics.

E. Hermeneutics and Liturgical Text

Like its non-liturgical counterparts, a liturgical text is a text precisely because it is a work larger than a sentence that has order and unity about it. The liturgical text is a closed sequence of discourse; it has a beginning and an end and an

---

[92]P. RICOEUR, "Speaking and Writing" in *Interpretation Theory*, p. 35.

[93]Ibid., p. 36.

[94]In writing we speak of a "split reference" where there is both an ostensive, descriptive reference detected in the grammar as well as an unostensive reference that cannot be said in a direct, descriptive way. See Ibid., p. 37.

internal logic that connects them. Any hermeneutics of a liturgical text is concerned with uncovering this inner logic as a structure unique to that text.

The various layers of meaning that may be uncovered in language, discourse, text, and written text are especially significant with respect to the liturgical text. As written, a liturgical text can be taken up and used again and again by a worshipping community because of the semantic autonomy proper to written text. But also, because it is celebrated, that text emphasizes event, lending it an historical dimension part and parcel of its meaning.

Since it is a text, the three components of any text also figure into uncovering the depth meaning of a liturgical text. But each of these components reflects its own special flavor when they contribute to the formation of a liturgical text. The composition component is now no longer the work of a single speaker or author, but rather the composite work of a whole tradition of worshipping communities who have shaped the text. The literary genre that generated a liturgical text incorporates a creative use of numerous genres (for example, hymns, narration, and poetry) that renders a genre unique to liturgical texts. Finally, style is especially particularized by the community who celebrates a liturgical text.

In determining the meaning of a liturgical text, we must not only take seriously the process of recovery of meaning and the components of text, but we must do so within the specialized milieu in which the liturgical text is celebrated. The "reading" of a liturgical text is, in actuality, its celebration. From this, certain questions arise: Is the recovery of the meaning of a liturgical text a wholly subjective venture depending on its particular celebration by a local worshipping community? Or is there an objectivity about its meaning that threads its way into each celebration, minimizing a conflict of interpretations? These questions lead us in the direction of identifying a methodology that respects both questions. In his *method* of textual hermeneutics, Ricoeur takes up these kinds of questions. Chapter Three addresses Ricoeur's *method* of textual hermeneutics.

CHAPTER THREE

RICOEUR'S METHOD OF TEXTUAL HERMENEUTICS

Chapter Two's explorations into the recovery of meaning unveil new possibilities for approaching meaning and pave the way for a fresh approach to liturgical texts from within the texts themselves. By defining meaning as the dialectic of sense and reference, Ricoeur shows an interplay between the ideal objectivity of the sense of meaning and the priority of the mode of existence of the reference of meaning. The recovery of meaning through internal structures is not accomplished apart from language's function of mediating reality.

The task of this present chapter is to outline Ricoeur's *method* for eliciting meaning from a text. Ricoeur creatively uses the linguistic tools at hand, linking these tools into a workable method to be applied to a variety of texts. Through his helpful distinction of meaning as sense and reference, he respects the integral objectivity of a text itself to deliver up its own meaning and gives credence to a reality underpinning texts. The first part of this chapter addresses the key dialectic of Ricoeur's method, that of explanation and understanding, which embraces both this objectivity and the modes of existence at the heart of texts. The second part presents the three moments of Ricoeur's method of textual hermeneutics which concretize the explanation-understanding dialectic in a workable methodological approach to texts. The chapter includes a preliminary application of the three moments of the method to liturgical texts. Finally, we set out an agenda for testing the proposed liturgical methodology on a select liturgical text.

A. Explanation-Understanding Dialectic

The key dialectic of Ricoeur's method, explanation and understanding, is related to the key dialectic of the textual moment, sense and reference. By placing emphasis on this latter dialectic, Ricoeur claims that in addition to an objective sense of a text, there is a referential meaning that links a text to reality. For Ricoeur, the sense of meaning lies in the linguistic structure itself and is recovered through a scientific approach to a text, for example, by utilizing structural analysis; this is the explanation pole of the methodological dialectic which Ricoeur calls the "methodic" pole. Scientific, explanatory methods, however, cannot uncover the referential meaning of a text. A "nonmethodic" pole is required that points to this extralinguistic reality; this is the understanding pole of the methodological dialectic.

Ricoeur's method of textual hermeneutics flows from these two poles, explanation and understanding, the methodic and nonmethodic poles, respectively. They are central to Ricoeur's textual hermeneutics because they allow for a recovery of both sense and reference from within a text itself. The methodic pole focuses on explanation which is an analytic moment of the text; the nonmethodic pole focuses on understanding which derives from the interpreter's way of existing.

For Ricoeur, there is no opposition between explanation and understanding. He sees the central problem of hermeneutics as overcoming the opposition between explanation and understanding that Romanticist hermeneutics had posited.[1] For the latter, explanation and understanding each represent "a distinct and irreducible mode of intelligibility."[2] That is, they are not in a dialectical relationship, but they are mutually exclusive modes

---

[1]See P. RICOEUR, "The Task of Hermeneutics" in *Hermeneutics and the Human Sciences: Essays on Language, Action and Interpretation*, ed. and trans. J.B. Thompson (Cambridge: Cambridge University Press, 1981), p. 43. The eighteenth century marked the development of hermeneutics into a philosophical problem. In reaction to the emphasis of the Enlightenment on reason, Romanticism emphasized *life*. In this latter vein, Romanticist hermeneutics tried to reach the thought which produced a discourse (see P. RICOEUR, *Cours sur l'herméneutique* [Louvain: Institut Supérieur de Philosophie, 1971-1972, mimeograph], p. 77) by appealing to a living relation with the creative process (see Ibid., p. 71). It thus sought to understand the author even better than the author understood her/himself. The Romanticist hermeneutical problem takes the coherence of history as the expression of life as fundamental (see Ibid., p. 82). Romanticist hermeneutics also responded to another cultural fact of its time, positivism, whereby it undertook to ground the human sciences in an epistemology and methodology as objective as that of the natural sciences (see Ibid., pp. 82-83). This sets up an opposition between explanation and understanding in which hermeneutics can be none other than an epistemological concern.

[2]P. RICOEUR, "Explanation and Understanding" in *Interpretation Theory: Discourse and the Surplus of Meaning* (Ft. Worth: The Texas Christian University Press, 1979), p. 72.

of methodology and reality. Explanation belongs properly to the natural sciences and understanding belongs to the human sciences. This opposes two methodologies and "two spheres of reality, nature and mind."[3] Against this opposition, Ricoeur sees explanation and understanding as a dialectic, as having "relative moments in a complex process called interpretation."[4] For Ricoeur, interpretation is "the theory of operations of understanding in their relation to the interpretation of texts."[5] Since, according to Ricoeur, understanding is a nonmethodic moment in touch with the reality underpinning texts, hermeneutics is essentially concerned with exposing this reality as a proper object of interpretation. Yet, the reality is exposed through the help of the methodic, explanatory pole.

Ricoeur overcomes the opposition between explanation and understanding by retaining an analytic of language (explanation) *directed to* a text whose very structure points to a way of existing (understanding) in terms of the text's objectification of the signs of self-existence. The structured language of a text is the level at which understanding operates. As an analytic device Ricoeur's method of textual hermeneutics disclaims analysis of individual linguistic signs or symbols and regards more complex works, texts. It can thus integrate the positive contributions of linguistics, structuralism, and philosophy of language into a single, larger framework.[6] In

---

[3]Ibid., p. 73.

[4]P. RICOEUR, "Explanation and Understanding: On Some Remarkable Connections Among the Theory of the Text, Theory of Action, and Theory of History" in *The Philosophy of Paul Ricoeur: An Anthology of His Work*, ed. C.E. Reagan and D. Stewart (Boston: Beacon Press, 1978), p. 150.

[5]P. RICOEUR, "The Task of Hermeneutics" in *Hermeneutics and the Human Sciences*, p. 43. The present analysis reflects Ricoeur's later philosophical journey in which text is his focus. In his earlier work, Ricoeur's indirect ontology was unfolded in terms of an analytic of language at three levels: the semantic, reflective, and existential levels (see P. RICOEUR, "Existence and Hermeneutics" in *The Conflict of Interpretations: Essays in Hermeneutics*, ed. D. Ihde [Evanston: Northwestern University Press, 1974], pp. 11-24).

[6]See D. PELLAUER, "The Significance of the Text in Paul Ricoeur's Hermeneutical Theory" in *Studies in the Philosophy*

this, the text as the object of hermeneutics no longer delivers up layers of meaning of symbols. Its interpretation involves the self-implicating task of understanding.[7] The latter is a recognition of the signs of our self-existence within the language of a text. The task of understanding, then, concerns our mode of existence.

The proper object of hermeneutics is *any human work* that has a structure analogous to the structure of a text resulting in understanding which operates differently in different modes of discourse. In oral discourse, "mutual understanding relies on sharing the same sphere of meaning."[8] In other words, mutual understanding is possible because of the shared ostensive reference of the interlocutors. Here, understanding and explanation almost coincide since the dialogical situation allows for the give-and-take of questions and answers between the interlocutors which can verify the interpretation.

When oral discourse gives way to writing, "the development of explanation as an autonomous process proceeds from the exteriorization of the event in the meaning."[9] Because of this exteriorization, a text can be approached on its own ground where explanation is precipitated by understanding in addition to being directed toward understanding. There is a movement from understanding as a "naive grasping of the meaning of the text as a whole"[10] to explanation to understanding as a "sophisticated

---

of Paul Ricoeur, ed. C.E. Reagan (Athens: Ohio University Press, 1979), p. 112.

[7]See, for example, P. RICOEUR, "Existence and Hermeneutics" in *The Conflict of Interpretations*, p. 13, for his early linking of hermeneutics directly to deciphering the different layers of meaning of symbols. His later approach to interpretation is in line with his text theory and is defined in terms of the dialectic of explanation and understanding. The important thing to keep in mind is that, for Ricoeur, interpretation has an ontological moment (see P. RICOEUR, *Cours sur l'herméneutique*, pp. 57-63).

[8]P. RICOEUR, "Explanation and Understanding" in *Interpretation Theory*, p. 73.

[9]Ibid., p. 74.

[10]Ibid.

mode of understanding, supported by explanatory procedures."[11] Explanation is "the *mediation* between two stages of understanding."[12] It is helpful to further clarify the mediating role of explanation.

Understanding-explanation-understanding is concretized in the hermeneutical enterprise as guess-validation-appropriation. The first instance of understanding (also called "pre-understanding") can be merely a guess because there is no longer present the shared meaning of discourse. To guess is to generate a new event. In guessing, the meaning of a text is construed as a whole, as individual, and as having potential meanings that can be actualized in different ways.[13] This requires verification, which is the aim of explanation.

Explanation is the validation of the guess which is not a question of empirical verification but an argument that one interpretation is more probable than another. This is a new way of looking at things from the sense of meaning of writing itself, opening up a possible world.[14] This new and possible world is the text's reference of meaning. Text is never a static, dead document since it requires an interaction-response on the part of the reader. A text that is, indeed, "read" is a text that gives way to human action. The very reading of a text is a human act because of the requirements the text places on its reader which leads to the second instance of understanding (also called "self-understanding").

The second instance of understanding is a self-understanding; that is, it is the making of our own

---

[11]Ibid.

[12]Ibid., p. 75; italics mine.

[13]See Ibid., pp. 74-78.

[14]Ricoeur sees a new way of looking at things resulting from structural analysis, the intermediary between the naive interpretation of the guess and the critical interpretation of understanding. See P. RICOEUR, "Explanation and Understanding" in *Interpretation Theory*, p. 87. Elsewhere, Ricoeur notes that "the function of structural analysis is to lead from surface semantics ... to the ultimate 'referent' ... " (P. RICOEUR, "The Model of the Text" in *Hermeneutics and the Human Sciences*, p. 217).

(appropriation) a "possible world and of a possible way of orientating oneself within it,"[15] the creating of a new mode of existing. It would seem that we are trapped in the perennial hermeneutical circle, where our anticipation of meaning is projected into the actual interpretation. Since there is more at stake in Ricoeur's methodology than this, he is able to claim self-understanding as a *new* mode of existing. We return to the key dialectic of the textual moment, sense and reference. Text is referential, but "referring is not something done by an expression; it is something *done by someone* when *using* an expression."[16] That is, the interpreter chooses to "actualize the potential non-ostensive references of the text in a new situation, that of the reader."[17] For Ricoeur, the hermeneutical circle is not a vicious one because the interpreter chooses *possibilities* to be *actualized* when s/he makes them her/his own.

The process of interpretation begins with our recognition of the potential meanings of a text construed as a whole. It ends with one or more of those meanings becoming our own. "In this process the *mediating* role played by structural analysis [explanation] constitutes both the justification of this objective approach and the rectification of the subjective approach."[18] In Ricoeur's method of textual hermeneutics, the art of interpretation is a dynamic process.

B. Three Methodological Moments

Ricoeur's insistence that interpretation is a *process* highlights the activity character of his method. "Activity," here, has a broad extension. It implicates the lived experience which the author draws upon in her/his creative task and in which the reader participates in a moment of pre-understanding. It implicates the capacity of the text itself to incorporate a

---

[15]P. RICOEUR, "Explanation and Understanding" in *Interpretation Theory*, p. 88.

[16]P. RICOEUR, "Language and Ontology" in *Main Trends in Philosophy*, ed. P. Ricoeur (New York: Holmes & Meier Publishers, Inc., 1979), p. 123; italics mine.

[17]P. RICOEUR, "The Model of the Text" in *Hermeneutics and the Human Sciences*, p. 215.

[18]Ibid., p. 218; italics Ricoeur's.

language of human action in the very language of the text whose sense is uncovered in the moment of explanation and, finally, "activity" implicates the receiving of the text by a reader in a moment of new self-understanding. For Ricoeur, the power of a text is to conduct one from the side of the author to the side of the reader in a dynamic hermeneutical process. In this, a text is a mediating faculty. At stake is the transition from the situation of the author to the reception of a work by the reader. The entire hermeneutical process implicates human action: a complete work derives from the human activity of the author and culminates in the human activity of the reader. The task of textual hermeneutics is

> to reconstruct the set of operations by which a work lifts itself above the opaque depths of living, acting, and suffering, to be given by an author to readers who receive it and thereby change their acting. ... Hermeneutics ... is concerned with reconstructing the entire arc of operations by which practical experience provides itself with works, authors, and readers.[19]

The reconstructing derives from the text, is mediated by it, and unites three distinct methodological moments: participation, distanciation, and appropriation. These three moments concretize the explanation-understanding dialectic, circumscribing Ricoeur's method of textual hermeneutics.

1. Participation: Pre-understanding

Participation implies a pre-understanding of the world of human action, perceived from two vantage points. From one vantage point, participation is "an entirely positive condition which would be better expressed by the concept of belonging."[20] Belonging is basically our being given over to ourselves. From another vantage point, participation can be exteriorized because it can be communicated over time and distance so that we recognize that we are not the starting point of our own life. Participation's two vantage points of belonging and communication are the focus of the next two paragraphs.

---

[19] P. RICOEUR, *Time and Narrative*, Volume 1, trans. K. McLaughlin and D. Pellauer (Chicago: University of Chicago Press, 1984), p. 53.

[20] P. RICOEUR, "Phenomenology and Hermeneutics" in *Hermeneutics and the Human Sciences*, p. 105.

a. Belonging. Belonging

> designates the nonmethodic pole, dialectically opposed to the pole of explanation in every interpretive science, *and* it designates the indicator, no longer methodical but verifying, of the ontological relation of belonging of our being to beings and to Being. The rich ambiguity of the word *understanding* is that it designates a moment in the theory of method, the one we call the nonmethodic pole, *and* the apprehension, at a level other than scientific, of our belonging to the whole of what is.[21]

This belonging is grasped as a structural whole, answering the question "why" in addition to the question "who" or "what." The unity of goals, motives, and agents is first grasped as a "belonging-to" which results in our being thrust into situations not chosen and being affected by things not of our own making.[22] Ricoeur is not perpetrating his own brand of determinism here. He is simply asserting that a text is a human mediation of the objectification of the signs of self-existence. Text advances our participation in life from interiorization to exteriorization. Human mediation permits a projection outside of self as works of the artist, legislator, educator; that is, as texts. Our point is, these objectifications of human existence derive from our participation in human existence. Some originary human experience or event gives rise to any text.[23] This originary experience or event is never lost to a text because

---

[21]P. RICOEUR, "Explanation and Understanding" in *The Philosophy of Paul Ricoeur*, p. 165; italics Ricoeur's. In his pre-linguistic philosophy Ricoeur had already investigated the notion of participation as a dialectic of affirmation and negation leading from a joyful affirmation of our existence to a recognition of our finitude, with "feeling" as the link. See P. RICOEUR, *Fallible Man*, Philosophy of the Will, Part II: Finitude and Guilt, Book I: *Fallible Man*, trans. C. Kelbley (Chicago: Regnery, 1965), pp. 123-202.

[22]See P. RICOEUR, "History and Hermeneutics," *The Journal of Philosophy* 73 (1976, trans. D. Pellauer), 686.

[23]A note on "originary": Ricoeur's use of the French term "*originaire*" is sometimes translated "originating" and at other times "originary." The use throughout this volume is "originary" because we feel it better expresses the dynamic characteristic of Ricoeur's hermeneutics.

participation ensures a certain "readability" to the extent that readers share a common "belonging-to," a common tradition. This leads to the second vantage point of participation, that the meaning of a text is communicated through past, present, and future.

b. Communication. Human action is never a solitary endeavor; "to act is always to act 'with' others."[24] Belonging is intersubjective and intratemporal. Belonging as "pre-understanding" is the subject's participation in being as apprehended through any cultural object. "Belonging-to" is mediated by *externalizations*: historical marks, texts, rites, inscriptions, documents, archives, etc. Externalization is an intensification of an experience which is objectified. Pre-understanding or belonging is intersubjective and intratemporal because it is communicated by the monuments which constitute tradition.[25]

Tradition implies a certain "connectedness," "a rule-governed sequence."[26] These rules are not the same rules that govern the connectedness of objects in the natural sciences, but rather history is torn away from the natural sciences in that it has its own rules of intelligibility which govern the sequence of connectedness. We can articulate the transmission of tradition in terms of such categories as the human agents who begin the flow of events of the particular tradition, interpretation of the actions in terms of motives, regulation by institutions, founding of such institutions, and the continuation, termination, or renewal of the tradition. The operative principle of the inter-subjectivity is the requirement that all temporal fields within temporality be analogous, which means that all "can ascribe their experience to themselves."[27] In other words, externalization in tradition is possible because there is first a belonging-to characterized by the ascription of experience to ourselves.

In the above remarks on tradition, there is an emphasis on a "sedimentation" aspect of tradition that guarantees a paradigmatic structure part and parcel of tradition. In

---

[24]P. RICOEUR, *Time and Narrative*, p. 55.

[25]See P. RICOEUR, "History and Hermeneutics," 686-693.

[26]Ibid., 687.

[27]Ibid., 688.

addition, tradition has a certain "innovation" about it that introduces a kind of singularity with respect to tradition. Any externalization of action emplotted in a text requires a preliminary competency on the part of the reader in order to identify the structures of that action. The innovation built into the ambiguity of the linguistic articulation of action makes it a wholly human making (*faire*) so that the act of reading demands an involvement that is also a human making.[28] A text asks the reader to guess its meaning in terms of both its whole (its sedimentation) and its parts (its innovation). But a guess as to the meaning of a text is just that: a guess. It selects meaning out of many possible meanings. The pre-understanding or "preliminary competency" or methodological guess as to the meaning of a text is not an isolated methodological moment. It is mediated by the second methodological moment, distanciation.

2. Distanciation: Explanation

Ricoeur calls *distanciation* an objectification of the relation of belonging.[29] Distanciation is the counterpart of the moment of participation because there is necessarily a distance between the remoteness and proximity characteristic of historical tradition.[30] A text attempts to overcome the chimera of objectification of meaning versus historical situation which gave rise to meaning:

> Text is much more than a particular case of intersubjective communication: it is the paradigm of distanciation in communication. As such, it displays a fundamental characteristic of the very historicity of human experience, namely that it is communication in and through distance.[31]

---

[28]Cf. P. RICOEUR, *Time and Narrative*, p. 34.

[29]See "Explanation and Understanding" in *The Philosophy of Paul Ricoeur*, p. 166.

[30]See P. RICOEUR, "Phenomenology and Hermeneutics" in *Hermeneutics and the Human Sciences*, p. 110.

[31]See P. RICOEUR, "The Hermeneutical Function of Distanciation" in *Hermeneutics and the Human Sciences*, p. 131.

Distanciation is "constitutive of the phenomenon of the text as writing."[32] In distancing the text from the situation of its writer, the text enjoys an autonomy which allows it to be present to the situation of the reader. This autonomy privileges the text with a diversity of meaning to be recovered in the hermeneutical process. Though the "text's career escapes the finite horizon lived by its author,"[33] it is rescued by the numerous horizons of its infinite number of possible readers. The "opportunity for multiple readings is the dialectical counterpart of the semantic autonomy of the text."[34] Distanciation allows the meaning of a text to traverse the historical situation of the writer to the historical situation of the reader, lending a new proximity to the text, "a proximity which suppresses and preserves the cultural distance."[35]

Ultimately, interpretation is directed to the dialectic between a way to talk about things and the things themselves. Things themselves are the concern of pre-understanding and self-understanding. The text derives from human activity and culminates in further human activity. The moment of distanciation is a necessary one in that it mediates these two activities in its way of talking about things.

Distanciation allows a text to be brought to a level of intelligibility on its own terms and supplies an analytic moment. For Ricoeur, a science of text can only be established in the moment of distanciation. This explanatory, analytic moment regards the internal structure of a work itself "without any regard for the two sides of the text."[36] Yet, it is not severed from the two sides. As explanation, the moment of distanciation is a validation of the initial guess as to meaning which characterizes the hermeneutical moment of participation where new worlds are opened up to a reader. These possibilities confront

---

[32]Ibid., p. 139.

[33]P. RICOEUR, "Language as Discourse" in *Interpretation Theory*, p. 30.

[34]Ibid., p. 32.

[35]P. RICOEUR, "Speaking and Writing" in *Interpretation Theory*, p. 43.

[36]P. RICOEUR, *Time and Narrative*, p. 53.

the reader in such a way that a text may be *applied* to the situation of the reader so that the moment of distanciation is not cut off from the other side of the text, the moment of appropriation. Distanciation mediates these two sides of a text.

Participation and appropriation are singular activities involving author and reader through the text. Distanciation, however, allows for a wide range of modes that fulfill its mediating function. The interpreter, therefore, is free to choose any analytic mode that best suits the particular text being examined. For Ricoeur, structuralism, linguistic analysis, the critique of ideology, for example, are all mediations between participation and appropriation. The guiding thread for a choice of explanatory mode is the nature of the text itself: its composition, genre, and style. Any one mode may serve as the analytic; indeed, applying more than one mode to a text may emphasize different aspects. For example, applying a communications theory to a text might emphasize a dialogical aspect, while a critique of ideology might emphasize its historical traits.

A science of text is not aimed at univocal meaning, but rather at mediating the moment of participation and appropriation. It is now time to look more closely at the moment of appropriation.

3. Appropriation: Self-understanding

The fullest meaning of a text is reached only in the third moment, appropriation. According to Ricoeur, appropriation is making our own the meaning of a text: "To appropriate is to make what was alien become one's own."[37] What is appropriated is the meaning of the text as the world of possibilities opened up to the reader. Appropriation implies a change in the reader, a change which is a human act.

Human acts express human realities: "Social structures are ... attempts to cope with existential perplexities, human predicaments and deep-rooted conflicts."[38] It is because human

[37] P. RICOEUR, "Phenomenology and Hermeneutics" in *Hermeneutics and the Human Sciences*, p. 113.

[38] P. RICOEUR, "The Model of the Text" in *Hermeneutics and the Human Sciences*, p. 220.

action culminates in appropriation of the world of action that Ricoeur can maintain that action involves making a change in the world. Action makes a change in the world because action means a change in the subject.

Several features characterize appropriation. First of all, since appropriation is linked to distanciation, "appropriation no longer has any trace of affective affinity with the intention of an author."[39] Thus, a second feature: appropriation is the subjective counterpart of the objectification (distanciation) characteristic of the work. The subjective response proper to appropriation is not a response to the author, but rather it is a response to the text. As such, a third feature of appropriation emerges: the vis-à-vis of appropriation is the reference, the world of the text. This world of the text is not *behind* the text, tied in with the intention of the author, but it is embedded in the depth-meaning of the text "as that which the work unfolds, discovers, reveals."[40] Appropriation concerns the way a text addresses a reader. The act of reading actualizes appropriation.

a. Reading as the Dialogue of Worlds. The text finds its completion in the act of reading. In this process of reading, the text releases the objective meaning as an event present to the reader in the act of appropriation.[41] As we said above, "to

---

[39]P. RICOEUR, "The Hermeneutical Function of Distanciation" in *Hermeneutics and the Human Sciences*, p. 143.

[40]Ibid.

[41]It would take this study too far afield to explore adequately current research in the reading process, though such insights are valuable additions to flesh out our own methodology. See, for example, W. ISER, "The Reading Process: A Phenomenological Approach" in J.P. Tompkins, ed., *Reader-Response Criticism: From Formalism to Post-structuralism* (Baltimore: Johns Hopkins University Press, 1981), pp. 50-69; W. ISER, *The Act of Reading: A Theory of Aesthetic Response* (Baltimore: Johns Hopkins University Press, 1981); U. ECO, *The Role of the Reader: Explorations in the Semiotics of Texts* (Bloomington: Indiana University Press, 1979); H.R. JAUSS, *Toward an Aesthetic of Reception*, trans. T. Bahti, Intro. P. de Man, Theory and History of Literature Volume 2 (Minneapolis: University of Minnesota Press, 1982). These authors stress reading is a dynamic process unfolding between reader and text.

appropriate is to make 'one's own' what was alien."[42] It actualizes the meaning of the written text specifically as addressed to a particular reader.

What must be appropriated in a text is the world of possibilities addressed to the reader. The process of appropriation lends to reading an event character that allows a kind of dialogical situation to ensue between the world of the text and the world of the reader. Appropriation is the reader's "answer" to the text's possibilities, unfolded in the world of real human action.[43]

The relationship of text and reader is a dialectical one. Because meaning is addressed to someone it opens up a process by which the making present of new modes of being (the proposed or possible world before the text) offers the reader *new possibilities* for self-understanding. As Ricoeur says,

> by 'appropriation', I understand this: that the interpretation of a text culminates in the self-interpretation of a subject who thenceforth understands himself better, understands himself differently, or simply begins to understand himself.[44]

Ultimately, the goal of appropriation is self-understanding resulting from making our own the world of possibilities lying in the depth-meaning of the text.

b. Self-understanding through Text. The explanation-understanding dialectic begins in a kind of "pre-understanding" which is an initial participation in experience. This pre-understanding is informed by explanation, which is an uncovering of the sense of meaning of the text, the analytic moment of distanciation. There is, then, a dialectical relationship between participation and distanciation, between pre-understanding and explanation. This dialectic culminates in understanding, not the same understanding as the pre-understanding but a new understanding that has been informed by

---

[42]P. RICOEUR, "Speaking and Writing" in *Interpretation Theory*, p. 43.

[43]See P. RICOEUR, "Appropriation" in *Hermeneutics and the Human Sciences*, p. 185.

[44]P. RICOEUR, "What is a Text?" in *Hermeneutics and the Human Sciences*, p. 158.

explanation. Moreover, this new understanding is self-understanding. This is to say that the understanding which is the moment of appropriation is the result of the interpreter's way of existing being challenged by the possibilities opened up by the reference of the text and validated in the explanatory moment. In the moment of appropriation, the new possibilities that are made our own actually lead to a change in the self; hence, a new self-understanding is a new mode of existing. As appropriation, understanding is the fusion of horizons "which occurs when the world of the reader and the world of the text merge into one another."[45] All understanding is self-understanding:

> Interpretation therefore is not something absolute, resulting from the existence of text, but stems from the possibility of explicating in a number of ways our understanding of the relationship between our situation and our possibilities. It is this initial bipolarity which creates the hermeneutic situation, in the sense that it is always possible to understand more fully and to interpret in a different way the ontological condition of the existence which we represent.[46]

Through the appropriation of the world of the text, a document of life rooted in existence and reality, an interplay of situation and possibilities occurs which leads to a new situation with new possibilities.

This new self-understanding calls for a critique of the illusions of the subject.[47] The reader brings to the text an ego that "is based on prejudices which are linked to our position in the relations of force of society ... [and] by hidden

---

[45]P. RICOEUR, "Appendix: From Existentialism to the Philosophy of Language" in *The Rule of Metaphor: Multi-disciplinary Studies of the Creation of Meaning in Language*, trans. R. Czerny with K. McLaughlin and J. Costello, S.J. (Toronto: University of Toronto Press, 1977), p. 319.

[46]P. RICOEUR, "Phenomenology and Ontology" in *Main Trends in Philosophy*, p. 130.

[47]Ricoeur borrows from two masters of suspicion, Freud and Marx, in this. See P. RICOEUR, "Appropriation" in *Hermeneutics and the Human Sciences*, p. 191; also, *Cours sur l'herméneutique*, pp. 222-228.

interests."[48] Fundamental to appropriation is the relinquishment of this ego so that the projection of the world of the text takes precedence over a projection of the reader into the text. Thus, appropriation is the process by which a new mode of existing is revealed to the reader who then receives "a new mode of being from the text itself."[49] The process by which a new mode of existing is appropriated may, indeed, be a kind of distanciation of self from self. As Ricoeur puts it, "I exchange the *me*, *master* of itself, for the *self*, *disciple* of the text."[50] Through the text one is offered a new mode of existing, a new self-understanding. Losing the old self to find a new self conferred by the work defines the act of appropriation; the ego gives way to a new self.[51] In this, there is a celebrative (playful) transposition of the text.

Play transforms those who participate in it because play has its own way of life; it is "something other than the activity of a subject."[52] Play has a kind of existence of its own that occurs without the effort or intentionality of a subject. To play is to play with or at something. Thus, "worlds are proposed in the mode of play" which the player confronts through "recognition rather than cognition."[53] The playfulness of the text mediates the playful transformation of the author in the text[54] and the playful transformation of the reader through the latter's recognition of the possible world of the text. A text is a celebration because the seriousness of a utilitarian

---

[48]P. RICOEUR, "Appropriation" in *Hermeneutics and the Human Sciences*, p. 191.

[49]Ibid., p. 192.

[50]P. RICOEUR, "Phenomenology and Hermeneutics" in *Hermeneutics and the Human Sciences*, p. 113; italics Ricoeur's.

[51]See P. RICOEUR, "Appropriation" in *Hermeneutics and the Human Sciences*, p. 190. Ricoeur is indebted to H.G. Gadamer for this theme. See Ibid.

[52]Ibid, p. 186.

[53]Ibid., pp. 186 and 187.

[54]The author never totally disappears from the text; the author's meaning remains as a dimension of the text, but it is disguised, assumes different "voices." See Ibid., p. 188.

preoccupation with subjectivity[55] gives way to the playfulness of a possible, proposed world and the transformation that the recognition of that world brings about.

A fecundity of meaning is uncovered in textual hermeneutics where participation-distanciation-appropriation makes available the "given-ness" of experience through an analysis of the textual linguistics as possible new modes of being in terms of new self-understanding. This fecundity is a consequence of the text being a document of life.

C. Textual Hermeneutics and Liturgical Text

Severed from speaker or author, a written text poses special problems and rewards for the interpreter. The liturgical text is no exception.

Textual hermeneutics is an appropriate method for liturgical studies because the latter has as its legitimate aim the "analysis of the data of the liturgical experience and tradition of the Church."[56] That data is none other than the liturgical texts themselves. The human experience of liturgy results in traditions that have been concretized in liturgical texts as the signs of those traditions, texts which can be submitted to analysis in order to recover the meaning of liturgical tradition.

Ricoeur's textual hermeneutics is also appropriate because his approach to text is not to text as a dead document. Text is an essential mediation between temporal exigencies. On the one hand are the past originary events which gave rise to the text and the future possibilities opened up by the world of the text. On the other hand is the present historical context of the text-users. The liturgical text confronts the gathered community (the *ekklesia* of the present historical context) with new modes of understanding in terms of the possibilities of the world opened

---

[55]See Ibid., p. 186. For a more extended discussion of play as a strategy, see P. RICOEUR, *Sémantique de l'action* (Louvain: Université Catholique de Louvain--Cercle de Philosophie, 1971), polycopy, pp. 91-104. See also *Cours sur l'herméneutique*, pp. 216-222.

[56]A. SCHMEMANN, *Introduction to Liturgical Theology*, trans. A.E. Moorhouse (New York: St. Vladimir's Seminary Press, 1966), p. 12.

up by the liturgical text. The liturgical text is unique in that as text it both embodies and distances itself from the originary events which gave rise to it, and it is also a text that is celebrated ("read") each time within a different historical context which situates the interpretation and creates new possibilities. Thus the liturgical community is confronted with new modes of understanding itself in faith.

Since textual hermeneutics has a broad extension because its methodology can be applied to any and all documents of life which have structures analogous to texts, the operative hypothesis here is none other than a methodological choice: textual hermeneutics can be fruitfully applied to liturgical texts. Approaching liturgical studies through a different methodology opens up the possibility for a fresh interpretation of liturgical texts (presumably) complementing the interpretations derived from other methodologies (for example, a historical-critical method). It remains to explore the implications of the three moments of Ricoeur's method of textual hermeneutics in terms of liturgical texts. We do so in a general and introductory manner in the three sections which follow. Chapters Five and Six of this study are a more comprehensive exploration.

1. Participation

Ricoeur sees participation as the pre-understanding of our experience. For him, "the interpreting self must interpret its own experience, which is a pre-comprehension--albeit non-conceptual--of that which is to be interpreted. ... lived experience is a pre-comprehension of what is to be articulated."[57] Given this premise, certain presuppositions are operative with respect to an interpretation of a liturgical text which point to the participatory moment.

First of all, and perhaps too obviously, participation is in the actual liturgical celebration itself. It is clear that because the originary Christian events are the transcendental foundation of any liturgical act, the domain of Christian action encompasses the goals and motives of the agents of that action. This is to say that liturgy presupposes a web of interconnectedness between an action and its meaning. Christian

---

[57]S. SKOUSGAARD, *Language and the Existence of Freedom: A Study in Paul Ricoeur's Philosophy of Will* (Washington, D.C.: University Press of America, 1979), p. 78.

pre-understanding of a liturgical celebration grasps its originary events in their singularity as events as well as weaves them together into a grasp of the meaning of the whole of the celebration.

Secondly, the interpreter guesses the meaning of the celebration. This is not a naive guess out of thin air, but an informed one that arises from the accumulated meaning of liturgy throughout tradition: we come to liturgy with a sense of what is going on. This is to say that liturgy's originary events are grasped through symbolic (sacramental) mediation. For Ricoeur, symbolic mediation is implicit or immanent before it is explicit or autonomous. Even before liturgy is articulated in a text governed by certain rules and norms (explicit symbols), it is already symbolically mediated as "a meaning incorporated into action and decipherable from it by other actors in the social interplay."[58] A Christian community participates in a liturgy that already imposes a certain readability on its actions.

Finally, the participatory moment of liturgical action presupposes a temporal dimension because what is presently taking place is the "present of the future, the present of the past, and the present of the present in terms of one another."[59] This telescoping of time ensures that no liturgical act is isolated, but participates in a whole Christian tradition of worshipping communities. The liturgical act is an emplotment of a tradition of Christian interpretations of liturgical celebrations. The community's celebration extends the limits of the cultic occasion or community beyond itself to embrace not only the actual communication of the cultic occasion, but also a virtual communication whereby the consequences of the liturgical act become a small but nonetheless real and permanent part of the ongoing Christian tradition.

2. Distanciation

While participation is the condition of possibility for the articulation of self-experience, distanciation allows for an analytical moment verifying the meaning of that experience. This second methodological moment sensitizes us to the need to distance self from self. Without distancing, the possibilities

---

[58]P. RICOEUR, *Time and Narrative*, p. 57.

[59]Ibid., p. 60.

presented by the text are lost to the "comfort" of a known interpretation. Distanciation allows the interpreter to consider all the possibilities opened up by the reference of the text and verify new possibilities commensurate with the interpreter's present situation.

Distanciation is an *explanatory* moment. As written, a liturgical text contains within itself linguistic marks which, when an analytical method is applied, uncover the experiences which gave rise to the articulation. As text, those marks cannot be analyzed as mere linguistic signs, but stand as part of a whole. An analytic of a liturgical text seeks to uncover the structure which constitutes the text as a *Christian text*. It is this Christian *text* which articulates different possibilities for understanding the tradition of Christian experience. The recovery is not a backward look into Christian tradition, but a recognition of new possibilities in the present liturgical celebration. The sedimentation feature of a text prescribes text as a paradigm, supplying the rules for subsequent revisions. These rules may change, but they change slowly and only after a long history of pressure from new innovations. Innovation itself remains under the watchful eye of rules, yet allows for each worshipping community to leave its mark on the tradition of liturgy. In this way each liturgical act is unique while at the same it time remains within the general flow of tradition.

3. Appropriation

Through participation and distanciation the worshipping community is presented with meaning which embodies the tradition of experiences. In the dialectic of participation and distanciation possibilities are presented to the Christian community and verified for the present situation. In authentic celebration of liturgy, these possibilities lead to new self-understanding. Is not the purpose of a liturgical text in a worshipping community to present possibilities for self-understanding to the community? Further, is not the challenge to let go of the ego that is brought to the celebration (one side of the text) in order that, through the text's celebration, a new self might emerge (the other side of the text)?

Just as text finds its completion in the act of reading, so does the liturgical text find its completion in liturgical celebration. The arc between participation and appropriation is mediated by the celebration of the liturgical text. If liturgical celebration does not call forth appropriation, then the mediating role of the liturgical text is not complete. Only when the text mediates its two sides can liturgy be said to be a complete act.

D. Agenda

Ricoeur's textual hermeneutics shows promise as a methodology suitable to liturgical texts. Since they are written texts, liturgical texts can be submitted to the analytic moment of distanciation. This affords liturgical texts the possibility of being approached through a science of text suited to liturgical studies and which articulates the possibilities inherent in the text itself. But this moment of distanciation is a mediating moment, connecting the two sides of the liturgical text: the tradition of Christian experiences and the new self-understanding which is offered for appropriation. In all of this, liturgy as a *celebration* is emphasized; that is, liturgy is not merely a cultic occasion, but derives from and affects human activity beyond the parameters of those occasions. Thus, the study of liturgical texts from the perspective of textual hermeneutics is not the study of dead documents, but rather the interpretation of documents of Christian life. A study of liturgical texts is really an encounter with Christian life. In its deepest sense, liturgy is a language of faith.

Chapters Five and Six are an initial application of Ricoeur's method of textual hermeneutics to a select liturgical text.[60] These chapters are not meant to be exhaustive interpretations; that would cloud the real purpose of this work, which is to seek in Ricoeur's textual hermeneutics a methodology suitable for uncovering the possibilities of meaning of liturgical texts. The purpose of these two chapters is to indicate the promised fruitfulness of Ricoeur's methodology and its viability for liturgical studies.

Chapter Four, which immediately follows, is directed toward outlining concrete tools of analysis appropriate for uncovering the possibilities of the meaning of liturgical texts in their methodological moment of distanciation. While there are many possible directions this analytic could take (for example, the text could be analyzed vis-à-vis A.J. Austin's constative and

---

[60]The select liturgical text is the eucharistic text, which here means the Roman rite of the Eucharist as contained in the *Roman Missal*, not just the eucharistic prayer. This is addressed again in Chapter Five, below.

performative statements), two approaches seem particularly appropriate for an analysis of liturgical texts. One approach focuses on the action character of liturgy. That direction is an expansion and application of speech-act theory, as explicated by Ricoeur, especially in his *Sémantique de l'action*. Speech-act theory is especially applicable because it allows for analysis not only in terms of propositional content, but in terms of the force and effects that action has while remaining within the linguistic parameters. The second approach is a utilization of the communication theory of Roman Jakobson that focuses on the dialogical character of liturgy. Further, Jakobson's theory allows for an analysis of both the various divisions of liturgical texts and an analysis of texts as wholes. Finally, it is a theory to which Ricoeur himself refers rather frequently in his works.[61] These two theories complement each other, especially since Ricoeur's analysis of a semantics of action fleshes out criteria for applying Jakobson's theory to a text in a more objective way.

---

[61]See, for example, "Speaking and Writing" in *Interpretation Theory* (pp. 25-44) where Ricoeur shows what happens to the writing that takes the place of speaking in terms of Jakobson's communication components.

CHAPTER FOUR

THEORETICAL ANALYTIC OF SELECT ACTION AND COMMUNICATION THEORIES

Liturgists have traditionally employed conceptual, historical, and/or pastoral methodologies when studying liturgical texts. These tried-and-true approaches have rested on the liturgical texts themselves as the deposit of data. In these approaches, however, there is an ever-present danger of bringing a preconceived liturgical theology to bear on the meaning of a liturgical text. If a methodology proper to liturgical theology should vary, then we could expect the theological expression itself to vary. The methodology suggested by this study allows meaning to emerge from an analysis of a text and lets *that* meaning point toward a liturgical theology. In other words, texts speak for themselves.

In our present approach, the textual moment is primary; the key dialectic is that of sense and reference, as indicated in Chapter Two.[1] This suggests that while the sense of meaning opens up the linguistic structure of a text to explanation, even in this analytical moment there are hints that this is not all there is to a text. There is a residue pointing to the reference of meaning which opens up to understanding the possible world of a text.

This chapter demonstrates the explanatory moment of Ricoeur's method of textual hermeneutics in order to uncover the sense of meaning. The chapter is divided into three major parts. In the first two parts, two complementary approaches particularly appropriate to the analysis of liturgical texts are presented. First, Ricoeur's semantics of action (borrowed from Anglo-Saxon linguistic theory), seeks to recover human action through a text. This approach defers to the action character of liturgy, which has a broad extension. At one level, action is captured by the very language of the text itself, especially recognized in the predicate.[2] Sentences are more than propositional content; they also carry force and effects incumbent on the interlocutors. At

---

[1]See above, Chapter Two, pp. 71-73.

[2]This is the level at which language theory usually operates.

a deeper level, action points to the human activity (experience) from which the text derives (the moment of participation) and points to the culmination of the act of reading the text in human activity (the moment of appropriation).[3]

The second part, utilizing Roman Jakobson's communication theory, builds on his insight that communication is not simply someone sending a message to someone, but it is a complex process involving not only the interlocutors and the message that passes between/among them, but also the code used to send the message, the means of gaining and keeping the interlocutors' attention, and checking up on whether the message is "heard." Jakobson refers to all these elements as communication factors, and relates certain functions to each. Further, Jakobson claims that since all the factors/functions are not equally emphasized in the process of communication, they form a hierarchy, the analysis of which underscores the dynamic of communication. With respect to communication unfolded in a text, Jakobson's factors and functions of communication and their hierarchical ordering of sets and subsets help to uncover the foci of various sections of a text and ultimately of the text as a whole, making apparent the movement in the text from beginning to end. Our own particular interest lies in applying Jakobson's theory to liturgical texts, focusing on the dialogical character of liturgy.[4]

The third part of this chapter sets out criteria for an analysis of a liturgical text. Using Jakobson's suggested criteria as a basis, the criteria presented here in outline form are amplified within the framework of Ricoeur's semantics of action and adapted for a liturgical application. We present the criteria as concretely as they allow so that evidence in the text can be uncovered with as little interpreter's bias as possible.

---

[3]This is the level suggested by a reference, addressed in the participation and appropriation moments of Ricoeur's method of textual hermeneutics. These are not two mutually exclusive levels of action. It is not difficult to recognize that the performative force and effects of the language of the text certainly contribute to the action that describes appropriation. Yet, we do not wish to limit appropriation to performative force and effects. We understand the action of appropriation to encompass a broader notion of action.

[4]A convergence of communication theory with a semantics of action is evident here in terms of performativity's implication of interlocutors, mentioned in the preceding paragraph.

At the same time, it must be admitted that neither the criteria for explanation nor their practical application in the next chapter are exhaustive. They simply open up a way to recover the meaning of a liturgical text that complements the results of other possible analyses. In the following exposé, our starting point is an analysis of the semantics of action because that analysis leads to a communication dimension of the select text through the verb's relationship to its grammatical subject and object.[5] This demonstrates that the two theories chosen for the analytic are not mutually exclusive but actually implicate one another.

A. Ricoeur's Textual Indicators of Action

Ricoeur claims that human action can be objectified in a way similar to the fixation of the meaning of discourse through writing.[6] In this, the characteristics of texts suggest parallel characteristics of action permitting a science of action paralleling a science of text. In other words, since action is inscribed in a text and recoverable therein, textual analysis of

---

[5]"Subject" and "object" in this chapter refer to the grammatical parts of speech.

[6]See P. RICOEUR, "The Model of the Text: Meaningful Action Considered as a Text" in *Hermeneutics and the Human Sciences: Essays on Language, Action and Interpretation*, ed. and trans. J.B. Thompson (Cambridge: Cambridge University Press, 1981), pp. 197-221. This fixation or objectification is possible because action has the structure of a locutionary act; that is, its propositional content can be identified and re-identified as the same (p. 204). Action has a fixation in meaning by inscribing the "done" of acting. We can speak of an action leaving a trace, a "mark" (p. 205) as its objectification. Second, it also develops consequences of its own (p. 206) which indicates an action can be detached from its agent. Third, it has a "durable relevancy" (p. 208) that can be re-inscribed in different social contexts. Finally, human action is addressed to an infinite range of "readers" (p. 208) who judge action through subsequent history. In these four characteristics of discourse transposed to action (fixation of meaning, autonomy from agent, durable relevancy, and judgment by history), the model of the text suggests ways in which important action surpasses the immediacy of its originary situation and develops consequences that endure through history.

action at this level is a matter of focusing on what in a text indicates action. Grammatically, Ricoeur develops this primarily in terms of the predicate (verb). There are different ways that predicates function, both in themselves and in relation to other key parts of the sentence. This is our next concern, developed in five points: (1) Predicates and Relations; (2) Transitive Verbs; (3) Objects of Action Verbs; (4) Illocutionary Force; and (5) Perlocutionary Effects. There is a progression in these sections that leads from a consideration of the verb in itself to a reflection on how the action of the verb leads us outside the text.

1. Predicates and Relations

Ricoeur's analysis of textual indicators of action begins with a comparison/contrast of action predicates and relations, which are of two kinds: predicate relations and relations of attribution.[7] His intent is to more clearly indicate exactly what he means by "action predicate."

Action predicates and predicate relations are alike in that both name two (or more) terms. For example, "He took bread" is an action predicate with the two terms "He" and "bread." "He is the Word" is a predicate relation with the two terms "He" and "Word."[8] In these propositions, the order of the terms of the statement may be logically reversed with appropriate grammatical changes without changing the sense of the statement. Thus, "Bread was taken by Him" is a reverse statement which still makes sense. Greater clarification emerges when action predicates are *contrasted* with relations.

Predicate relations "are irreducible to all the kinds of predicates which may follow the copula 'is.'"[9] Another kind of relation is possible, a relation of attribution. The reversal of terms that is possible with action predicates or predicate

---

[7]See P. RICOEUR, *Sémantique de l'action* (Louvain: Université Catholique de Louvain--Cercle de Philosophie, 1971), polycopy, pp. 58-60.

[8]Cf. Ibid., p. 58. The examples are our own, taken from or referring to the select liturgical text.

[9]P. RICOEUR, "The Model of the Text" in *Hermeneutics and the Human Sciences*, p. 204.

relations is not possible with relations of attribution, which really have only one term. For example, "He is holy" is a relation of attribution; this statement cannot be reversed because "holy" cannot be a grammatical subject. We would have to introduce a new term such as "holy one." Here, "is holy" is the whole predicate, so that only one term is named, "He."

The class of action predicates is not reducible to predicate relations. In predicate relations, the terms are two existing entities. Action predicates, on the other hand, can link intentional objects; for example, mental acts such as "admire" and "worship." An even more important distinction, however, concerns not the "abbreviated state" of the predicate relation but the "elliptical state" of an action predicate. For example, the abbreviated state of a predicate relation is given in the example, "He is the Word." This is a complete statement; we need add nothing to satisfy the hearer's curiosity for more information. In another example illustrating the elliptical state of an action predicate, a statement like "He took bread" allows for any number of complements that add information to the bare proposition, such as "in his hands," "on a plate," "with a crust," an illustration of the elliptical state of an action predicate. Actually, the number of these variables is unlimited. Action predicates have a variable polydicity because they are elliptical in the sense that they embrace a multitude of information that can be added to the action utterance enhancing the sense of meaning.[10]

Action predicates are a larger class than predicate relations. There are similarities between them: both action predicates and predicate relations are larger classes than relations of attribution. Action, in the present discussion, refers to the broadest category, action predicates.

Ricoeur brings out other ways action may be inscribed in a text.[11] Our next consideration focuses on the effects of action predicates on other parts of the sentence; that is, on action predicates as transitive verbs.

---

[10]See P. RICOEUR, *Sémantique de l'action*, p. 59.

[11]See P. RICOEUR, *Sémantique de l'action*, pp. 61-67. In this whole discussion, Ricoeur draws heavily on the work of A. KENNY, *Action, Emotion and Will* (London: Routeledge & K. Paul, 1963), Chapters 7-9, pp. 151-202 (see *Sémantique de l'action*, p. 57).

2. Transitive Verbs

Transitive verbs are action predicates that have objects; transitive verbs relate subject and object. They can be classed as states, performances, or activities based on their *temporal* behavior.[12] Verbs of state and activities both occur for a time or *during* time; performances, on the other hand, occur *in* time. The former two classes can be prolonged indefinitely or stopped; the latter can be complete or incomplete. If a performance is completed, it always brings about a state. This implicates the consequences of performances. Performance statements are of the form "doing in such a way that p" (*faire en sorte que p*); for example, "assembling the community such that the community now exists." In this statement "assembling" is a performance verb; "exists" is a static verb (verb of state). Ricoeur's point here is the importance of the "means-end" relationship, especially for ethics as well as for a strategy of action derived from calculating the consequences of action.[13]

The ethic or strategy of action lies in the *language* of action (of the form "doing in such a way that p") and, as such, is the fundamental form for *voluntary* action utterances. Since only performatives can be put in the imperative mood, only

---

[12]See P. RICOEUR, *Sémantique de l'action*, p. 61. Ricoeur makes an initial distinction among the three classes of transitive verbs in terms of their temporal continuity or non-continuity. In this initial distinction, the verbs of state are non-continuous and are opposed to the performances and activites, which are continuous (see Ibid.). He then distinguishes between performances and activities in the way they move from the present to the perfect tenses. A performance has the form "assembling the community implies that the community has *not* been assembled." An activity takes the form "the community is living in Christian fellowship implies the community has lived in Christian fellowship." In the performance, the perfect is negative; in the activity, the perfect is not negative. For a fuller treatment of these statements, see A. KENNY, *Action, Emotion and Will*, pp. 171-175. The real distinction Ricoeur is unfolding is the uniqueness of the performances and so his presentation in *Sémantique de l'action* is limited to this end.

[13]See P. RICOEUR, *Sémantique de l'action*, p. 62.

performances can be voluntary.[14] This form ("doing in such a way that p") also suggests an answer for an inquiry about the truth of an act of discourse. The truth of a statement lies in the establishment of p. This suggests a purely linguistic definition of change: "X changes if some statement on X changes its truth value."[15] Hence, "doing in such a way that p" implies "giving truth that p."[16] Performances have a linguistic truth that is inherent in the very form of the performance statement.

Analysis in a different direction leads to another conclusion about the relation of performance and static verbs. In a purely conceptual analysis, event is understood broadly as that which happens in relating grammatical subject to object.[17]

---

[14]We cannot command a state, nor can we volunteer to be in a state. The same is true for activities. For example, we cannot command a community to live in Christian fellowship. Either the community is living in fellowship or it is not. If we wish a community to live differently from how it is actually living, we may command the community to live differently, but then this is really a performance, since what is precisely commanded is not the *living* in fellowship but a *change* of life that results in living in fellowship, which is a performance (and so can be commanded).

[15]P. RICOEUR, *Sémantique de l'action*, p. 63. My translation of the original French: "*X change* si quelque position sur X *change sa valeur de vérité* ... "

[16]Ibid. My translation of the original French: "faire en sorte que p" and "rendre vrai que p."

[17]The conceptual analysis is actually the first, more immediate (see *Sémantique de l'action*, p. 8) step in uncovering a semantics of action. Here, Ricoeur explores the fact that the language which describes human action is not the same language that is used to describe movements in nature (see Ibid., p. 5). Movement is of the type: "The celebrant raises the bread," and can be observed by a spectator. However, action is of the type "The celebrant raises the bread so the community can adore it." Here, it is not enough to simply observe the movement "raise the bread" but to that movement must be added the point of view of the agent (see Ibid.). Hence, action includes intention, mark, reason to act, motive, desire, preference, choice, agent, responsibility (see Ibid., p. 3). The import of this distinction is to move from a consideration of the natural world to the *meaning* of the world (see Ibid., p. 12). This is uncovered in a

In a more limited sense, however, event is understood as that which results in a change in the object. Again, this can be noted in a purely linguistic analysis. Performances have a passive voice. It makes sense to speak of action from the point of view of the grammatical object.[18] This points to a much more important reason for the distinction between performance and static verbs than the simple difference between classes of verbs: the linguistic rule of change and the linguistic event are both defined in terms of the object. They are constitutive of the very notion of verbs of action and are inscribed in the very grammar of those verbs. It is helpful, then, to search further into the linguistics of the objects of action verbs.

3. Objects of Action Verbs

The sense of the grammatical object derives from the grammar of the verb because objects complete the sense of the verb.[19] Or, to accept the scholastic adage (as Ricoeur does), objects specify acts. If we say "I worship God" we specify quite a different act from "I worship money." But there is another way objects specify acts; that is, according to whether the object is formal or material.

---

logical analysis of the propositions which describe action. In asserting that the sense of an action is in its force of desire (see Ibid., p. II-21), Ricoeur proceeds to where meaning and force coincide (see Ibid., p. 16). This is the real kernel of a theory of action (and hence our own development solely in terms of a semantics of action) for "it is in the relationship between disposition to and power of in which finally resides the ultimate difficulty of a theory of action" (Ibid., p. II-50. My translation of original French: "c'est dans la rapport entre *disposition à* et *pouvoir de* que réside finalement la difficulté ultime de la théorie de l'action"). This difficulty is addressed in applying the categories of speech-act theory to action, the main portion of our own treatment here. A third level of analysis of a theory of action is a discursive analysis of the fact that one proposition leads to another. Ricoeur develops this within a theory of decision and play (see Ibid., Chapter 6, pp. 91-104).

[18]See Ibid., p.63. Ricoeur uses "patient" here rather than "object."

[19]See Ibid., p. 64.

Formal objects identify the entire sphere of logically possible objects. Thus, for the verb "to worship," the formal object is "any object I esteem." On the other hand, material objects identify particular things. Thus, "God" is a material object of "to worship." Further, any given verb designates its formal object; the verb describes the genus of its formal object. As such, the formal object restricts the material object and "delineates the ideal shape of the sense of the verb."[20] The formal object can be logically derived from the verb but the material object cannot. Thus, "to worship" logically implies that who/what is worshipped must be worthy of esteem. But "to worship" does not logically imply any specific material object such as God. We could ask "worship whom/what?" and then the reply would specify the material object. The material object adds to the formal object an identifiable reference. While the formal object can be derived from the verb, the material object cannot.

Since we can identify the formal object through the verb, we might ask if there might be a more precise specification of the formal object? We need to consider more closely the nature of the verb. To begin, both non-psychological and psychological acts have a subject-verb-object form as, for example, in "The community worshipped God" and "The community feared God," respectively. On the surface these two propositions have the same grammatical form, but actually they are very different. The first specifies an effective action, the second, a mental act. In the non-intentional (non-psychological) act, the change affects the object. This is not the case with an intentional (psychological) act. There the change is in the subject. Moreover, there is not the same degree of existence between subject and object because, actually, the example sentence says "The community feared *that* God would ..." The truth of the mental proposition is uncovered in what comes after the word "that."[21] It is not sufficient to look only to the propositional content. Psychological verbs carry an illocutionary force incumbent on the subject and perlocutionary effects incumbent on the object.

---

[20]Ibid. My translation of original French: "dessine le contour notionnel du sens du verbe."

[21]See Ibid., pp. 65-66.

4. Illocutionary Force

The illocutionary force is what *we do in* speaking. To place this in the above context, Ricoeur wants to show that voluntary intention resides in language as declaration of intention.[22] Thus, language carries within it a *force* that derives from the intentionality of the locutionary act. This force is called the "illocutionary force" of the speech act.

Ricoeur does not accept A.J. Austin's simple substitution of "locutionary" and "illocutionary" for "constative" and "performative," respectively.[23] This, because it leads to insurmountable typological problems. Beginning at the level of manifestation, if we try to divide the constatives and performatives by types we find that, in a sense, every constative has a performative aspect. For example, even in a proposition like "God is holy" there is an assertion that the speaker is giving affirmation to holiness as an attribute of God. So Austin introduced the notion of "illocutionary" to mean what is implied *apart from* the internal propositional content of the statement. He then outlined five classes of illocutionary acts: verdicts, decrees, promises, behaviors or attitudes, and expositions. In effect, we could type distinctions without end. If, instead, we type illocutionary acts from the level of constitutive rules, we surpass ordinary language by a metalanguage and solve the typology problem. This needs further clarification.

Beginning at the level of rules, each type is regulated by an *essential condition*; for example, the essential condition of a promise is that the promise "counts as."[24] This "counts as," the constitutive rule, permits the identification of the illocutionary force of the proposition. It is the heart of the intention itself, where the speaker, through the illocutionary

---

[22]See Ibid., p. 68.

[23]See Ibid., p. 69. "Constative" refers to the propositional content of a statement and "performative" refers to its force and effects.

[24]See Ibid., p. 75. Ricoeur's discussion focuses on the promise, since it (plus intention) best expresses the human act of willing, which is the context for the development of his theory of action. But the method of locating the essential condition can be extended to any illocutionary act (see Ibid., p. 76).

force, is placed under the obligation to do such and such. The intention is not there in terms of the speaker's introspection, but it is there in terms of the semantic implication of the *use* of language.

This essential condition is the center of two other conditions. There are preparatory conditions which are mental or psychological conditions. Where the essential condition has the form "S has the intention *that*," the mental condition has the form "S has the intention *of*." Though the mental intention is subordinate to the verbal (essential) intention,[25] the mental act is at the base of what is expressed.[26] The third condition follows after the mental and essential conditions, and distinguishes the illocutionary act from the perlocutionary act.

5. Perlocutionary Effects

The illocutionary act is distinguished by what we do *in the saying*: "I promise" binds the speaker to a promise. The perlocutionary act is distinguished by what happens *in the doing*: "I promise" results in a promise being kept. The third condition, then, is a condition of recognition by others that the illocutionary force places an obligation to *do* something on the object. In this there is an inter-subjectivity so that in the speech-act the locutionary, illocutionary, and perlocutionary aspects of the single speech-act are inseparable.[27] The link between grammatical subject and object is the predicate. It is the latter which is the key to the change on subject and object favored by the speech-act.

Ricoeur's recovery of action from a text converges on action predicates which are performance transitive verbs. This very specific action predicate is the one which most clearly shows the relationship of predicate to subject and object, pointing to illocutionary force and perlocutionary effects. Performance transitive verbs are those which demand a change in subject and

---

[25]Because the essential condition rests in *semantics*. If the mental intention were logically prior, it would be impossible to get out of psychologism.

[26]See P. RICOEUR, *Sémantique de l'action*, pp. 78-79.

[27]Ibid., pp. 79-88.

object. With intersubjectivity being a constituent part of a speech-act, our next consideration is the act of communication itself.

B. Jakobson's Communication Factors and Functions

Just as the above remarks show that there is more to a verb than the simple elementary school definition "A verb is an action word," so this next section demonstrates that there is more to an act of communication than the simple "someone says something to someone." Roman Jakobson is a linguist who recognized that there is more involved in the communication process than an addresser conveying a message to an addressee. Jakobson extends this traditional triadic model to include three additional communication factors (components of communication): every communication involves an addresser, addressee, and message; but also a context, a means of contact, and a code.[28] The meaning of a communication act can only be uncovered when all these factors are taken into consideration.

Ricoeur's remark that Jakobson's "model calls for a philosophical investigation, which may be provided by the dialectic of event and meaning"[29] sets an agenda for its liturgical application. To the extent that liturgy is language and communication, we can isolate the communication factors as well as uncover in that analysis a dialectic of event and meaning. An analysis of the language of the liturgical text within Jakobson's communication theory paves the way not only to describe more concretely what is involved in perceiving liturgy as communication; but (and even more importantly), it also paves the way to understand how the very meaning of liturgy is bound up in its action character.[30]

---

[28]See R. JAKOBSON, "Closing Statement: Linguistics and Poetics" in *Style in Language*, ed. T.A. Sebeok (Cambridge: The M.I.T. Press, 1960), pp. 350-377.

[29]P. RICOEUR, "Language as Discourse" in *Interpretation Theory: Discourse and the Surplus of Meaning* (Fort Worth: The Texas Christian University Press, 1979), p. 15.

[30]Cf. J. LADRIERE, "The Performativity of Liturgical Language," trans. J. Griffiths, *Concilium* 9-1 (1973), p. 50: "The expression of faith in worship relies upon various registers which may be reduced to three: those of vocal, gestural and

There is more to Jakobson's communication theory than identifying the six factors that make up a communication act. To these six factors, Jakobson parallels six communication functions (how the factor affects the meaning of the communication): the addresser factor is paralleled in the emotive function, the addressee factor in the conative function, the message in the poetic, the context in the referential, the contact in the phatic, and the code in the metalingual.[31] In the following schema of factors and functions the upper case text indicates communication factors, and the lower case text in parenthesis indicates functions.[32]

CONTEXT
(referential)

MESSAGE
(poetic)

ADDRESSER - ADDRESSEE
(emotive) (conative)

CONTACT
(phatic)

CODE
(metalingual)

---

symbolic expression. *Vocal expression* is one form of language use, which may involve singing. *Gestural expression* is a form of body language--the body as a meaningful force. *Symbolic expression* is a way of using things (places, clothes, lights, and so on) which endows them with a referential capacity over and above their direct meaning. These three forms of expression are mutually supportive, and any full analysis of expressive worship obviously ought to take into account the complex ways in which they interact" (italics Ladrière's).

[31]See R. JAKOBSON, "Closing Statement" in *Style in Language*, pp. 350-377.

[32]See E. HOLLENSTEIN, *Roman Jakobson's Approach to Language: Phenomenological Structuralism*, trans. C. Schelbert and T. Schelbert (Bloomington: Indiana University Press, 1976), p. 154.

T. Hawkes suggests the model is a significant advancement in communication analysis:

> The central point to emerge from Jakobson's account of communication is that the 'message' does not and cannot supply all of the 'meaning' of the transaction, and that a good deal of what is communicated derives from the context, the code, and the means of contact. 'Meaning' in short resides in the *total* act of communication ...[33]

Even the visual presentation of the model suggests implications. The line connecting addresser and addressee intimates a relationship between them that cannot be broken if communication is to take place. What connects them is the message. However, this message is not isolated: what stands above it (to which it refers) is a context, and what lies below it (which establishes attentiveness) is the contact. Underlying the whole schema is the code, the medium of communication.

Jakobson holds that in different acts of communication different functions are primary; "the nature of the message is finally determined by the fact that it takes on the functional character of whichever of the six elements involved happens to be dominant."[34] Jakobson speaks of a "set" (*Einstellung*) toward one or other function which determines its primary position in a hierarchy of functions, but "the accessory participation of the other functions in such messages must be taken into account by the observant linguist."[35] This relative hierarchy of the functions taken as a whole determines the meaning of the communication. For Jakobson, the key to describing an act of communication lies in identifying the relative hierarchy of set and subsets that characterizes the communication. The set of a communication act is an emphasis on one of the factors/functions while the other five factors/functions figure in a supportive role to the main emphasis. The communication is directed toward the factor/function of its set. For example, if the set of an act of communication is directed toward the addresser, then the

---

[33]T. HAWKES, *Structuralism and Semiotics* (Berkeley: University of California Press, 1977), p. 83.

[34]Ibid., p. 84.

[35]R. JAKOBSON, "Closing Statement" in *Style in Language*, p. 353. See also R. JAKOBSON, *The Framework of Language*, Michigan Studies in the Humanities, No. 1 (1980), p. 82.

point of the communication is to reveal the emotional import of the addresser. All other factors/functions operate within this overriding emphasis and must be interpreted in this light.

According to Ricoeur, the model of Jakobson

> is interesting in that it (1) describes discourse directly and not as a residue of language; (2) describes a structure of discourse and not only an irrational event; and (3) it subordinates the code function to the connecting operation of communication.[36]

Its positive contribution lies in recognizing that the message cannot supply all the meaning, that discourse is structural, and that *langue* is in the service of *parole*.

We now present Jakobson's six communication factors and functions (1) in terms of Jakobson's initial descriptions and (2) with comments, explanations, and amplifications by other selected authors *paying special attention to Ricoeur's correctives.*[37] In addition, (3) we tailor this communication/linguistic data to liturgical application. Finally, Jakobson's insistence that in communication there is always a set toward one particular factor/function with the others contributing to the meaning of the communication in a relative hierarchy (4) will be outlined.

1. Addresser/Emotive

For Jakobson, "the so-called EMOTIVE or 'expressive' function, focused on the ADDRESSER, aims a direct expression of the speaker's attitude toward what he is speaking about."[38] Note that the emotion involves what the addresser is speaking about,

---

[36]P. RICOEUR, "Language as Discourse" in *Interpretation Theory*, p. 15.

[37]It should be noted that, though the importance of Jakobson's model is universally accepted, he himself wrote little on the subject and few others have added to the theory through analysis and/or commentary on the factors and functions (see J. LYONS, *Semantics* [Cambridge: Cambridge University Press, 1977], Vol. 1, p. 54).

[38]R. JAKOBSON, "Closing Statement" in *Style in Language*, p. 354.

not an emotion directed to the addressee. This emotive function is most clearly seen in interjections, though this must be understood in the broader sense of not just pithy words (Tut! Tut!), but also in one using expressive features ("gestures? Yes, but also elongated phonemes, etc."[39]). E. Holenstein adds that a set toward addresser reveals the personal attitude, status, or emotional state of the speaker; it indicates the attitude of the speaker *toward the words spoken.*[40] I.A. Richards places emphasis on someone directing, sending a message.[41] This is first-person discourse. The stress here is on the *source* of the message as conveying emotion that affects the meaning of the communication. Within the context of speech-act theory, a set toward addresser is indicated by the illocutionary force of the speech act. Certain types of performatives evidence this force at work: affirmation or negation, thanking, promising, approving, deciding, etc.[42] In these performatives, the addresser binds her/himself to a certain kind of action by the very utterance itself.

Liturgically speaking, the addresser could involve several possibilities: the presider, deacon (if one is present), proclaimers of the word, commentators, and the assembled community. Theologically speaking, one could even argue that the addresser in the Liturgy of the Word is Christ himself, since it is his word which is proclaimed.[43] Over and above the question of who is speaking, the more important questions are when and why is there a set toward the addresser in liturgy? The answer

---

[39]Ibid. See also L.R. WAUGH, *Roman Jakobson's Science of Language* (Lisse: The Peter de Ridder Press, 1976), p. 25.

[40]See E. HOLENSTEIN, *Roman Jakobson's Approach to Language*, p. 54.

[41]See I.A. RICHARDS, "Functions of and Factors in Language," *Journal of Literary Semantics* 1 (1972), 27.

[42]See J. LADRIERE, "The Performativity of Liturgical Language," p. 53.

[43]See *The General Instruction of the Roman Missal* in *Documents on the Liturgy 1963-1979: Conciliar, Papal, and Curial Texts* (Collegeville: The Liturgical Press, 1983), Document #208, pp. 465-534, #9: "When the Scriptures are read in the Church, God himself speaks to his people and it is Christ present in his word, who proclaims the Gospel."

evokes a realization that the attitudes and emotions expressed by the addresser affect the meaning of the communication and that this is what is primary in the specific act of communication when the set is toward addresser.

2. Addressee/Conative

For Jakobson, "orientation toward the ADDRESSEE, the CONATIVE function, finds its purest grammatical expression in the vocative and imperative ... "[44] He goes on to note that imperative sentences differ from declarative sentences most notably in that the former cannot be determined to be true or false nor can they be converted into interrogative sentences. A set toward the addressee attempts to make what is contained in the communication more or less evident to the person being addressed. This is second-person discourse. A set toward the addressee is indicated by a perlocutionary act. The emphasis here is on the promotion of an effect because perlocutionary language leads to results. Hence, a set toward the addressee is an invitation to activity. It is evidenced in performative utterances which are aimed at producing a particular effect in the addressee: persuading, commanding, enlightening, inspiring, petitioning, etc.[45]

Jakobson's use of the term "conative" rather than the term "vocative" to describe an addressee's correlative function implies "that it is primarily as an instrument in the satisfaction of the speaker's wishes and desires that the addressee is invoked."[46] Hence, even though a set toward addressee is an indication of desired effects on that addressee, the emphasis is not separate from the addresser's wishes or desires. The effect produced in the addressee accrues some benefit for the addresser. Analysis of addresser/addressee factors indicates that there is a close relationship between them in the communicative act. If the set is toward one, the other will be directly and closely affected. If the set is toward the addresser, the import of the communication lies in the attitude

---

[44]R. JAKOBSON, "Closing Statement" in *Style in Language*, p. 355.

[45]See J. LADRIERE, "The Performativity of Liturgical Language," p. 53.

[46]J. LYONS, *Semantics*, p. 52.

of the speaker *as directed to* the addressee. If the set is toward the addressee, the import of the communication lies in the effects the addresser's attitudes and emotions *seek to have on* the addressee. When determining the hierarchy of functions, it is not sufficient just to highlight a set toward addresser or addressee without also showing how the other is implicated as well.

As with the addresser, in liturgy the addressee is sometimes God, sometimes the presider, and at other times the assembled community. Most frequently, however, the addresser/addressee pair is between the assembled community as addresser and God (named in various ways) as addressee. This "dialogue" characterizes liturgy as prayer. When the set of this dialogue is on addresser, the prayer emphasizes the attitudes and emotions of the community. Here, prayer as praise, adoration, and thanksgiving is paramount. When the set is on the addressee, the prayer emphasizes the desires of the addresser (usually the community) to whom the addressee (God) is to respond. Here, the prayer is that of supplication. An analysis of the addresser/addressee pair not only points to liturgy as prayer, but it also indicates the kind of prayer language that is used.

3. Contact/Phatic

Jakobson asserts that

> there are messages primarily serving to establish, to prolong, or to discontinue communication, to check whether the channel works ("Hello, do you hear me?"), to attract the attention of the interlocutor or to confirm his continued attention ("Are you listening?" or in Shakespearean diction, "Lend me your ears!"--and on the other end of the wire "Um-hm!").[47]

A set for contact "may be displayed by a profuse exchange of ritualized formulas, by entire dialogues with the mere purport of prolonging communication."[48] This set asks, checks out, whether contact between/among interlocutors is being maintained. Holenstein sees contact as the physical channel or psychological

[47] R. JAKOBSON, "Closing Statement" in *Style in Language*, p. 355.

[48] Ibid.

connection which maintains the communication.[49] Richards rewords Jakobson to see contact as the physical and mental conditions which let the addresser and addressee come into and continue communication; it keeps the parties "in touch."[50]

In liturgy, contact establishes a relationship between the presider and the assembled community.[51] This not only strengthens the presider's role as president of the assembly, but it also establishes the "here and now" reality of liturgy. Another consideration arises, however, if we consider contact in terms of ritualized formulas. This is ordinarily understood to mean such queries as "How are you?" where the addresser does not expect a medical report by way of an answer. When contact is made in liturgy through such ritualized formulas as "The Lord be with you," the question arises as to whether contact is established not so much between the presider and community (who are obvious interlocutors) as between God and the community (who are the usual interlocutors when the set in the liturgical text

---

[49]See E. HOLENSTEIN, *Roman Jakobson's Approach to Language*, p. 155.

[50]See I.A. RICHARDS, "Functions of and Factors in Language," 28.

[51]Not unimportant in the present discussion is the fact that the early notion of Church (community) was not so much as a static, spatially-defined, enumerated entity or body, but as a *gathered* assembly called by God for worship. The emphasis in this latter notion of Church is on action rather than passion. In the Greek Septuagent, *ekklesia* translates *qe hal*, which means "the *assembly* of God, the *meeting* of God" (C. VAGAGGINI, *Theological Dimensions of the Liturgy: A General Treatise on the Theology of the Liturgy*, 4th ed., trans. L.J. Doyle and W.A. Jurgens [Collegeville: The Liturgical Press, 1976], p. 279; see also the article " ἐκκλησία " by K.L. SCHMIDT in *Theological Dictionary of the New Testament*, ed. G. Kittel and G. Friedrich, trans. G.W. Bromiley [Grand Rapids: Wm B. Eerdmans Publishing Company, 1964-1976], Vol. III, pp. 501-536). In this action sense of community as a gathered assembly for worship, language is "the location in which and the instrument by means of which the community is constituted" (J. LADRIERE, "The Performativity of Liturgical Language," 59). In liturgy, then, the phatic function of language is not only an "attention-getting" device, but (much more importantly) it actually constitutes the community.

is toward addresser or addressee). If this were the case, then there would be a strong affinity between contact and context in the liturgy.

4. Code/Metalingual

According to Jakobson, "whenever the addresser and/or the addressee need to check up whether they use the same code, speech is focused on the CODE: it performs a METALINGUAL (i.e. glossing) function."[52] Centered on language (French: *langue*), the code is "the corpus of possible messages."[53] Further, "any overall code is multiform and comprises a hierarchy of diverse subcodes freely chosen by the speaker with regard to the variable functions of the message, to its addressee, and to the relation between the interlocutors."[54] In other words, "the code is not static but dynamic, a diversified, convertible code, with differentiations as to functions and as to time and space factors."[55] Hence, code is a "semiotic entity rather than a material one."[56] It is "the system ... which underlies and makes possible that and every other message"[57] and "requires the collective concensus of the

---

[52]R. JAKOBSON, "Closing Statement" in *Style in Language*, p. 356. Note that U. ECO ("The Influence of Roman Jakobson on the Development of Semiotics" in D. Armstrong and C.H. Van Schooneveld, eds., *Roman Jakobson: Echoes of His Scholarship* [Lisse: The Peter de Riddler Press, 1977], p. 48) brings out two different uses of code, which he says Jakobson always keeps distinct: the code within a system which relates signifier to signified and the code between systems.

[53]R. JAKOBSON, *Selected Writings II*, Five Volumes (s'Gravenhage: Mouton & Co., 1962-1979), p. 705. See also U. ECO, "The Influence of Roman Jakobson on the Development of Semiotics" in *Roman Jakobson: Echoes of His Scholarship*, p. 48: "There is a code only when there is an ensemble of forecasted possibilities based upon the correlation of a given signifier to a given signified."

[54]R. JAKOBSON, *Selected Writings II*, p. 719.

[55]L.R. WAUGH, *Roman Jakobson's Science of Language*, p. 23.

[56]Ibid.

[57]Ibid.

individual speakers."[58] L.R. Waugh's conclusions are echoed in Richards, who describes the code as a "system of sounds, marks, related to parts that can make up the messages"[59] and this must be fully or at least in part the same for addresser and addressee. A set toward the code tries to show by explications or through examples how terms (language) are being used.

One departure of Ricoeur from Jakobson involves the metalingual function. Jakobson limits the code to the language system, as a function over and against the other functions. Ricoeur, however, extends the metalingual function to the reflective capacity of language to designate itself and its other. In this, the metalingual function is particularly related to the referential function. Both functions point to language's mediation of reality.[60] This has important consequences for a liturgical application.

In liturgy, the code is identified as the language that is used. However, this must be understood as more than use of the vernacular, or even more than use of religious or sacred language. The set toward code in liturgy is concerned with finding out if the code is used/understood in the same way by all who participate in the liturgy. Thus, this set is determined by the *concurrence* of the assembled community with what is being communicated. The "checking up" on whether the code is understood is more than just a common agreement on the sense of *langue*, but in liturgy a set toward code implies an involvement, a commitment, to what is commonly understood. Code is expressed through such utterances as acclamations, faith statements, and commitment ceremonies and in this the metalingual function is the community's affirmation of the reality being mediated by language.

---

[58]Ibid. See also P. RICOEUR, "Language as Discourse" in *Interpretation Theory*, p. 3, who sees code as "systematic and compulsory for a given speaking community."

[59]I.A. RICHARDS, "Functions of and Factors in Language," 27.

[60]See P. RICOEUR, "Metaphor and Philosophical Discourse" in *The Rule of Metaphor: Multi-disciplinary Studies of the Creation of Meaning in Language*, trans. R. Czerny with K. McLaughlin and J. Costello, S.J. (Toronto: University of Toronto Press, 1977), p. 304.

5. Message/Poetic

Being of primary interest to Jakobson, the workings of the poetic function are both more accessible in his writings as well as more illusive. Here we come to the heart of communication. For Jakobson, the poetic function is the dominant, determining function of verbal art.[61] It is an aesthetic, artistic function[62] although we must be careful to recognize that the poetic function is not equal to poetry: "Any attempt to reduce the sphere of poetic function to poetry or to confine poetry to poetic function would be a delusive oversimplification."[63]

The poetic function operates in two ways. First, "by promoting the palpability of signs, [it] deepens the fundamental dichotomy of signs and objects."[64] For Jakobson, the message is necessarily arbitrary because the focus is on the "message for its own sake at the expense of the reference"[65] and hence on the elucidation of the sign which promotes the dichotomy of signs and objects. Second, the poetic function "projects the principle of equivalence from the axis of selection into the axis of combination."[66] The poetic function, for Jakobson, plays on mere equivalence of terms. Thus, the message is contingent, implying that the process of combination offers no surprises: "the message

---

[61]See R. JAKOBSON, "Closing Statement" in *Style in Language*, p. 356.

[62]See R. JAKOBSON, *Selected Writings II*, pp. 558 and 662.

[63]R. JAKOBSON, "Closing Statement" in *Style in Language*, p. 356. The poetic function applies not only to poetry but to any artistic, creative use of language in general (see J. LYONS, *Semantics*, p. 54).

[64]R. JAKOBSON, "Closing Statement" in *Style in Language*, p. 356.

[65]See P. RICOEUR, "Language as Discourse" in *Interpretation Theory*, p. 36. See also P. RICOEUR, "The Hermeneutical Function of Distanciation" in *Hermeneutics and the Human Sciences*, p. 141: " ... poetic, where language seems to glorify itself at the expense of the referential function of ordinary discourse."

[66]R. JAKOBSON, "Closing Statement" in *Style in Language*, p. 358; italics Jakobson's. See also P. RICOEUR, "Metaphor and Reference" in *The Rule of Metaphor*, p. 223.

has the ground of its communicability in the structure of its meaning."[67] As Richards puts it, a message is a meaning selected from a limitless possible field.[68] It is in this context that Jakobson says "poetry and metalanguage ... are in diametrical opposition to each other: in metalanguage the sequence is used to build an equation, whereas in poetry the equation is used to build a sequence."[69] Thus "the message is a temporal event in the succession of events which constitute the diachronic dimension of time."[70] Waugh nicely summarizes message as "the unique, semelfactive [instantaneous, momentary, singular], single act of speech."[71] The set toward message is a set toward the linguistic symbols in themselves. For them to have meaning, they must be *interpreted* by the addressee.[72]

Ricoeur rejects Jakobson's eclipse of reference in the poetic function: "My contention is that discourse cannot fail to be about something. In saying this, I am denying the ideology of absolute texts."[73] Except for a few very sophisticated texts in modern literature, Ricoeur maintains that even texts whose emphasis is on message still refer to a world. To this end he distinguishes between texts with ostensive-descriptive references (for example, discourse) and non-ostensive-descriptive references (for example, non-poetic, non-fictional texts) which point to a situational reference as opposed to texts with a non-ostensive and non-descriptive reference (poetic texts) which point to a non-situational reference. It is not a question of *whether* a

---

[67]P. RICOEUR, "Language as Discourse" in *Interpretation Theory*, p. 16.

[68]See I.A. RICHARDS, "Functions of and Factors in Language," 36-37.

[69]R. JAKOBSON, "Closing Statement" in *Style in language*, p. 358.

[70]P. RICOEUR, "Language as Discourse" in *Interpretation Theory*, p. 3.

[71]L.R. WAUGH, *Roman Jakobson's Science of Language*, p. 23.

[72]See I.A. RICHARDS, "Functions of and Factors in Language," 38.

[73]P. RICOEUR, "Speaking and Writing" in *Interpretation Theory*, p. 36.

text refers to a world, but rather it is a question of *how* the text refers to a world. A descriptive text precipitates a situation while a non-descriptive text does not. The distinction is between a situation (whether real or imaginary is unimportant at the moment) opened up by descriptions including space-time references and a non-situation that has no "connection to the unique space-time network common to ostensive and non-ostensive discription [*sic*]."[74] In either case, there is a world because there is reference. Further, for Ricoeur the term "world" indicates

> the ensemble of references opened up by every kind of text, descriptive or poetic, that I have read, understood, and loved. And to understand a text is to interpolate among the predicates of our situation all the significations that make a *Welt* out of our *Umwelt*. It is this enlarging of our horizon of existence that permits us to speak of the references opened up by the text or of the world opened up by the referential claims of most texts.[75]

Even poetic texts, for Ricoeur, enlarge our horizon of existence in their own non-situational way.

The Liturgy of the Word emphasizes message and its interpretation. But while Jakobson would support the increased dichotomy between sign and object (that is, between Scripture and reality), Ricoeur would maintain that the proclamation must be about something, so it must refer to a world. This is evident when that message is not only proclaimed, but *interpreted*. The interpretation is aided, however, by the context. There is a relationship between the poetic and referential functions.

6. Context/Reference

Asserting that a set toward the context is the leading task of numerous messages, Jakobson sees this as a denotative, cognitive function.[76] For Jakobson, "in referential language the

---

[74]Ibid., p. 36.

[75]Ibid., p. 37.

[76]See R. JAKOBSON, "Closing Statement" in *Style in Language*, p. 353. See also *Selected Writings II*, p. 705: "referential, conceptual component"; p. 719: "cognitive, referential function."

connection between *signans* and *signatum* is overwhelmingly based on their codified contiguity,"[77] and here Jakobson and Ricoeur part company again. Jakobson would maintain that a set toward reference seeks to manifest the *signatum.* Waugh suggests Jakobson is saying that the referential function is ideational, that it informs about ideas or the outside world.[78] It seems that Jakobson makes no claim about that *signatum* in terms of its prerogative to unveil reality. The task of a set toward reference is simply to "designate objects and bestow them with meaning."[79] Thus, for Jakobson, the context is "something the addresser is thinking of, talking about; [that] which the addressee can think of, more or less, as the addresser does."[80] It makes what is spoken more "seizable." Richards uncovers a special problem with respect to referent: "referent, so defined, is dual: both a bare denotation (extension) AND the character being ascribed to it."[81] Then he raises two questions concerning the character being ascribed to the referent: "Is the referent what would be, were it as the statement represents it as being? Or is it what would make that representation true, if true, and false, if false?"[82] This takes us to the heart of the problem. Richards continues his probing:

> CONTEXT links this trouble [duality of the referent] with at least two others. Any attempt to describe how we come to

---

[77]R. JAKOBSON, "Closing Statement" in *Style in Language*, p. 372.

[78]See L.R. WAUGH, *Roman Jakobson's Science of Language*, p. 25.

[79]E. HOLENSTEIN, *Roman Jakobson's Approach to Language*, p. 156.

[80]I.A. RICHARDS, "Functions of and Factors in Language," 27.

[81]Ibid., 34.

[82]Ibid. O. RIBOUL (in *Langage et idéologie* [Paris: Press universitaires de France, 1980], pp. 46-51) comments that it is only the referential function to which true or false can be applied. On p. 51 he charts a *valeur* (import, force) for each of the factors/functions: referential--truth; emotive--sincerity; conative--legitimacy; poetic--beauty; phatic--politeness; and metalingual--correction. These forces and their opposites (falsehood, insincerity, etc.) could be added to the criteria listed in the next section.

> know anything through experience, become able to refer to it, think of it, talk of it, etc., has somehow *to connect present thinkings of, pointings to, etc., with past originative occasions.* Through one nomenclature or another it has to take account of recurrence.[83]

In other words, Richards is saying that the sequence of past meanings affects the present meaning of the *signatum*; when speaking of context or reference, this must be taken into account. So the context is twofold: both the *process* of past recurrences which affects present meanings and the immediate *surroundings* of the *signans* in the given communication act.

Herein is a pivotal problem. Though the analysis thus far has remained on an epistemological level, a sense of "something more" prevails which is never explicated. Ricoeur, therefore, pushes the referent to the level of reality. For Ricoeur,

> the sense of the meaning is the ideal object which is intended. This meaning is purely immanent to discourse. The reference is the truth value of the proposition, its claim to reach reality. Through this character discourse is opposed to language which has no relationship with reality. Words refer to other words in the round without end of the dictionary. Only discourse, we say, intends things, is applied to reality, expresses the world.[84]

What is essential is that meaning is recovered only in use. While the reference of oral language results from monstrations common to the interlocutors,[85] in texts the "referential function is supported by the sentence ... which intends to say something true or something real, at least in declarative discourse."[86] Though language in itself separates signs from things, language in use compensates for this:

---

[83]I.A. RICHARDS, "Functions of and Factors in Language," 34; italics added.

[84]P. RICOEUR, "Philosophy and Religious Language," *Journal of Religion* 54 (1974), 78-79.

[85]See P. RICOEUR, "Language as Discourse" in *Interpretation Theory*, p. 35.

[86]P. RICOEUR, "What is a Text? Explanation and Understanding" in *Hermeneutics and the Human Sciences*, p. 148.

> Language is not a world of its own. It is not even a world. But because we are in the world, because we are affected by situations, and because we orient ourselves comprehensively in those situations, we have something to say, we have experience to bring to language. ... This notion of bringing experience to language is the ontological condition of reference, an ontological condition reflected within language as a postulate which has not [*sic*] immanent justification ... [87]

Limit-experience is connected with limit-expression, which has important ramifications within the religious sphere:

> The limit-expressions of religious language are appropriated in the redescription of that which we might correlatively call the *limit-experiences* of man, and that these limit-experiences, redescribed by the limit-expressions of religious language, constitute the appropriate *referent* of this language.[88]

Ricoeur is saying that religious language has within its very configuration the possibility of being in touch with the religious reality to which it is directed. Thus, while "religious language discloses the religious dimension of *common* human experience"[89] on the one hand, on the other hand it also discloses the human dimension of common *religious* experience. Language in use is a model for theologically relating human experience and religious experience.

Liturgically speaking, there is a set toward reference in that text where the focus is on a sequence of disclosures that open up the text's relationship to reality. As descriptive text, it is necessarily situational.

We suspect that just as addresser/addressee hold in tension an essential contiguity, so do message and context. A set toward message is a commitment to redescribe reality because the scope of the poetic function is "the power of making the redescription

---

[87]P. RICOEUR, "Language as Discourse" in *Interpretation Theory*, pp. 20-21.

[88]P. RICOEUR, "Biblical Hermeneutics," *Semeia* 13 (1975), 108; italics added.

[89]Ibid., 128; italics Ricoeur's.

of reality correspond with the power of bringing the fictions of the imagination to speech."[90] In religious terms, this is to say that a set toward message is a recognition of the power of bringing into line reality and its expressions precisely in terms of the redescription arrived at in the very process of interpretation. A set on message renders the text primary with respect to offering a redescription of reality. On the other hand, a set toward context measures the adequacy of the text over and against the reality it discloses. This renders reality as primary with respect to interpreting the text and shapes and controls that very interpretation. In either case, there is a contiguity between message and context that cannot be disrupted precisely because of the relationship between limit-expression and limit-experience.

Having layed out Ricoeur's action theory and Jakobson's communication model and having made preliminary suggestions about their applicability to liturgical texts, we now set out the linguistic criteria that are the interpretive tools for applying these theories to a liturgical text.

C. Criteria for a Liturgical Analytic

An analysis of a liturgical act as communication is difficult because each liturgical celebration is a unique communication event. Analysis, therefore, cannot be extrapolated to indicate implications for all liturgical acts as specific events. Yet, liturgical principles and theological indications can be universalized. Analysis, then, focuses only on what is common to all liturgical acts: the liturgical text.

The criteria for this analysis of liturgical texts are a combination of the linguistic indications of action inscribed within a text and communication factors/functions that may be operative. Since there has already been an extensive presentation of Ricoeur's semantics of action and Jakobson's communication model, the criteria for analyzing the select Eucharistic text are presented in outline form. Our intention is to keep the criteria specific enough to be recognizable in a text with as little ambiguity as possible. The linguistic criteria are grouped together under some common headings. Each criterion is marked with a black dot ("●") so it can be quickly identified and so that the various criteria can be clearly separated from the categories under which they have been grouped.

---

[90]Ibid., 107.

Six categories adequately group the criteria. (1) "PRONOUN USE" refers to the actual inclusion of first ("I," "me," "my," "we," etc.), second ("you"), or third ("he," "she," "it," etc.) person pronouns in the text. (2) "VERB USE" includes such items as illocutionary or perlocutionary verbs, moods (conditional, optative, subjunctive, indicative), and voice (active or passive). (3) "GRAMMAR USE" emphasizes construction of a sentence beyond subject-verb-object, including such examples as use of interjections, adverbs, particular word order, etc. (4) "TYPOGRAPHY USE" refers to elements that are part of the printed appearance of the text, such as exclamation points, question marks, or use of italics. (5) "EXPRESSIVE FEATURES" includes any vocal expression (such as voice inflection) or bodily action (gestures) which gives a textual indication of feeling or emotion. Finally, (6) "LITERARY GENRE" includes the devices normally accepted in the literary field as genre (such as narrative, poetry, etc.).

Most of the criteria listed are general and might apply to any field in which a text might be written to express content. Some criteria, however, would apply specifically to the field of liturgy. For example, "signs of reverence" in general transposes to "bow," but it may transpose to "genuflection" for a specifically liturgical context. Where these criteria are uniquely liturgical, they are included in square brackets in the following list. What follows, then, is a listing of each of Jakobson's communication factors/functions with respective linguistic criteria augmented by Ricoeur's action theory. Since all of these criteria have been mentioned earlier in the chapter, further comments would only be redundant. The criteria are listed here in point form in order to pull together concrete criteria for analyzing a text which may have been lost in the density of the above exposé and to provide a handy quick-reference for the reader as s/he follows the ensuing analyses of Chapters Five and Six.

1. Addresser/Emotive

PRONOUN USE

- First Person ("I," "we," etc.)

VERB USE

- Performative Verbs of Illocutionary Force

- Intentional (verb denoted as a mental act)
- Passive voice a possibility, denoting action *by* a subject

Examples:
  - Affirmations
  - Negations
  - Praising
  - Thanking
  - Promising
  - Approving
  - Deciding
  - Doubting, etc.

- Predicate relations
- Specific moods
  - Hortatory
  - Conditional
  - Subjunctive
  - Optative

GRAMMAR USE

- Interjections

TYPOGRAPHY USE

- Exclamation points
- Question marks

EXPRESSIVE FEATURES

- "Feeling" expressions or words revealing attitude or emotion
- Songs
- Gestures
- [● Extended hands]

2. Addressee/Conative

PRONOUN USE

- Second Person ("you")

VERB USE

- Performative Verbs of Perlocutionary Effects

- Non-intensional (denoting an effective action)
- Action that affects the addressee
- Passive voice a possibility, emphasizing action "done to"
- Truth value lies in the performance or non-performance of an action
- Examples:
    - Persuading
    - Petitioning
    - Enlightening
    - Inviting to activity
    - Inspiring, etc.

- Specific moods
    - Imperative verbs:[91]
        - Commanding
        - Intending, etc.

GRAMMAR USE

- Statements with no propositional truth value; they cannot be converted into a question
- Non-declarative statements

---

[91] J. LADRIERE indicates that "imperative formulations involve a non-expressed performative" ("The Performativity of Liturgical Language," 57). Note that Ricoeur (see above, p. 98) sees imperatives as perlocutionary performatives. Ricoeur does allow for at least a limited inscription of the perlocutionary. With Jakobson's communication factors/functions, a greater specification is permitted. Hence, with an emphasis on addressee, we see the imperative as indicating a perlocutionary performative, though Jakobson's insistence on a *hierarchy* of functions implies that the addresser is also significant in an imperative. This hierarchy suggests a refinement of Ricoeur rather than a contradiction in the classification of inscribed indicators. Other refinements involve including some performative verbs under criteria for addressee (thus implying perlocutionary force), and adverbs as indicating context.

EXPRESSIVE FEATURES

● Pointed finger
[● Joined hands]
[● Lifting of gifts]

3. Contact/Phatic

EXPRESSIVE FEATURES

● Exchange of ritualized formulas or responses

[● "The Lord be with you." "And also with you."]

● Touch
● Eye contact
● Inclusive gestures
[● Extended hands]
[● Showing the gifts]
[● Voice volume]
[● Facing the people]

4. Code/Metalingual

GRAMMAR USE

● Definitions
● Concurrence giving evidence that the code is being understood

[● Acclamations]
[● Faith statements]
[● Commitment ceremonies]
[● Vows, promises]

TYPOGRAPHY USE

● Quotation marks

5. Message/Poetic

GRAMMAR USE

● Stress on sense/words
● Repetitions or rephrasing

- Formal introductions and conclusions
- Instructional material

  [● Homily]

TYPOGRAPHY USE

- Italics

LITERARY GENRE

- Poetry
- Artistic or creative expression
- [● Proclamation]

EXPRESSIVE FEATURES

- Signs of reverence
- Position of honor
- [● Incense]
- [● Candles]
- [● Bows]
- [● Genuflections]

6. Context/Reference

PRONOUN USE

- Third person ("him," "her," "it," etc.)

VERB USE

- Use of past tense which connects present circumstances and meanings to past originary events and meanings
- Verbs of state
- Attributive relations
- Stress on event
- Specific moods
  - Indicative

GRAMMAR USE

- Demonstratives ("this," "that," etc.)
- Declarative statements

THEORETICAL ANALYTIC

- Adverbs of time and place
- Descriptive texts

LITERARY GENRE

- Narration
- Apocalyptic
- Parables
- Proverbs
- Metaphors

CHAPTER FIVE

PRACTICAL ANALYTIC OF SELECT EUCHARISTIC TEXT

The preceding theoretical analytic can only promise a recovery of the sense of meaning from the linguistics of a text. It remains for us to actually demonstrate a practical analytic directed to a select text. When the conclusions of a practical analytic support the claims of a theoretical analytic, the latter can be said to be a viable methodology.

Chapter Five is divided into four parts. Since our practical analytic needs a text and a methodology, the first part of this chapter addresses these two factors in two sections. The first section discusses various "texts" that must be taken into account when referring to any liturgical text, but in particular to the eucharistic text. The discussion proceeds from a consideration of the broadest application of the term "text" (as an actual liturgical celebration) to a more delimited use of text (as written text). "Written text" requires even further clarification. The written text of the eucharistic rite is an expanded text which includes the "proper" parts of the eucharistic rite (for example, the presidential prayers and readings). "Written text" is also a more restricted text consisting of only the "ordinary" of the rite (which we take as our select text). The relationship among these uses of "text" is considered as well as their relationship to other documents which enhance our explanation. The second section of this first part of the chapter demonstrates certain principles that are operative when applying the methodology. We address such areas as our divisions of the select text, its overview of action, and the hierarchy of sets and subsets and their interrelationships.

The second part of Chapter Five uncovers the linguistic sense of the select text through an analysis of that text. We divide the eucharistic text according to four divisions: the Introductory Rites, the Liturgy of the Word, the Liturgy of the Eucharist, and the Concluding Rite. Each division is analyzed, summarized, and critiqued according to the semantics of action and communication factors and functions that are apparent at a linguistic level.

The third part of the chapter raises questions about the genre which generated the text. While this exploration points to the genius of the text as a composite work, at the same time it leads us into the fourth part of the chapter, a conclusion, which intimates that an explanation of sense already indicates a reference implicating understanding.

A. Text and Methodology

This first part of Chapter Five explores the relationship between the written text which is our own immediate object of inquiry and the broader living text that is actually the eucharistic rite. The meaning of a liturgical text can never be gleaned only from an explanation of a written text because the written text does not capture the full dimension of dynamic re-presentation of Christian possibilities unfolded in an actual celebration. Nevertheless, an explanation of the written text affords clues which open up these Christian possibilities. Exploring the relationship of the various delimitations of the eucharistic text in turn calls for a clarification of methodological procedure with respect to that liturgical text. We now turn our attention to these two tasks.

1. Text: Operating Relationships

Ordinarily, when we speak of "liturgy," we refer to an actual liturgical celebration in which we participate and we posit the fullness of the liturgical text to be an actual liturgical celebration. Even though a liturgical text is a "linguistic fact," it is "designed for celebration."[1] Several important consequences are implied by this presupposition.

A first consequence is that each liturgical celebration is a unique, unrepeatable event. It takes place with a specific presider and assembly, at a given time, in a particular place. Liturgical celebration, as an historical event, unfolds once and for all in its own singular way. If we would choose to study a liturgical text in its fullness, we would do so by observing and then describing actual celebrations. Indeed, much of the contribution of an anthropology of religious ritual is gleaned from on-the-scenes research such as this which has the distinct advantage of capturing innovative elements proper to particular celebrations.[2] As a second consequence, the descriptive reporting

---

[1]25 January 1969 Instruction *Comme le prévoit*, Document #123 in *Documents on the Liturgy 1963-1979: Conciliar, Papal, and Curial Texts* (Collegeville: The Liturgical Press, 1982), #27.

[2]See Chapter 1: "Interpreting Ritual in the Field" in R.L.

characteristic of such research points to *layers of meaning* inherent in the celebration and shows the fecundity of the language and action of the celebration.[3] In a third consequence, the unfolding of the action in an actual liturgical celebration indicates the diachronic character of every celebration. A fourth consequence of viewing liturgical text in its fullness as celebration is that liturgy is seen to be grounded in a particular cultural ethos. In this respect, liturgy is part of cultural, historical existence rather than alongside it or outside it.

While the consequences of assuming "liturgical text" to be identical to "liturgical celebration" are many and advantageous, observation of a number of liturgical celebrations (for example, Eucharist) reveals that while some elements identify any given celebration as particular, nonetheless there is a discernible structure that underlies all celebrations of the same rite. Eucharist, for example, always unfolds as gathering and introducing, reading, preaching, praying common prayers, gift-giving, praying anaphora, eating and drinking, dismissing. There is in this a liturgical tradition derived from particular celebrations yet witnessing to a form recognized and accepted by liturgical communities as prescriptive. An important note is that the progression is not from prescription to description, but the reverse. The prescriptive text derives from that which is normative in a tradition of celebrations.[4] "Prescriptive," then, does not imply an unchangeable text nor an invariable manner of celebration since the history of liturgical texts shows that they have undergone numerous changes over the centuries. "Prescriptive" here implies a text that bears the structural form (i.e., that which is normative) of a tradition of celebrations.

GRIMES, *Beginnings in Ritual Studies* (Washington, D.C.: University Press of America, 1982), pp. 1-17. See also M. COLLINS, "Liturgical Methodology and the Cultural Evolution of Worship in the United States," *Worship* 49 (1975): 100-101.

[3]See, for example, Chapter 1: "Thick Description: toward an Interpretive Theory of Culture" in C. GEERTZ, *The Interpretation of Cultures: Selected Essays* (New York: Basic Books, Inc., Publishers, 1973), pp. 3-30.

[4]We use "normative" in relation to tradition to refer to the common form that has survived through the centuries of celebrations and revisions. We use "prescriptive" in relation to the celebration of an actual rite.

It is also true that the present celebrations of a liturgical text remain in the line of tradition that continues to give shape to and defines the prescriptive text. Thus, the prescriptive text changes (or at least it ought to) as the tradition changes and requires new forms. The relationship between actual celebration and prescriptive text is an essential one precisely because of the interaction of celebrations through a tradition and an identifiable, common form.

But where do we turn to find a prescriptive text? We find a tradition of liturgical celebrations in churches, schools, convents, monasteries, hospitals, homes for the aged, prisons, family homes, in any space where there is Christian community gathered for the purpose of celebration. What is their prescriptive text? The answer to this question is that the prescriptive text is a written text found in those books (for example, missals and other books of rites) which are approved by the authorities responsible for liturgical celebration. But even this statement is not as simple as it may seem. Let us consider the case of the eucharistic text.

The prescriptive eucharistic text is actually a collection of parts gathered from several sources. Thus, in addition to what we call the "ordinary" in the eucharistic rite, the prescriptive text also includes the propers for the day (the antiphons for the Introductory Rites and Communion Rite and the Presidential Prayers) which are usually located elsewhere in the *Roman Missal*, other variable texts such as prefaces and blessings, the day's scripture readings found in the lectionary and the responses which are also in the lectionary or *Graduale Romanum* or *The Simple Gradual*.[5] But this is still not all that is necessary or helpful for a liturgical celebration. The written text likewise includes a number of instances calling for interpolations to the text: songs, at the greeting and introduction, the verses for the Lord, Have Mercy (Form C), the Homily, General Intercessions, invitation to the Lord's Prayer, announcements, all those instances where the presider is invited to use "these or similar words." Interpolated texts are prepared by the presider or members of the community for each celebration. Sometimes, too, unofficial books of pastoral aids suggest texts for interpolations. We can see that even the written liturgical text is more extensive than a single document, encompassing a

---

[5]The *General Instruction of the Roman Missal*, Document #208 in *Documents on the Liturgy*, #36; hereafter cited as "GIRM" with paragraph number and included in parenthesis within the text.

number of texts gathered from various sources. Finally, the promulgation of the present written liturgical text was accompanied by the *General Instruction of the Roman Missal*, a document which replaces the rubrical instructions in the edition of the *Roman Missal* prior to its current revisions.[6] Therefore, our prescriptive liturgical text not only includes the various kinds of texts of the celebration itself (songs, antiphons, prayers, responses, readings, acclamations, etc.) but it also includes instructions on how the celebration is generally to be enacted.

There probably does not exist a written text of a eucharistic rite that includes a prescription on absolutely every word and action of the celebration. If such a text did exist, there would in all likelihood be so much attention paid to "getting things said and done right" that the celebrative, worship character of liturgy would be lost. This brings us back to the relationship of written text to its celebration, a relationship that we maintain is essential, but not absolute in all the various aspects of the celebration. A unique feature of a written liturgical text is that it exists for the sake of celebration. Other written texts can be appreciated in themselves as written texts. Even drama, which is a text written precisely to be performed, can be appreciated as a literary work in itself without its performance. But in the case of a written liturgical text, its very appreciation (especially in our sense of appropriation) is through its enactment. The liturgical text may be written, but its intent is to be celebrated and its fullness is known only in its celebration.

While our intent is to maintain that the fullness of liturgical text is its celebration, we do not wish to minimize the value of the written text nor the relationship of this prescriptive text and its celebration. We have already indicated how the prescriptive text derives from a tradition of celebration and makes explicit a common form. Further, the relationship is essential for at least two other reasons, one generative and the other methodological in nature.

First, though derived from tradition, the liturgical text is also generative of that tradition. As prescriptive, the text is to be taken seriously as that form of celebration which locates the particular celebration event within ongoing tradition. This

---

[6]See the decree *Ordine Missae* promulgating the revised *Roman Missal*, Document #203 in *Documents on the Liturgy*.

keeps the event character of liturgy from degenerating into unrelated episodes of celebration. In other words, if a celebrating community is not faithful to the prescribed text, they place themselves outside the tradition and by so doing compromise liturgy's meaning. Second, a methodological reason arguing for an essential relationship between text and celebration is that without a written text, there can be no distancing from the participation presupposed by the celebration. The written text allows this distancing (the moment of distanciation, in Ricoeur's methodology) so that an analytical in addition to a descriptive explanation of the text is possible.

We are now in a position to identify the select liturgical text that is the object of our present study. The text we chose is the eucharistic text with Eucharistic Prayer II. Our choice of Eucharistic Prayer II for this analysis in no way suggests that it is a paradigmatic anaphora. Our analysis could be applied equally to the eucharistic rite using any of the eucharistic prayers. We select Eucharistic Prayer II because it is based on the early third-century Anaphora of Hippolytus (the earliest surviving example of a eucharistic prayer), because it is short, and because it embodies the classical elements of a eucharistic prayer.

With the hermeneutics set in motion by our analysis, the choice of a different text would result in uncovering different possibilities of worlds to be appropriated. Indeed, even our analysis of the select text has different repercussions for worshipping communities since appropriation is a matter of a dialogue of the world of the text *with* the world of the reader (liturgical participants, in our case). However, the purpose of our analysis is not to incorporate the full variety of the possibilities of a eucharistic text. We exclude the "propers" with their specific antiphons, readings, and prayers as well as the many instances where the text may be interpolated. We intend to remain more structural and examine the rite for its relationship of various elements. Our purpose is to show what may happen when our proposed methodology is actually applied to a text. Because of this limited purpose, our select text is also limited to what is usually considered to be the "ordinary" of the Mass. To this end, the "proper" parts of the eucharistic rite are discussed only insofar as they are part of the structure of the rite, but they are not considered in themselves. To use an extended text that would include the propers would not greatly affect our structural conclusions, but it certainly would lengthen the analysis. In some cases, when the select text does not give sufficient information to judge its semantics of action or communication factor/function, the written text pushes us outside itself so we look to other authoritative texts for help. For example, the homily is listed in the select text as an element of the rite, but there is no indication as to its nature or function so we look elsewhere (to the *General Instruction of the Roman Missal*) to round out our explanation.

2. Methodology: Operating Principles

Certain principles are operative in our practical analytic. In this section we put forth those principles in five paragraphs: a. Manner of Application; b. Division of Text; c. Hierarchy of Sets and Subsets; d. Interaction of Parts; and e. Method of Procedure.

a. Manner of Application. Our methodology is an analytic applying a conflation of Ricoeur's semantics of action and Jakobson's approach to communication. To illustrate, we include on Page 134 the first page of the Appendix. The text on the left hand side is the approved English text (ICEL translation) of the *Missale Romanum* (*editio typica*). On the right hand side of the page the structural indications of the text are given, either in terms of the communication factors of Jakobson's theory or in terms of performative verbs of Ricoeur's semantics of action.

The first step in the analysis is to work with the select text, applying the analytic at the level of words or phrases by underscoring certain ones and assigning a number to them. Words or phrases are underscored and numbered because they satisfy one of the criteria outlined above in Chapter Four. For example, signs of reverence are expressive features indicative of a set on message. In the sample text, the third paragraph has "reference," "kisses," and "incenses" underscored and numbered with a "5" above to show a set toward message. Likewise, in the first paragraph the infinitives "to help," "to become," and "to prepare" are underscored and marked above with a "2" to indicate they are performative, perlocutionary verbs satisfying the addressee factor of non-intensional verbs (that is, they are not mental acts) denoting an effective action. If there is no underscoring and no number assigned to a word, then none of the criteria has a direct application.

This first step of the analysis only deals with words or phrases of the select text and appears as the annotated, left hand column of the Appendix. The next step of the analysis involves generating the right hand column which gives the structural indications of the text according to our select analytic tools. This process comprises the analysis of the

APPENDIX

SELECT EUCHARISTIC TEXT

INTRODUCTORY RITES	CONTACT
The purpose of these rites is[6] to help[2] the assembled people to become[2] a worshiping community and to prepare[2] them for listening to God's word and celebrating the eucharist. [Note: See General Instruction, No. 24.]	Addressee Perlocutionary Context
ENTRANCE SONG[1]	Addresser
After the people[6] have assembled, the priest and the ministers go to the altar while[6] the entrance song is being sung[1]. When the priest[6] comes to the altar, he[6] makes the customary reverence[5] with the ministers, kisses[5] the altar and (if incense is used) incenses[5] it[6]. Then, with the ministers, he[6] goes to the[6] chair.	Context
GREETING[3]	Contact
After the entrance[6] song, the priest and the faithful remain standing[6] and make the[6] sign of the cross[6], as the priest says:	

SIGLA: 1=ADDRESSER; 2=ADDRESSEE; 3=CONTACT;
4=CODE; 5=MESSAGE; 6=CONTEXT

chapter's second part. Here, linguistic units larger than words or phrases (such as sentences, paragraphs, and whole prayers) are examined for their significant communication factors and accompanying action. These are indicated as communication factors and performative verbs in the right hand column in light type. The communication set of the largest divisions of the select text appear in upper case boldface, identifying the action and communication set that best describes each division as a whole. In our example page above, the boldface text "**CONTACT**" indicates the set of the Introductory Rites as a division.

b. Division of Text. The boldface text marking the largest divisions of our select text brings us to our second operating principle, the divisions of the text. The eucharistic rite is divided into four divisions: Introductory Rites, Liturgy of the Word, Liturgy of the Eucharist, and Concluding Rite. We follow the *General Instruction*: "The Mass is made up as it were of the liturgy of the word and the liturgy of the eucharist ... [and] certain rites to open and conclude the celebration" (GIRM #8). At this point in our synchronic analysis, we allow the *General Instruction* to be our guide and so we make no distinction or comment about the relative importance of the four divisions to each other, though we note that the *General Instruction* does not seem to give equal importance to all four. This problem is taken up in the Critical Reflection of the Concluding Rite. We do point out here, however, that there is no consistency among different editions of the eucharistic text with respect to the typographical presentation of the divisions.

c. Hierarchy of Sets and Subsets. Since so much emphasis is placed on the hierarchy of factors and functions in the following analysis, some preliminary examples using Jakobson's concept of set and hierarchy with respect to the select liturgical text may be helpful. The relationship of sets and subsets is an important operating principle for our methodology.

While we speak of a *set* in a text that shapes the meaning of the communication and concommitant action, in general there are other important factors and functions that are subsets of that communication so that it is more proper to speak of a *hierarchy* of factors/functions. For example, while the set of the Gloria is toward the addresser because of its emotive function, there are also significant numbers of occurrences of the second person pronoun indicating a subset on addressee. In fact, the occurrences of addressee are even more numerous than that of addresser. Then why is the set of the Gloria on addresser? This question can only be answered by reviewing the concommitant action. If we examine the structure of the prayer, the occurrences of addressee are found in the middle portion of the prayer which is supplicatory. The supplicatory tone is indicated by two performative verbs: "have mercy" and "receive." This central supplicatory portion, however, is framed by verbs which indicate the real tenor of the prayer. The Gloria opens with five performative, illocutionary verbs: "[give] glory," "[give] peace," "worship," "give thanks," and "praise." All of these illocutionary performatives point to an emphasis on the emotive state of the addresser. The Gloria concludes with three verbs of predicate relation which give the reason (they are introduced by the causative "for") for confidence in the perlocutionary effect of the supplication which forms the middle portion of the prayer: Lord Jesus Christ is the "Holy One," the "Lord," and the "Most High." The inclusion of the definite article in each case ("the") ensures that these are used as nouns rather than as adjectives and, therefore, they are predicate relations rather than predicates of attribution. Here, the import of these verbs is not to establish the event of the context, but rather to express the emotive state of the addresser: the sentiments are addressed to someone considered special, which makes the perlocutionary language of the middle section reasonable. Our analysis establishes the communication set of the Gloria as addresser, but also points to two subsets (toward addressee and context) which contribute to the overall sense of the prayer. Indeed, if the subset toward addressee were not present, the prayer genre would not be explicit.

Another good example to demonstrate how set and subsets form a hierarchy of factors/functions is the Profession of Faith. Here, the set is toward code because of the profession character of the prayer, initially suggested by the fourfold occurrence of the verb "believe." However, each verb is preceded by a first person plural pronominal subject "we" and is followed by a preposition ("in") introducing a contextual statement on the economic Trinity and the four marks of the Church. The code word indicating commitment is thus framed by who is making the profession and in whom/what that profession consists. Though there is a significant occurrence of first person pronouns which point toward addresser and of third person pronouns, past tense verbs, and adverbs of place which indicate the importance of context, in a wider perspective the overall action of the division confirms a set toward code for the Profession of Faith. Coming toward the end of the Liturgy of the Word, the Profession of Faith is "a way for the people to respond and give their assent to the word of God heard in the readings and through the homily and for them to call to mind the truths of faith before they begin to celebrate the eucharist" (GIRM #43). Hence, the addresser and context express and support a set toward code for the Profession of Faith rather than being a primary focus themselves. Yet addresser and context are not unimportant, because they identify both the person(s) and context of the profession. The meaning of the act of communication, then, is realized not only by the Profession of Faith's set on code, but it is given a richer connotation when explained by a hierarchy with the subsets addresser and context.

These two brief analyses illustrate how it is not sufficient in an analysis of a text to simply point to the set because the subsets also help shape the meaning of the communication. An examination of the concommitant action helps uncover the hierarchy of sets and subsets.

d. Interaction of Parts. A fourth operating principle in our analysis deals with a different aspect of the explanation of a text. A textual explanation is not complete when only its component parts are analyzed. The interaction of those parts is also a vital part of the explanation. Any dividing of a text to aid analysis must in turn re-integrate parts into the whole. Parts of a text must be looked at in relation to other parts. For example, using the two analyses from above, a comparison of the Gloria and the Profession of Faith is enlightening. The Gloria is dialogical and, with the typical prayer sentiments expressed through the verbs (praise, adoration, thanksgiving, and petition), it is truly prayer. One can say that prayer genre is characterized by a dialogical structure with the presence of performative verbs. A similar emphasis can be observed in the Eucharistic Prayer, where the set is toward context but the text also witnesses to the importance of the addressee (God) and addresser (the assembled community). The Lord's Prayer is another example. We suspect that in all prayer, no matter toward what the set is, the addresser and addressee play an important part in the shape of the prayer. This says at least two things about prayer: as addressed to God, prayer is conative but as focused on addresser, prayer is emotive.[7] The characteristics of a prayer genre are noticeably absent in the Profession of Faith since there are no references to addressee. The Profession of Faith has a purpose other than prayer, which would further support its set toward code. Thus, while an initial examination of a text may expose several factors/functions operative on the

---

[7]On this theme, see D.E. SALIERS, *The Soul in Paraphrase Prayer and the Religious Affections* (New York: Seabury Press, 1980), passim.

basis of the linguistic evidence, a comparative examination can usually help in determining a set and subsets so that a hierarchy of factors/functions can be established without sacrificing the objectivity of the linguistic evidence.

Another example of parts cooperating to form a whole is how analysis of our four divisions of the select eucharistic text indicates a parallel occurrence that serves to frame the divisions: each of the divisions begins with or has near its beginning a set toward contact, and each division concludes with a set toward code. Two divisions (the Introductory Rites and the Liturgy of the Eucharist) conclude with a proper prayer, to which the community's final word is "Amen" ("So be it," a code phrase). First, the Introductory Rites (after the ministers have assembled) begin with the Greeting and conclude with the Opening Prayer. Since the nature and purpose of the Introductory Rites do not indicate a movement toward code, it is not surprising that the concluding code is the simple "Amen," though it is significant that the code was not omitted. Second, the Liturgy of the Eucharist begins with contact in the form of the presentation of the gifts, and ends with the simple "Amen" of the Prayer after Communion. But the metalingual function figures much more importantly in this division, appearing also at the "Holy, Holy, Holy," the Eucharistic Acclamation, and the great Amen, which, as a sung acclamation, has a more solemn tone than the other "Amen" responses of the eucharistic rite. These periodic occurrences of the metalingual function throughout the Liturgy of the Eucharist show code as an important subset of the division.

In the Liturgy of the Word and the Concluding Rite there is movement in the divisions themselves toward code as a climax and in these divisions the code is more complexly expressed than the simple "Amen" of the Introductory Rites and the Liturgy of the Eucharist. First, the Liturgy of the Word begins with contact in the form of announcing the reading ("A reading from . . . "). The Liturgy of the Word concludes with the General Intercessions. The community gives expression to the petitions, usually by a response said together after each intention, after which the community responds "Amen" to its concluding prayer. This seems like a rather weak metalingual climax until we look to the Profession of Faith with its more elaborate set toward code which follows immediately upon the readings and homily. Since the Profession of Faith is the community's assent to the readings and homily which are the heart of the Liturgy of the Word (GIRM #33), we suggest that the Liturgy of the Word climaxes in the metalingual Profession of Faith. Second, the Concluding Rite begins with contact in the form of a formal greeting ("The Lord be with you." "And also with you.") and concludes with a dismissal that is more than simply giving the congregation a signal to leave: the "dismissal of the assembly ... sends each member back to doing good works, while praising and blessing the Lord" (GIRM #57). The presider's "Go in the peace of Christ" (or similar words) and the community's "Thanks be to God" are in this instance indications that the eucharistic act is not concluded in the cultic occasion, but there is an ongoing acclamation of its action by the manner of living beyond the confines of the ritual action.

e. Method of Procedure. Our procedure for determining the sense of each of the four divisions is to first describe the overall action that shapes the division, state and describe the major set of the division, and then validate these "guesses" through analysis where the major subsets of the division are shown to support and amplify the sense suggested by the set of that division. Our operating principle here uses as its model an inverted pyramid: we move from an hypothesis about the sense of a division as a whole to validating this by analyzing its smaller linguistic units.

B. The Sense of the Select Text

Having delineated our text and stated certain operating principles, this second part of Chapter Five is directed to uncovering the sense of the select eucharistic rite through an analytic comprised of Ricoeur's semantics of action and Jakobson's communication theory. We proceed by presenting for each division an initial overview followed by analysis, summary, and critical reflection. A summary of the analytic data of the four divisions concludes this part of the chapter.

1. Introductory Rites

When we think of an introduction, we usually think of a simple, straightforward action or communication where people meet and/or an agenda is given. We suppose that the Introductory Rites of the eucharistic rite do this, except that an overview of the division shows it to be not simple at all to consist of diverse elements: ministers entering the worship space accompanied by song, the Greeting, the Rite of Blessing and Sprinkling Holy Water[8] or Penitential Rite, Lord, Have Mercy,

---

[8]Hereafter, shortened to "Rite of Sprinkling."

Gloria, and the Opening Prayer (GIRM #24). With so many diverse elements, it is not surprising that we find instances of all six of the communication factors as well as illocutionary and perlocutionary performative verbs. We focus on the opening actions of the division (the gathering and greeting) and guess that the Introductory Rites have a set toward contact. Our ensuing analysis supports this and shows how the other subsets specify the nature and purpose of the contact. This phatic function means that the language of the Introductory Rites serves to establish the communication act, underscoring this division's preparatory character. More importantly, though, this phatic function actually constitutes the community.[9] We look to the ensuing analysis to seek to support the contact set of the Introductory Rites.

a. Analysis. An initial indication that the Introductory Rites are crafted to establish contact comes from the language of the opening instruction ("The purpose of these rites is to help the assembled people to become a worshipping community and to prepare them for listening to God's word and celebrating the Eucharist"). This instruction uses a predicate of relation "is," followed by two sets of infinitives: "to help ... to become" and "to prepare."[10] The simple conjunction "and" implies an equality between the two infinitive clauses rather than any kind of causal relation between them. The implication, then, is that the desired effect of the Introductory Rites is twofold: community formation and preparation for listening and celebrating Eucharist.

The contact set of the Introductory Rites is corroborated by the gathering action of the community and ministers into the worship space. While the ministers are entering the worship space, the Entrance Song is sung. The *General Instruction* indicates a varied purpose for this song: "to open the celebration, intensify the unity of the gathered people, lead their thoughts to the mystery of the season or feast, and accompany the procession of priest and ministers" (GIRM #25). Though singing is a criterion for a set toward addresser because of the heightened emotion it expresses, the fact that here the

---

[9]See above, Chapter Four, Note 51, p. 111.

[10]The second infinitive is also part of a pair, if the clause is rewritten "to prepare ... to listen."

entrance song *accompanies* ("*while* the entrance song ... "; italics added) the entrance procession subsumes the emotive function to the phatic function.

The contact set of the Introductory Rites is further confirmed by the presider's greeting (with hands extended; for example, Form A: "The grace of our Lord Jesus Christ and the love of God and the fellowship of the Holy Spirit be with you all"; "And also with you") and introduction. The greeting in the form of a ritualized formula points to contact as intent. The simple conjunction "and" joining "extends his hands" with "greets all present" indicates that the extended hands here is an inclusive gesture underscoring contact with the community.[11] Moreover, the greeting shows that the contact is more than between presider and community: "through his greeting the priest declares to the assembled community that the Lord is present" (GIRM #28).

The Introductory Rites' phatic configuration is also confirmed by the three options following the entrance and greeting: (A) Rite of Blessing and Sprinkling of Holy Water, (B) Penitential Rite, and (C) celebration of one of the Liturgy of the Hours. The last option is only mentioned in the instructional text. Since it is not included as a rite after the prayer text of the Penitential Rite, we do not consider it here. The first option is permitted at the Eucharist of a Sunday. By and large, use of the Penitential Rite is the most common practice. However, the Rite of Sprinkling and the Penitential Rite have similar linguistic structures: both are prayer, with the expected dialogical emphasis on addresser and addressee. This is true no matter which of the several choices within the Rite of Sprinkling or the Penitential Rite are used. Beyond this, unique features of each option indirectly support the Introductory Rites' set toward contact.

In the Rite of Sprinkling, the only overt use of contact is in the invitation of the presider to pray ("Dear Friends, this water will be used to remind us ... "); the rest of the Rite is prayer. It basically has sets toward addressee with concomitant perlocutionary verbs as well as a set toward context in Form C.

---

[11]This is not the only meaning of the extended hands gesture. It would seem to indicate something different from an inclusive gesture when the hands are extended during a prayer. This is discussed in the Critical Reflection section below.

Especially striking is the narrative character exhibited in Form C, to be used during the Easter Season ("You chose water to show your goodness when you led your people to freedom ... and satisfied their thirst ... Water was the symbol used by the prophets ... You made the water of baptism holy by Christ's baptism ... "). Here the narrative section includes not only past tense verbs ("chose," "led," "satisfied," etc.) but also a change in pronominal use paralleling a change in verb tense: while the use of the second person pronoun continues throughout the prayer, the first person pronoun is not used in the narrative section. As soon as the verb tense changes back to the present, there is use of the first person pronoun (" ... by it [the water of baptism] you *give us* ... "; italics added). Since context situates an event, Form C of the Rite of Sprinkling indicates a situating of the community within a baptismal context ("this water will be used to remind us of our baptism"). This context is further concretized by the actual sprinkling of the community with the blessed water, a very physical form of contact. Forms A and B do not include contextual material. Other than the expected presence of first person pronouns which are necessary for a prayer genre, the overall emphasis is on addressee, especially supported by perlocutionary verbs. The subsets (addressee and context) suggest that contact is directed toward the assembled community and its purpose is to recall the baptismal event specifying the nature of the community.

As with the Rite of Sprinkling, all the forms of the Penitential Rite as well as the Lord, Have Mercy (used only when Form A is chosen because it is already part of Forms B and C) retain the dialogical character of prayer with set toward addresser or addressee. This rite begins with a choice of three forms by way of an introduction. All of them make clear that the confession of sin is for the purpose of preparing for the task at hand. In the form of an invitation, this is indirect evidence of contact in the Penitential Rite. All three forms use first person plural pronouns and illocutionary verbs, indicating a set toward addresser. The introduction is followed by a confession, again with an option for three forms. Form A has set toward addresser, supported by both first person (in this case singular) pronouns and illocutionary verbs. It is interesting to note that except for the Sign of Peace, the two uses of direct address ("and to you, my brothers and sisters") are the only times in the rite that there is direct communication among the community members. This is a rather clear indication of contact in the Penitential Rite. Forms B and C begin with a set on addressee, indicated by use of direct address, second person pronouns, and perlocutionary verbs. However, both forms end with an absolution with set on addresser, using both first person plural pronouns and illocutionary verbs. All three forms also end with the phatic "Amen," implicating addresser and indicating that the focus of the contact is the liturgical community.

The Gloria shares the dialogical, prayer genre of the Rite of Sprinkling and the Penitential Rite but it has no internal linguistic evidence that would support a set toward contact for the Introductory Rites. As we discussed in the first part of the chapter above, the Gloria has a set toward addresser whose sentiments are praise, adoration, and thanksgiving underlying the prayer as a whole.

The Opening Prayer, which concludes the Introductory Rites, begins with a phatic "Let us pray." Its invitation, with a primary set toward contact, is in the hortatory mood and it indicates a subset toward addresser (the presider). The invitation does more than establish attention because it also sets the agenda for the time which follows. After a time of silence, the presider prays the opening prayer, to which the community assents with "Amen." This prayer has a threefold structure: (1) address to God; (2) thematic petition; (3) mediatorial conclusion ("Through Christ ...," whichever form; GIRM #32). Both the thematic content of the prayer and the address to God sustain the overall preparatory, phatic purpose of the Introductory Rites.

b. Summary. The strongest evidence for the phatic set of the Introductory Rites is contained in the initial gathering of the ministers and the greeting and introduction by the presider. Other linguistic indications throughout the Rites support and sustain a configuration of the Introductory Rites toward a phatic function while the subsets specify the nature of the contact set.

Three subsets figure predominately. Context is especially evident in the opening instructions but, more significantly, it is the set of the "In the name of the Father, and of the Son, and of the Holy Spirit." Since it precedes the greeting, this seems to establish the reference point for what follows: it is in God's name that the action is performed. By implication, the contact characterizing the Introductory Rites is between God and the assembled community. The other two dominant subsets, addresser (Penitential Rite) and addressee (Rite of Sprinkling) also indicate that the contact is between God and community since these are the interlocutors of the prayer dialogue.

c. Critical Reflection. Our method offers tools for determining elements commensurate with a division's communication set, and in it this can show criteria for determining a rite's structural form and meaning. We offer several reflections on our explanation of the Introductory Rites.

In terms of determining the set of the Lord, Have Mercy, there is a discrepancy between the ritual text of the *Roman Missal* (where they are referred to as "invocations") and the *General Instruction* (where they are referred to as "acclamations"; see GIRM #30). Linguistically, as invocation they have a set toward addressee because of the direct address ("Lord"). The illocutionary force of the performative "have mercy" implicates addresser and also completes the requirements for a prayer genre. If they are considered as an acclamation, then the set is toward code and there could be some linguistic justification for a set toward code, if we recall that the Lord, Have Mercy is always used. Further, in Forms B and C the Lord, Have Mercy follows an interpolation acknowledging sinfulness and/or God's mercy and love and so a metalingual affirmation of these interpolations is structurally consistent because it draws the community into the action. It seems, then, that both interpretations make linguistic sense, with no linguistic evidence to determine whether the Lord, Have Mercy is invocation or acclamation.[12]

In terms of linguistic affinity with the set of the Introductory Rites, the Gloria is problematic. Indeed, it has been suggested that perhaps the Gloria is better transposed to another position in the eucharistic rite.[13] With set on addresser, and no subset on contact at all (recall that contact is the set of the Introductory Rites), little can be said to argue from communication analysis for supporting the Gloria's present position in the eucharistic rite. Its addresser set is found in the Preparation and Communion, so the Gloria would find

---

[12]G. DIX (in *The Shape of the Liturgy*, 2nd ed. [Westminster: Dacree Press, 1945]) suggests three approaches to the use of the Lord, Have Mercy by differing churches: as a remnant for a former litany (p. 454), treated as a hymn musically (p. 461), or as prayers for catechumens (p. 478). All three of these would support the interpretation that the Lord, Have Mercy is an invocation. This is a good example of how a dialogue with history can draw us to certain conclusions when the linguistic evidence is inconclusive.

[13]See, for example, D. DUFRASNE, "Les chances du 'Gloire à Dieu,'" *Communautes et Liturgies* 64-1 (1982), who suggests that historically it has been found at the beginning, at the Preparation, at the Sign of Peace, and before Communion (p. 26).

better linguistic affinity in either of these sections. Further, the *General Instruction* refers to the Gloria as an "independent rite" (GIRM #17a); there is a hint even in this appelation that it does not necessarily relate to the other elements in the Introductory Rites.

Another critique of a specific point deals with the extended hands gesture. This gesture is used twice in the Introductory Rites. In the first instance, as we noted above, it is an inclusive gesture associated with contact between the presider and assembly. In the second instance, it accompanies the presider's praying the Opening Prayer, where it seems to emulate the traditional Jewish prayer posture of lifted arms. It would seem that the different communication sets call for a distinction in gesture between *extended* hands and *lifted* hands, bringing out different meanings for the gesture: when it is an inclusive gesture, it points to a phatic function and when it accompanies prayer, it points to an emotive function evidencing the heightened sentiments of the addresser.

A critical look at the use of first and second person pronouns in the eucharistic rite is also telling. The usual pronominal use is plural, even when the presider recites a prayer alone. This underscores the truly communal character of liturgy. But there is no consistency in plural pronominal usage, with a rather significant number of first person singular pronominal utterances. Two instances of this first person pronominal usage are uttered by the liturgical assembly: at the prayer "I confess to almighty God and to you, my brothers and sisters ... " in the Penitential Rite and at the community preparation for Communion ("Lord, *I* am not worthy ... "). More numerous examples of first person singular utterances are by the presider: in the Liturgy of the Word at the proclaimer's preparation for the Gospel ("Almighty God, cleanse *my* heart ... "); in the Preparation at the washing of the presider's hands ("Lord, wash away *my* iniquity ... "); in the Communion Rite at the private preparation of the presider for Communion (" ... free *me* from all *my* sins ... " or " ... Let it not bring *me* condemnation ... "); at the presider's reception of Communion ("May the body [blood] of Christ bring *me* to everlasting life"); and, finally, at the cleansing of the vessels after Communion ("Lord, may *I* receive these gifts in purity of heart ... "). In all but one instance of this first person singular pronominal usage (the presider's reception of Communion excepted), the theme is forgiveness of sin or unworthiness.

The preceding remarks on first person singular pronominal usage bring up another point touching on the role of the presider. With respect to the prayers and other parts assigned to the presider, the *General Instruction* categorizes them in a three-fold manner: the presider prays the presidential prayers in the name of the community (GIRM #11); he exercises an instructive, introductory, or concluding role for the community (GIRM #12); or he prays privately (GIRM #14). We ask why the liturgical text includes prayer intended to help the presider's "attention and devotion" when such prayers are not specified for the assembly? It would seem that the number of first person singular and/or optative utterances by the presider in face of his more general use of first person plural utterances, whereby he is speaking in the name of the entire community, suggests (from a linguistic viewpoint) an inconsistency in the role of the presider: Does he speak/pray *only* in the name of the community, or sometimes for community and sometimes for himself?

We conclude our critical reflection with one final observation about the Introductory Rites. The invitation to the Penitential Rite undoubtedly establishes its preparatory character, specified in the rite as recalling sins and seeking forgiveness. While this does emphasize a certain disposition toward the eucharistic action taking place, it is also eschatological in tone: all forms end with "May almighty God have mercy on us, forgive us our sins, and *bring us to everlasting life*" (italics added). This eschatological tone is perhaps already suggested by the "In the name ... " It is the Lord's gathering, inserting an eschatological dimension into the language. Both the baptismal theme of the Rite of Sprinkling and the mercy theme of the Penitential Rite are shaped by this eschatological context, and give a sense of dynamic presence to the Introductory Rites. It would seem, then, that this calls for a change in the celebration of the Penitential Rite so that the forgiveness of sins is for the more immediate purpose of coming into God's presence *now* so that the "now" of mercy reaches backward from the eschatological context rather than the mercy validating an eschatological context. Indeed, the Rite of Sprinkling also ends on an eschatological note ("make us worthy to sit at this table in his heavenly kingdom"), but this is rightly expressed within the present eucharistic situation ("through the Eucharist we celebrate").

2. Liturgy of the Word

We saw above that the Introductory Rites focus on persons (God, presider, assembled community) by means of a contact set. After the Opening Prayer (which concludes this division), there is a noticeable shift in the enactment: in focus from several persons (God, presider, assembled community) to reader; in posture from standing to sitting and standing; in activity from preparation to receptivity; in locus from the presider at his chair to the lectionary (the Word of God) at the lectern; in atmosphere from entry, greeting, and introducing to active listening.

The posture accompanying the unfolding action of the Liturgy of the Word also points to a shift in emphasis and to differing types of activities: receptivity during the first two readings, Responsorial Psalm, and Homily when the community is seated; affirmation and alertness during the Gospel Acclamation and Gospel, the Profession of Faith, and the General Intercessions when the community is standing.

Though the readings (three of them on Sundays and solemnities, two readings on other days) form the main part of the Liturgy of the Word, other actions round out this division: the chants help the people make God's word their own, the Homily explains the readings, the community affirms their adherence to the word through the Profession of Faith, and, finally, having been nourished by the word the community prays for their and others' needs in the General Intercessions (GIRM #33). From this it appears clear that actually the entire Liturgy of the Word focuses on or flows from the word that is proclaimed. This convergence of all the elements of the division on the word suggests that the set of the Liturgy of the Word is on message. We recall from Chapter Four that "message" according to Jakobson's communication theory does not mean "information," but artistic expression. Let us look at the implications of this more closely before beginning our analysis.

A set toward message is a set toward the artistic symbols in themselves. The poetic function calls for an interpretation in order to uncover meaning. Further, according to Ricoeur, the poetic function has an "extratextual" vehemence (reference) which implies a relationship between the word proclaimed and human cultural existence. In this case of Scripture as a poetic text, its reference is descriptive, pointing to a real situation.[14] We turn now to our analysis of the text to uncover the textual indicators of a set toward message. We will see how this poetic

---

[14]See above, Chapter Four, pp. 115-116. I am only interested in pointing to the textual indications of reference in this part of the analysis. Reference and the possibilities of the world of the text are discussed below in Chapter Six.

function also incorporates indications of its reference into the linguistics of the text.

a. Analysis. We organize our analysis according to several broad indices that the Liturgy of the Word is configured with a set on message. The first indicator derives from considering the elements of a "minimal" Liturgy of the Word: pared down to its barest essentials, the Liturgy of the Word consists of a reading, a response, and a Gospel. Since the response is related to the reading ("the psalm as a rule is drawn from the Lectionary because the individual psalm texts are directly connected with the individual readings ... ," GIRM #36)), we can conclude that the focus is the word. But does this necessarily imply, then, a set toward message? Further support for a set toward message is the fact that, with proper scripture readings, this is the only instance in the eucharistic rite where there is a varied and changeable use of literary genre including parables, proverbs, oracles, myths, poetry or, in short, of all those artistic expressions which indicate a set on message.

Another index we might examine to confirm a set on message is the formal introductions and conclusions for the readings. Each of the scripture selections is formally introduced. The two first readings are introduced simply with "A reading from ... " The Gospel is more elaborately introduced to draw attention to its importance and to set it apart from the other readings. The introduction to the Gospel begins with the Alleluia and its verse. More immediately, the Gospel is introduced by the phatic "The Lord be with you" with its response. This is followed by "A reading from ... " to which the community responds "Glory to you, Lord," though we note that there is no community response to the "A reading from ... " of the other two scripture readings. All the scripture selections are concluded formally: "This is the Word (Gospel) of the Lord" with the appropriate response "Thanks be to God" or "Praise to you, Lord Jesus Christ."

The formula "The Lord be with you" with its response is used only three other times in the entire eucharistic rite: it is one of the optional forms of greeting in the Introductory Rites, it opens the Preface Dialogue, and it is the greeting at the beginning of the Concluding Rite. We wish to draw further attention to this, and also to look at other special features (GIRM #35) which surround the Gospel in order to see what this says about the communication process.

Three other instances where "The Lord be with you" and its response are used occur at the beginning of divisions: the

Introductory Rites (as one of the options for the Greeting), the Liturgy of the Eucharist, and the Concluding Rite. As a phatic formulary, "The Lord be with you" with its response draws attention to the action of a new division, an action different from that of the previous division. In so doing, the contact helps refocus the communication process with its concomitant action. In other words, it points to a shift in the communication process. If we apply this premise to the Gospel, even though here the formulary does not introduce a division, we might say it is nonetheless a way to indicate a shift setting the Gospel apart from the readings which precede it.

Several other features draw attention to the Gospel as a special part of the Liturgy of the Word over and above its unique introduction and conclusion. The Gospel is proclaimed by a special minister, either a deacon or a priest. When the gospel proclaimer is someone other than the presider, he requests a blessing from the presider who responds with "The Lord be in your heart and on your lips that you may worthily proclaim his gospel. In the name of the Father, and of the Son, and of the Holy Spirit." (Even when the presider is the one who proclaims the Gospel, he prepares himself for the proclamation with the prayer "Almighty God, cleanse my heart and my lips that I may worthily proclaim your gospel"). Other elements point to the special significance of what is taking place and highlight the importance of the Gospel: signing of the gospel book with a cross before its proclamation, incensing the book (optional), kissing it after the proclamation, and the optional accompaniment by acolytes with lighted candles.

Analysis argues that the Gospel itself is the central feature of the Liturgy of the Word. The use of the second person pronoun in the introduction and concluding response to the Gospel ("Glory to *you*, Lord"; "Praise to *you*, Lord Jesus Christ") indicates speaking *to* someone (Lord Jesus Christ). This second person address does not accompany the introduction nor conclusion of the other readings. Clearly, the linguistic intention is twofold. It communicates a set toward addresser because of the use of emotive verbs ("glory" and "praise"). It also communicates an actual presence evidenced by a set toward addressee indicated by second person pronouns and direct address. With this being said, we conclude that all the action preceding the Gospel leads up to it and all the action following the Gospel flows from it, directing attention to the Gospel as message with textual indicators that its reference is a person (the Lord Jesus Christ). The rite is configured with a moment of interpretation for the reference, the Homily. As a commentary on the word (GIRM #9 and #33), the Homily is especially focused on the Gospel as central to the Liturgy of the Word. But the Liturgy of the Word is more than hearing the word and having it explained because the communication calls for a response. The Profession of Faith is such a response, with set toward code. A metalingual set is indicated because of the profession character of the prayer given credence by the quadruple use of the verb "believe."[15] This division concludes with the General Intercessions whereby the "fullness" of the word ("having been fed by this word," GIRM #33) leads the community to make supplications on behalf of themselves and others. Even with emphasis on addresser and addressee (because of their supplicatory nature), there are still indicators pushing the interpreter outside the text which we draw from the *General Instruction* (GIRM #45). The General Intercessions involve the assembled community in two ways. First, the community exercises a priestly function by interceding for all humanity. In this, the reference is about *who* the community is (a priestly people). Second, through the General Intercessions the community reaches beyond itself and its own needs and embraces all of humanity; in this, the reference is about *what* the community can do (intercede for all).

b. Summary. The focus on the readings, and especially the Gospel, indicates message as the communication set of the Liturgy of the Word. Two major subsets, contact and code, lend it an action character: the contact before and after the readings unites the community with the proclamation and the codes make public the community's assent.

The metalingual subset is especially important in relation to the poetic function of the whole division. In fact, we might distinguish two different exercises of the metalingual subset. As characterizing the Responsorial Psalm and Gospel Acclamation, code is an affirmation of a particular message but, as Profession of Faith, code is an affirmation of a composite message. This latter conclusion draws the Liturgy of the Word through the General Intercessions (which carry the message beyond the immediate community toward others and their needs) into the next division, the Liturgy of the Eucharist. Before the analysis of this next division, however, we pause to put forth a few critical remarks with respect to the present division.

c. Critical Reflection. Structurally, the Liturgy of the Word as it stands in the present rite is coherent and balanced,

---

[15]See above, pp. 136-137, where we present more extensive analysis.

moving through proclamation, response, affirmation, reaching out to others. If, however, in a particular celebration only the minimum is enacted (with the Homily, Profession of Faith, and General Intercessions omitted), both the coherence and balance are jeopardized. Even though the major set (message) and two notable subsets (contact and code) would still be recognizable in the abbreviated structure, certain important elements from a communication point of view would not be present. We saw above that a poetic reference must always be an interpreted reference. Without the interpretation that is provided by the homily, there is danger that the interpretation will not be explicit. Also, though there is metalingual affirmation for the particular readings, affirmation of the broader message would not be explicit. Perhaps the Profession of Faith might be a more concise statement for simpler celebrations of Eucharist, but the communication structure indicates it is an essential element of the rite. Finally, the General Intercessions allow for an extension of the fruits of the word just received beyond the parameters of the present cultic occasion. Without this element, the encompassing and opening aspects of the action at this point in the rite do not receive structural expression.

We draw attention to one final critical reflection: the *General Instruction* refers to the Responsorial Psalm and Gospel Acclamation as "independent rites" (GIRM #17a). As metalingual functions, we would see them as definitely related to the readings and not "independent" at all.

3. Liturgy of the Eucharist

In this next division, we once again detect a noticeable shift in the enactment: in focus from lectionary and its space (proclamation area) to altar; in objects from lectionary to bread and wine; in activity from receptivity back to preparation; in atmosphere from active listening to active offering. Within the division itself, moreover, there are shifts in action indicating a natural division of the Liturgy of the Eucharist into three parts (GIRM #48), each concluding with a phatic "Amen" response: the Preparation of the Altar and of the Gifts[16] ("Amen" is the response to the Prayer over the Gifts); the Eucharistic Prayer ("Amen" is the response to the Doxology); and the Communion Rite ("Amen" is the response to the Prayer after Communion). Each of these parts has its own major set which configures the particular action for that part.

---

[16]Hereafter referred to simply as "Preparation."

The set of the Preparation is toward addresser. This emotive function is especially evident through the participatory of the community and expresses their sentiments. The action fashions the attitude of the community during the preparation of the altar and gifts into one of blessing and offering.

The set of Eucharistic Prayer II is toward context. This referential function is especially evident through the institution narrative and points toward the remembrance of Jesus' redemptive activity. The action of offering is configured within this context.

The set of the Communion Rite is toward addresser. This emotive function is especially evident in the community's nourishing activity of eating and drinking.

We propose that the set of the Liturgy of the Eucharist as a whole is toward context. The analysis below seeks to verify this referential function by examining the communication subsets and the movement of action within the three parts. Especially helpful for verifying the referential function of the Liturgy of the Eucharist is an examination of the relationship of the three parts to each other.

a. Analysis. Our analysis unfolds by first examining each of the three parts of the Liturgy of the Eucharist we outlined above to verify the major sets and subsets. In the summary below we examine the relationship of these three parts to support our hypothesis that the set of the Liturgy of the Eucharist as a whole is toward context.

1) The Preparation is the first part of the Liturgy of the Eucharist. It has lengthy introductory instructions and further instructions throughout which configure the action and aid in determining its set.

The initial action of the Preparation indicates an emphasis on contact: the ministers place the corporal, purificator, chalice, and missal on the altar where the action is that of preparation. The community's participation is expressed by bringing the gifts forward in procession.

The text indicates two options for carrying out these participatory actions. First, a song may accompany the phatic actions. The text of the Preparation begins with the instruction, "After the liturgy of the word, the offertory song is begun." The use of an indicative rather than a verb in the conditional or optative mood suggests that singing a song at this time is the usual (preferred?) procedure. This is supported by an instruction which directs the presider to pray "quietly" the blessing over the bread. Again the verb is indicative rather than conditional or optative in mood. In this option, the emphasis is on the participatory action of the community. The second option is specified by an instruction whose verbs are in the conditional and optative moods: "*If* no offertory song is sung, the priest *may say* the preceding words in an audible voice; then the people *may respond*: Blessed be God for ever" (italics added). The same situation ensues for the blessing over the wine. In this option, the emphasis is on the emotive sentiment ("blessed") of the community. In either case, the set is on addresser. In the case of the first option, the song and procession point to the emotive function. In the case of the second option, the verb "blessed" carries illocutionary force binding the addresser into a particularly emotive kind of relationship to the addressee,[17] the "Lord, God." This, along with the use of first person plural pronouns, indicates that the set of these blessing prayers[18] is toward addresser, with sentiments being directed toward addressee, "Lord, God."

A conative function characterizes the next section of the Preparation with set toward addressee. Following the blessings over the bread and wine, the presider prays two prayers quietly. He first addresses God, asking that God receive and be pleased both with the community as well as with their sacrifice. The second prayer is in the first person singular whereby the presider requests that he be cleansed of his iniquity and sin. Though there is use of first person (singular and plural) pronouns as well as emotive adjectives ("humble and contrite"), the formal address to God ("Lord God," "Lord") and the number of verbs with perlocutionary effects ("ask," "receive," "be pleased," "wash away," "cleanse") indicate a set on addressee.

---

[17]L. BOUYER (*Eucharist: Theology and Spirituality of the Eucharistic Prayer*, trans. C. Underhill Quinn [Notre Dame: University of Notre Dame Press, 1968]) remarks that "blessing" God is really a proclamation of the wonderful works of God (p. 29) and praise (p. 30). It is even more indicative of its illocutionary character that Bouyer goes on to say that "the *berakah* is a prayer whose essential characteristic is to be a *response*: the response which finally emerges as the pre-eminent response to the Word of God" (Ibid.; italics added).

[18]The combination of first and second person pronouns is one indication of a prayer genre. See above, p. 137.

The next section of the Preparation returns to a set on addresser. Before the washing of the presider's hands there is an optional rite where the presider incenses the altar and gifts, and then a deacon or other minister incenses the presider *and* the community. This sign of reverence draws attention to the gifts *and* community, as does the dialogue between presider and community which follows. The presider's address to the community ("Pray, brethren, that our sacrifice may be acceptable to God, the almighty Father") focuses on the theme of the acceptability of the gifts while the community's response ("May the Lord accept the sacrifice at your hands ... ") emphasizes God's praise and glory by the gifts being offered as well as the community's benefits through them. The verbs in the optative mood ("may be acceptable," "may ... accept") and the use of first person pronouns again points to a set on addresser. It is interesting to note that the presider's address uses first person plural pronouns which include him and the congregation (unless we consider it as the editorial "we"), while the community's response uses a second person pronoun "your hands," rather than "our hands." This dialogical situation is revealing. Here, the dialogue is not between the presider (and/or community) and God, but it is between the presider and the community. This suggests that it is the community which is really the addresser. If a song has been sung throughout the preparatory action and all the prayers have been prayed quietly by the presider, this dialogue could also be construed as establishing/sustaining contact. It is, therefore, a kind of preparation for the Prayer over the Gifts, which is itself a preparation for the eucharistic prayer (GIRM #53).

The Preparation has a twofold emphasis. The action character (with phatic function) of this section is sustained throughout. There is a clear shift in focus from the word of God of the previous division to the gifts of bread and wine of this division. This shift in focus accompanies a shift in set from the message of the Liturgy of the Word to the context of the Liturgy of the Eucharist. However, at this point in the rite, this referential function is merely intimated through the phatic function which not only redounds to the community but also begins to draw the community into the action that unfolds as the Liturgy of the Eucharist. The second emphasis of the Preparation stresses the participatory nature of the action. Here the communication set is toward addresser. It makes explicit what is implicit while the phatic function is sustained throughout. The set of the Preparation is toward addresser, with a sustained contact subset serving to link the community with the gifts of bread and wine which are a focus of the eucharistic prayer, the next part of the Liturgy of the Eucharist.

2) Eucharistic Prayer II has an overall set toward context supported by addresser, addressee, and code subsets. Our analysis shows how the subsets help point to reference as central to the eucharistic prayer.

Similar to the Preparation, Eucharistic Prayer II can also be divided into three sections, with a phatic function marking the delineation: the Preface which concludes with the phatic "Holy, Holy, Holy" acclamation; the pre-institution narrative and institution narrative which conclude with the phatic eucharistic acclamation; and the post-institution narrative which concludes with the phatic great Amen.[19] Our ensuing analysis shows that each section has an action that flows from prayer to narration to prayer to phatic response; in terms of the communication process, this pattern unfolds as ADDRESSER/ADDRESSEE--CONTEXT--ADDRESSER/ADDRESSEE--CODE. This pattern points to context as the main set. This is framed by addresser or addressee and culminates in phatic affirmation. Let us now turn to these three sections in more detail to see how the action and communication unfold.

The Preface Dialogue sustains contact with the community so predominant in the Preparation, though the accompanying hand gestures already intimate a shift is taking place: extended hands during the formulary "The Lord be with you" and its response which indicate an initial contact with the community; the lifted hands accompanying "Lift up your hearts" and its response "We lift them up to the Lord" which indicate an imperative and affirmative response to enter into the reference of the action. The final exchange returns to the phatic extended hands gesture, with the words "Let us give thanks to the Lord our God" and "It is right to give him thanks and praise" which emphasizes addresser. As the introduction to the Preface, and even to the whole eucharistic prayer, the Preface Dialogue is a

---

[19]I divide Eucharistic Prayer II structurally, as determined by phatic indicators. The *General Instruction* (#55) lists the elements of the Eucharistic prayer as eight: thanksgiving (Preface), acclamation ("Holy, Holy, Holy"), epiclesis, institution narrative and consecration, anamnesis, offering, intercessions, and final doxology. For the sake of clarity and brevity, we employ the term "pre-institution narrative" to include the prayer text preceding the institution narrative and the term "post-institution narrative" to include the prayer text following the institution narrative.

capsule foreshadowing of the action that is about to unfold: CONTACT/ADDRESSER--CONTEXT--ADDRESSER. In each section, context is the central focus framed by addresser/addressee.

The Preface itself is dialogical. The interlocutors are the presider (really, the community; note the use of first person plural pronouns) and God (addressed as "Father"). The dialogical feature is largely displayed at the beginning and end (use of first and second person pronouns and an illocutionary infinitive ["to give you thanks"] and illocutionary gerund ["proclaiming"]). The central portion of the Preface focuses on context. This is evidenced by the use of third person pronouns (all singular; their antecedent is Jesus Christ), past tense verbs ("made," "sent," "took," "was born," "opened," "revealed," "fulfilled," "won"), and an overall narrative genre which relates the Christian story. Use of a conjunction ("And so ... ") to begin the dialogical sentence following the referential central portion indicates a consequence of the context: the phatic Acclamation "Holy, Holy, Holy." This conjunction, in effect, directs the phatic focus of the Acclamation toward the reference of the Preface rather than toward the performative force of the dialogical text. The structural shape of this first section of Eucharistic Prayer II is CONTACT--ADDRESSER/ADDRESEE--CONTEXT--ADDRESSER/ADDRESSEE--CODE. The analysis has shown how the other subsets support the structurally central context as the focus of this section.

After the "Holy, Holy, Holy," the pre-institution narrative and institution narrative section of Eucharistic Prayer II begins with a prayer consisting of two short sentences. The first sentence has sets toward addressee, addresser, and context: the direct address of God ("Lord") suggests a set toward addressee; the emotive extended hands prayer gesture of the presider suggests a subset toward addresser; the verb is a relation of attribution confessing God's holiness and, as attribution, it is contextual. The second sentence is also an epiclesis with sets toward addresser, addressee, and context. An addresser set is indicated by a verb in the optative mood ("may become") and use of first person plural pronouns. The addressee set is indicated by use of a performative verb which expresses a perlocutionary intent ("Let your Spirit come"), by use of an explicit causative ("so that they may become ...), by use of the second person pronoun "your," and by the joined hands of the presider. The context of the preceding sentence is sustained by use of a demonstrative pronoun ("these") and third person pronouns ("them" and "they").

The institution narrative has a set toward context, as exhibited by past tense verbs and third person pronouns. There are first and second person pronouns in this narrative, but they are quotations of Jesus' words, and so continue the narrative genre. The one exception to this is after the presider takes up the cup and says "Again he gave *you* thanks and praise ... " (italics added). The "you" is the same "Lord" addressed above and sustains a prayer genre even in a narrative genre. But, in addition to this major referential focus, several subsets are operative: the narrative spoken with joined hands indicates a subset toward addressee; the reverencing gestures (bows and genuflections) draw attention to the bread and cup, symbols with poetic function and hence subset toward message; the showing of the consecrated host and wine indicates another subset toward contact. The institution narrative is concluded by a phatic imperative ("Let us proclaim the mystery of faith"; note that the addressee of the imperative is the community, a second departure[20] from the usual liturgical interlocutors, God and the community) and the community's proclamation (code). The structural shape of this section of Eucharistic Prayer II as indicated by the action and major sets is ADDRESSER/ADDRESSEE--CONTEXT--ADDRESSEE/MESSAGE/CONTACT--CODE. Once again, context is structurally central. We also saw how a referential function is sustained in the pre-institution narrative addresser/addressee emphasis. With subsets of message and contact drawing specific attention to the bread and cup as a focus of the central action of the institution narrative, the referential import of the poetic function also points to context as the overall set of this section of Eucharistic Prayer II.

Prayer genre characterizes the post-institution narrative section of Eucharistic Prayer II. With the extended hands of the presider, the use of first person plural pronouns (ten times), verbs in the optative mood ("May all of us share ... " and "May we praise ... and give glory ... "), and illocutionary verbs (we "thank," "offer," and "have mercy"), the indication is toward addresser as set. However, the direct address ("Father," and "Lord"), use of imperative verbs ("remember" [three times], "bring," and "make"), and second person pronouns (nine times) indicate a set toward addressee.

This prayer continues until the conclusion of the section at the Doxology. The Doxology begins with prepositions ("through,"

---

[20]The first departure occurs in the Preparation; see above, p. 154.

"with," and "in") and third person pronouns indicating a focus on context. After this introductory referential language, there is a change in pronoun from third to second person ("yours"). Though the source of the praise sentiments is obviously the worshipping community, there is no first person pronoun. This shows a set toward addressee for the Doxology as does the directive to lift up the bread and cup during the Doxology which emphasizes to whom the sentiments are directed ("almighty Father"). The conclusion to Eucharistic Prayer II is the community's great "Amen" with its set toward code.

The structural shape of the post-institution narrative section of Eucharistic Prayer II as indicated by the sets is ADDRESSER/ADDRESSEE--CONTEXT--ADDRESSEE--CODE. As in the two earlier sections, context is structurally central. Do the subsets support a set on context for the section as a whole? This section opens with a referential prepositional phrase ("In memory ... ") which actually establishes an anamnetic context for the entire action of offering and thanksgiving. Further, the intercessions for the living and the dead ("remember your Church ... " and "Remember our brothers and sisters who have gone ... ") lead the assembled community beyond themselves in "that the offering is made for the Church and all its members, living and dead" (GIRM #55g), thus revert back to the anamnetic context of the offering and thanksgiving mentioned above.

The subsets uncovered in Eucharistic Prayer II divide the prayer into three sections, with the code indicating where the cut-off point is for each. This may be schematized as follows:

Preface and its Acclamation	**Contact**	**Addresser/ Addressee**	**Context**	**Addresser/ Addressee**	**Code**
Pre-institution and institution narrative		**Addresser/ Addressee**	**Context**	**Addressee/ Contact/ Message**	**Code**
Post-institution narrative		**Addresser/ Addressee**	**Context**	**Addressee**	**Code**

If one abstracts the elements common to all three sections, the general pattern consists of context framed by addresser/addressee and culminating in code. Structurally, context is the central communication factor. However we have seen above how the subsets also sustain and support this major set of context for Eucharistic Prayer II. This is particularly brought out by the threefold occurrence of the phatic function culminating each section. In two of the three cases, it is a more elaborate code factor in the form of an acclamation ("Holy, Holy, Holy" and Eucharistic Acclamation). The entire communication process draws the community into the reference (major set is context supported by subsets) which they then affirm.

3) The Communion Rite for which we proposed a set toward addresser is the third part of the Liturgy of the Eucharist. An overview shows it is a complex rite and that there is no clear way to subdivide it. The *General Instruction* lists ten elements for this rite: Lord's Prayer, Rite of Peace, breaking of the bread, commingling, Lamb of God, personal preparation of the presider, showing the bread and reciting "Lord, I am not worthy ... ," reception of Communion accompanied by song, silent prayer or song of praise, and Prayer after Communion (GIRM #56). The *General Instruction* makes clear, however, that the purpose of the entire first part of the Communion Rite and the breaking of the bread is so that the community may receive the body and blood of the Lord (GIRM #56). This suggests preparation of the community for the central action of eating and drinking by the community. This initially confirms our hypothesis that the Communion Rite's major set is on addresser.

Except for its introduction and embolism, the Lord's Prayer exists independently of the eucharistic rite. The Lord's Prayer, which is attributed to the Lord who taught the disciples how to pray, has been part of the daily prayer pattern of the Church from early on.[21] With its petition for daily food (which also means eucharistic bread) and forgiveness "so that what is holy may be given to those who are holy" (GIRM #56a), its structural presence in the Communion Rite functions as preparation for the central action of eating and drinking. Analysis of the Sign of Peace which follows also bears out the preparatory intent of this first section of the Communion Rite.

The Sign of Peace begins with a prayer emphasizing addressee: use of direct address ("Lord Jesus Christ"), imperative verbs ("look not," "look" understood in the second clause, and "grant"), and second person pronouns. There is also one indication of context: the past tense verb ("said") recalls the historical situation of Jesus' presence with his disciples

---

[21]See Mt. 6:9-13 (Lk 11:2-4) and the *Didache* 8:2.

after the Resurrection.[22] It would seem that the exchange of peace among the addressers is within the context of the addressee (Jesus during a post-resurrection offer of peace). However, these addressee indications are nuanced by extended hands and the imperatives being followed by first person plural pronouns which point to addresser (in the second clause, "your church," though using a second person pronoun, is a synonym for the addresser, so it does not break the pattern). Moreover, the metalingual "Amen" at the end redounds to the addresser. The emphasis on addresser is further sustained by phatic indicators: formal address ("The peace of the Lord ... "; "And also with you") and a hortatory invitation ("Let us offer ... "). The language of the invitation places the actual exchange of a sign of peace within an action of offering. This would seem to presuppose that "peace" is already a condition of the believing community ("Look not on our sins but on the faith of your Church ... "), and to once again support a set toward addresser.

The Breaking of the Bread follows, with a set toward addresser since the bread is broken so that the community (addresser) may share in it. This action is accompanied by the Lamb of God. Here, the direct address ("Lamb of God, you") and imperative ("grant") indicate emphasis on addressee while the optative verbs "have mercy," the first person plural pronouns, and singing (though this is optional) emphasize addresser. This is followed by the commingling which is accompanied by a short prayer with an optative verb ("may ... bring") and first person plural pronoun, which also emphasizes the addresser.

The private preparation of the presider, said quietly, departs from an emphasis in the Communion Rite on addresser and departs from first person pronominal usage.[23] Here, the preponderance of direct address, second person pronouns, and imperatives indicates a subset toward addressee.

The next part of the Communion Rite, the Communion itself, begins with the presider showing ("taking ... raises") the host to the community and addressing them with a phatic demonstrative ("this") to which the community responds. Though there is use of direct address ("Lord"), a second person pronoun, and the imperative ("say") which emphasizes addressee, the tone of the

---

[22]See Jn 20: 19, 21, 26.

[23]See above, p. 145, where we first note this use of first person singular pronouns in face of the predominate plural usage.

prayer is marked by first person singular pronouns "I," a referential relation of attribution ("am not worthy"), and a statement of expected benefits ("shall be healed"), which emphasizes addresser. The optative verbs and first person pronominal use in the quietly-spoken prayers accompanying the presider's Communion do the same. The private, optative mood character of the presider's Communion stands in marked contrast to the public, processional, metalingual character of the community's Communion, where each communicant is shown the host (and cup) with the phatic "The body [blood] of Christ" to which each responds "Amen" and receives (and drinks). The Communion Song sustains the emphasis on addresser throughout this part of the Communion Rite.

After Communion, the cleansing of the vessels is accompanied by an optative mood and a first person singular pronoun which indicate an emphasis on the presider as addresser. This is followed by a period of silence ("all praise God in silent prayer," GIRM #23) or a song of praise, both of which have a set on addresser. The Communion Rite closes with contact ("Let us pray"), prayer, and the phatic response "Amen." The Communion Rite is complex, but the overall indication is that its set is on addresser. Addressee, code, and contact are operative subsets.

b. Summary. Analysis shows that the three parts of the Liturgy of the Eucharist (Preparation, Eucharistic Prayer, Communion Rite) have communication sets toward ADDRESSER--CONTEXT--ADDRESSER. The concomitant action develops around the community (addresser), especially in terms of offering gifts and eating and drinking. The action, however, is focused by the context (remembering the deeds of salvation) of the eucharistic prayer. This framing of the referential function between two emotive functions structurally demonstrates the eucharistic prayer as the central part of the Liturgy of the Eucharist around which the action is organized. As such, the action itself is to be interpreted within the referential thrust of the eucharistic prayer. The communication set of the Liturgy of the Eucharist as a whole is toward context.

c. Critical Reflection. While there is an overall direction to the action and communication in the Liturgy of the Eucharist which highlights and supports the centrality of the eucharistic prayer in this division, certain critical remarks are exacted by the complexity of the Preparation and Communion Rite.

Our analysis accepts the select text as it exists in its present form. Obviously, revisions over the centuries have introduced theological content and structural development which have resulted in the extended rite we know today. One example of conflated theological content is found in the Preparation: the post-Vatican II revision of the rite introduced two blessing prayers (noticeably indebted to Jewish meal *berakoth*) into the Preparation but also retained the sacrificial language of the tridentine rite in the prayers which follow. While a more adequate understanding of "sacrifice" than that of popular acceptance may well show the blessing and sacrifice themes richly complementary,[24] nonetheless these two themes remain juxtaposed in the present rite and prolong what is supposedly of a preparatory nature. We find in these latter prayers, too, use of first person singular pronouns, which introduces a dialogical ambiguity into what is usually first person plural, corporate language.

In the Communion Rite, while the elements preceding Communion are varied in subset, they all relate to the Communion Rite's set toward addresser. The exception to this is the first person singular prayers of the priest's preparation for Communion and their set on addressee and private nature pose structural problems. It would seem that the communication process would be more consistent if the action were simplified to include the Lord's Prayer, the Sign of Peace, and then immediately the Communion. We note, though, that the Sign of Peace has found itself at other places in the liturgy, notably at the Preparation.[25] But with its introductory prayer's set on addresser, the Sign of Peace does have linguistic affinity with the Communion Rite, so it is at least linguistically appropriate

---

[24]See, for example, R.J. DALY'S *Christian Sacrifice: The Judaeo-Christian Background before Origin*, Studies in Christian Antiquity 18 (Washington: The Catholic University of America Press, 1978).

[25]See G. DIX, *The Shape of the Liturgy*, p. 108. Another point to address in terms of the structure of the Communion Rite is the twofold action of eating *and* drinking. The rite indicates by a conditional clause that offering the cup is not the norm ("*If* any are receiving in both kinds ... "; italics added). Another indication of the tradition of receiving only the bread is that the text specifies only the host is raised during the "Lord, I am not worthy ... .") It would seem as though receiving both bread and cup ought to be the norm, if the action is to be truly complete and if the reference of the institution narrative is to be truly memorialized.

where it is. However, for the same reason (linguistic appropriateness) it could be placed at the Preparation, which also has a set toward addresser. Moving the Sign of Peace to the Preparation would allow the Communion Rite to more quickly arrive at its central action of eating and drinking. Then, the Lord's Prayer would be the immediate preparation for Communion with the eating and drinking immediately following.

Another point to address in terms of the structure of the Communion Rite is the twofold action of eating *and* drinking. The rite indicates by a conditional clause that offering the cup is not the norm ("*If* any are receiving in both kinds ... "; italics added). Another indication of the tradition of receiving only the bread is that the text specifies only the host is raised during the "Lord, I am not worthy ... .") It would seem that receiving both bread and cup ought to be the norm, if the action is to be truly complete and if the reference of the institution narrative is to be truly memorialized.

One last comment deals with posture during the eucharistic prayer. While ultimately left to conferences of bishops, the suggestion is to "kneel at the consecration" (GIRM #21). In light of the threefold division of Eucharistic Prayer II with each section culminating in code, it would seem that the assembly might kneel during the entire middle section; that is, from after the "Holy, Holy, Holy" until after the Eucharistic Acclamation. However, we question a change in posture that emphasizes this section at the expense of what precedes and follows it. Structurally, the integrity of the eucharistic prayer ought to be respected. One way to achieve this is to have only one posture (standing) throughout the entire eucharistic prayer.

4. Concluding Rite

This final division of the eucharistic rite also brings a shift in the action, from the altar back to the presider at his chair and the community. The most simple and brief of all the divisions, the action of the Concluding Rite unfolds as greeting, blessing, and dismissal (GIRM #57). Here, the emphasis is on code which, for our purposes, does not focus so much on the system of sounds and marks used to make up messages, but on language's capacity to designate itself and its other. In this, the code is related to the referential function because both point to language's capacity to mediate reality. In our particular case, a set toward code is a concurrence with the communication act that implies an involvement with or commitment to that action. We proceed to the analysis to seek to support this claim by examining how the text is configured for this purpose.

a. Analysis. The Concluding Rite may begin with the (optional) making of announcements. Usually it begins with the phatic formulary greeting "The Lord be with you." The Greeting is followed by a blessing in the optative mood with a choice of three forms: as a simple blessing, as a solemn blessing preceded by invocations to which the community responds "Amen," or as a prayer over the people followed by a blessing. In all three forms the community responds to the blessing with the metalingual "Amen." The Concluding Rite ends with the imperative dismissal with set on the community as addressee. There are three options: A. "Go in the peace of Christ"; B. "The Mass is ended, go in peace"; and C. "Go in peace to love and serve the Lord." The community responds "Thanks be to God" with set on code. The instructions for the dismissal make it clear that this is more than a simple dispersing of the community, and that it has a perlocutionary thrust: "The dismissal sends each member of the congregation to do good works, praising and blessing the Lord" (GIRM #57). Form C, "Go in peace *to love and serve the Lord*" (italics added), indicates this metalingual intent most clearly. Note, too, that the instruction is to love and serve the *Lord*. The first part of this instruction intimates that the set of the Concluding Rite is on code in terms of affirming the eucharistic action through a life that reflects its meaning. The second part of the instruction emphasizes the sentiments on the part of the worshipping community ("praising" and "blessing") that their living brings about. The action of the Concluding Rite proceeds from contact, through a focus on community with the blessing, toward the metalingual affirmation by the community. The culmination in code suggests this as the set of the Concluding Rite.

b. Summary. The entire communication thrust of the Concluding Rite redounds to the community (initial contact, blessing, and their affirmation) but its real import is community affirmation. The metalingual function of this division, moreover, is not an affirmation of something that takes place within the division, but rather of the whole action that has preceded it and follows it. This suggests that the eucharistic rite is not an eclectic conflation of disparate elements but that the various elements are organized in such a way as to lead somewhere: to the final metalingual response even though each division has its own unique sense to contribute to the meaning of the whole. The rite engages the assembly throughout and, finally, calls for an affirmation that carries the celebration beyond the cultic occasion. The communication set of the Concluding Rite is toward code.

c. **Critical Reflection**. Because the Concluding Rite is so short, and comes at the end of the whole eucharistic action, it might be easy to lose sight of its importance in relation to the other divisions. Structurally, the Concluding Rite not only completes the enactment of the eucharistic rite, but it is essential precisely in terms of its relationship to the other divisions. Its structural necessity ought to be carried over into the celebration.

The concurrence by the assembled community that marks the communication set of the Concluding Rite clearly indicates that the eucharistic action is an action *by* that assembly, not an action on their behalf. Yet, Eucharist as an action *of the assembled community* remains structurally ambiguous. For example, the more the presider is perceived as representing the community with focus on the presider as "priest," with the risk of alienating the action from the community, the more the enactment takes away from that act of appropriation which the Concluding Rite linguistically embodies. If this be the case, the import of the entire action is destroyed.

These reflections lead us to a second critical remark. We have already noted that the *General Instruction* perceives the Liturgy of the Word and the Liturgy of the Eucharist to be the central divisions, and relegates the Introductory Rites and Concluding Rite to peripheral roles (GIRM #8). Our own analysis would suggest that the Introductory Rites (which focus on presence of God and community) and the Concluding Rite (which focuses on concurrence with the action) are essential to the shape of the action itself. The action of the eucharistic rite, then, does not derive from just the Liturgy of the Word and the Liturgy of the Eucharist (although their centrality cannot be denied) but derives from the whole action from beginning to end. Structurally, this is borne out by the use of the Sign of the Cross both at the beginning and end of the rite, as a linguistic device of inclusion.

5. Summary

Having completed the analysis of each of the four divisions of the eucharistic rite with respect to their semantics of action and communication factors/functions, the divisions and their respective sets may be schematically presented in the following way:

PRACTICAL ANALYTIC

Introductory Rites - - - - - - - - - - - CONTACT

LITURGY OF THE WORD - - - - - - - - - - - - - MESSAGE

LITURGY OF THE EUCHARIST - - - - - - - - - - CONTEXT

Concluding Rite - - - - - - - - - - - - CODE

We note that no communication set is repeated, and that addresser and addressee are absent as a major set for any division. In addition to these major sets, each division also has important operative subsets which, as we show throughout our analysis, help to specify or focus the nature of the major set. Further, our schema above suggests that the Liturgy of the Word and the Liturgy of the Eucharist are central divisions. Each of their sets has referential import which points to the extralinguistic vehemence of the text. But the Introductory Rites and Concluding Rite (in their respective communication of presence and concurrence) also point beyond the text. Thus our synchronic analysis cannot remain within the text, but pushes us beyond. This becomes even clearer when we consider the relationship of the four divisions to each other.

So far in our analysis, we have asked the text to speak to us of its sense within the parameters of a semantics of action and communication theory. We reiterate again that through the sense uncovered here is not the whole meaning of liturgy, our analysis has allowed us a certain critical insight into the action and communication structure of the select text. Further, our analysis suggests that the divisions are not independent of each other, but that they are structurally related in such a way as to justify our speaking of a composite communication process from beginning to end. We pose key questions: Does the total liturgical action have a thrust toward an end? Do the various divisions of the eucharistic rite operate more or less as individual units, loosely holding together into some kind of whole, or does the rite have an internal structure that binds the units together into a purposeful and essential composition? Can our synchronic analysis identify the essentials of its generating process? These questions lead us to the third part of Chapter Five.

C. Liturgical Genre

We concur with the *General Instruction* that the central and most important divisions of the eucharistic liturgy are the

Liturgy of the Word and the Liturgy of the Eucharist. Their sets toward message and context, respectively, would support this since both of these communication factors point to a referential vehemence having an important capacity to refigure human existence. We take exception, however, to the *General Instruction*'s reductionist statement "There are also certain rites to open and conclude the celebration" (GIRM #8). Our analysis would suggest that the Introductory Rites and Concluding Rite are essential rather than peripheral. The contact and code sets do more than round out the rite. They situate the community as assembly before the Lord and mandate the community to continue living the celebration, actions intimately bound up with the meaning of the Liturgy of the Word and the Liturgy of the Eucharist. They also show that the eucharistic rite is not cut off from human cultural existence. If this be so, and we hypothesize that it is, then from our analysis we ought to be able to detect a generative factor operative in the production of the text. For Ricoeur, this generative factor in literature which is known as a "genre" is, along with composition and style, one of the components by which a text comes into existence. Without a generating genre, the liturgical text could be simply a conflation of disparate elements, in which case the Introductory Rites and Concluding Rite could be construed as "rounding out the rite." Our analysis indicates otherwise, and so we set ourselves upon a search for the generative factor at the origin of our present liturgical text. We add a note of caution, however. Our purpose here is not to define the genre which generates a liturgical text. To do so we would have to examine a number of liturgical texts, for a genre is only detected by examining many similar texts. Our intention here is simply to look to our select text for characteristics that speak to the uniqueness of what we might call a "liturgical genre."

Scattered throughout the previous analysis, there have been references to prayer genre and narrative genre.[26] Indeed, to some extent these genres have helped to uncover the sense of a specific portion of the select text. Did either of these genres generate the text as a whole? We think not.

We note in our analysis that prayer genre is always characterized in communication terms as having an addresser, an addressee, and performative verbs. Obviously, we are speaking

---

[26]Since all Scriptural possibilities for the readings are not analyzed, the multiple genres in Scripture have not figured in this discussion.

here in a religious context, where either the addresser or addressee is the Sacred. We analyzed numerous examples of this genre in our select text, though prayer genre is not evenly distributed throughout the four divisions: it is almost entirely lacking in the Concluding Rite; prayer concludes the Liturgy of the Word, but it does not figure predominantly there except in the Responsorial Psalm; prayer is used more extensively in the Introductory Rites; prayer is predominant in the Liturgy of the Eucharist even to the point that the central portion is entitled the eucharistic *prayer*.

The question remains: if there are numerous instances of a prayer genre throughout, and we even say that the celebration of the eucharistic rite is prayer, can we conclude prayer is the generating factor? If we return to the sets of each of the divisions, we see why our answer must be "no." Recall that the sets for the four divisions are CONTACT--MESSAGE--CONTEXT--CODE. Note that neither addresser nor addressee is the set of a division. Since its set characterizes the communication intent functioning in each division, there can be no addresser-addressee relationship between any two of the divisions. We conclude that at the level of the rite as a whole, the generating genre of the eucharistic rite is not a prayer genre, though certainly prayer genre is incorporated in the rite.

What about the narrative genre? At least we do have two divisions, the Liturgy of the Word and the Liturgy of the Eucharist, which point toward reference, the function characteristic of narrative genre. The Liturgy of the Word points to reference indirectly through its poetic function. The Liturgy of the Eucharist has as its communication function reference because of its set on context. We partially agree, then, with D.B. Stevick, who maintains that "one of the great organizing principles of liturgy is narrative ... we move through a liturgy of recital."[27] However, we must still account for the other two divisions. The narrative genre is an important part of the Profession of Faith, but it does not figure largely in the rest of the Introductory Rites and is entirely lacking in the Concluding Rite. We already guess that liturgical genre is not a narrative genre, though, again, narration is incorporated in the rite.

A more important indication that narration is not the eucharistic liturgy's generating genre is that while the rite

---

[27]D.B. STEVICK, "Language of Prayer," *Worship* 52 (1978), 551.

does unfold through a structure, it does not have a definitive end point from which we can read the story "backwards,"[28] a characteristic of narrative. While the ritual structure ensures us of an orderly and familiar celebration of the rite, the celebration of Eucharist does not converge on a "sense of an ending"; that is, the eucharistic liturgy does not "conclude." Rather, the rite moves through action toward a "sense of a beginning,"[29] which opens up space for appropriating new possibilities. A narrative has structural closure recognized in its retelling.[30] If we know the end of a story, we can read the story "backwards," and retell it to the same ending. Liturgy does not work in this way. We know its structure, but we cannot retell liturgy to the same ending. Liturgy's retelling is always an opening of space beyond the structure of the text to new possibilities. Thus, liturgy cannot be retold to the same ending. Rather than a structural closure, liturgy has a structural openness that guarantees a different "ending" to each celebration.

We pause at this point to clarify an equivalent use of language. We have been discussing "beginning" and "ending," and emphasizing that liturgy does not "conclude." Here, we are speaking of liturgy in a wide connotation that embraces the extralinguistic referential vehemence of the written text. We are saying, then, that liturgy in effect begins in human cultural existence and returns to that existence. Obviously, the cultic occasion has a beginning (with the Introductory Rites) and does draw to a "close" (at the Concluding Rite). But, while the *structure* of the rite has a beginning and closure, this is not in the sense of an ending to *liturgy*, but rather of a beginning due to the very nature of the act of appropriation called forth by the Concluding Rite's set toward code. The liturgical celebration implicates the human cultural existence of the celebrating community in an ongoing way because of its moments of participation and appropriation.

Are we doomed to conclude that the liturgical text is episodic with no generative factor? Our structural analysis

---

[28]See P. RICOEUR, *Time and Narrative*, Volume 1, trans. K. McLaughlin and D. Pellauer (Chicago: University of Chicago Press, 1984), pp. 67-68.

[29]This is my adaptation of Ricoeur's phrase: "sense of an ending."

[30]See P. Ricoeur, *Time and Narrative*, pp. 67-68.

belies this. Our sense of meaning already has shown that the Liturgy of the Word and the Liturgy of the Eucharist are central to the rite. They are linked together by message and context which are factors pointing to the referential import of the text. Moreover, we have argued that the Introductory Rites and Concluding Rite are not peripheral, but contribute two essential factors to the shape of the rite: the community phatically being drawn into the celebration and metalingually affirming the action. Our analysis, then, affirms that the rite is a composite. Further, the rite is configured not toward a "conclusion," but toward a "sense of beginning," as we said above. We suggest here that the genre which generates liturgical texts must at least be able to incorporate varied forms of discourse (such as prayer and narration) and configure the action toward our notion of a sense of beginning.

To follow up on these reflections at this point necessarily carries us beyond the semantics of the text toward its world of possibilities as opened up by the text's reference. This task is outside the scope of this chapter, so we leave for Chapter Six further consideration of the question of liturgical genre.

D. Conclusion

An important event takes place in the eucharistic rite. A community gathers into dynamic presence and celebrates God's saving actions presented as possibilities for Christian living. Even in our synchronic analytic of text, diachrony shows its face as a dynamic movement within the text which relates parts to a whole and carries us beyond the confines of the language of the text. Showing a rationale for the whole as we have done in discussing liturgical genre makes liturgy a whole rather than episodic and opens up spaces for meaning to unfold at differing levels. We must reintegrate our synchronic analysis into Ricoeur's broader framework of a hermeneutics of human existence.

Ricoeur places the explanatory moment *between* the moments of participation and appropriation. Before a fuller meaning can be attained, analysis must move beyond the realm of the linguistics of text to another level, that of reference. The sense of a liturgical text is uncovered in the composition and language of the text. But this is only half the story. The reference of the text must also be addressed. This is the task of the sixth and final chapter.

CHAPTER SIX

UNDERSTANDING THE EUCHARISTIC TEXT

Thus far in our discussion, we have said much about language and text. Let us summarize what we have accomplished in the preceding chapters in order to situate the work of this last chapter.

In Chapter One we showed that although language and text are not new concerns for liturgists, focusing on them with certain questions in mind points to the need of a new methodology that has those questions as its primary regard. We identified areas to which we might direct our attention: the relationship between verbal and nonverbal expressions, the use of language as discursive or nondiscursive, the consideration of cultural differences, the relationship text and human cultural existence. In short, we are interested in the basic question, What is the relationship of language (in our case, liturgical language or liturgy) and life?

We looked to Paul Ricoeur to help us address our questions when we asked in Chapter Two, Why is text a paradigm for the recovery of meaning? The key to our answer was found in the sense-reference dialectic by which Ricoeur can push the symbolic import of language beyond multivocity to include a reference to existence, to life. The process of interpretation, then, is more extensive than uncovering layers of meaning embedded in language because it includes the further task of pointing to human cultural existence.

The recovery of meaning is ultimately a recovery of our own existence. Why is this necessarily so for Ricoeur? Because for him language is a derived form. The import of this presupposition is that we can detect in language signs of our own self-existence. Ricoeur's method of textual hermeneutics, the subject of Chapter Three, contests the claim of the epistemology of the natural sciences to provide the only valid methodological model for the human sciences. Without denying the epistemological mode, Ricoeur's starting point is a hermeneutics of existence, which for him is a hermeneutics of understanding. This sets in motion the key dialectic of his method, explanation-understanding, which respects both the epistemology of explanation and the ontological vehemence of understanding. Ricoeur's hermeneutics of understanding seeks to accomplish the recovery of our own self-existence *through* the signs of our existence, language in use. In this way, the analytic of language in use (the explanatory moment) is a means to uncover a reference to human cultural existence (the moment of understanding).

In Chapters Four and Five we addressed the explanatory moment of Ricoeur's method of textual hermeneutics for our own liturgical purposes. We first outlined a theoretical analytic where we defined the parameters of our explanatory moment in terms of a theory of communication and a semantics of action. We then applied our analytic to a select eucharistic text in order to uncover its structure (the sense of meaning).

Having recalled the framework of our study to this point, we are now in a better position to lay out clearly the work of our present chapter, which is to address the methodological moment of understanding. We begin with a salient question: Why are we so concerned with a hermeneutics of existence with respect to liturgy? Our answer is that if we stop our work with Chapter Five, we have provided no means whereby we can relate the very meaning of the celebration itself to Christian living. Further, the relationship of a textual study of liturgy to its celebration would remain a suspended point. By completing our study with the understanding pole of Ricoeur's method, we can methodologically indicate how a hermeneutics of understanding helps to integrate our celebration of Eucharist into Christian living as well as underscore the importance of textual studies.

What is implied in this? What is an stake? We, with Ricoeur, maintain that through a moment of explanation directed to a sense of meaning we point to the reference of a text in terms of the experience which gave rise to the text and uncover a world of the text to be appropriated as new possibilities for Christian living. So far in the case of our select eucharistic text, we have explained the text but not "understood" it. We are now ready to turn to this interpretive task.

The work of explicating the reference of the select eucharistic text through its sense (uncovered in the practical analytic) leads to the essential task of this chapter: to integrate the moment of explanation within the larger framework of a hermeneutics of understanding. Our reflections are now pushed beyond the linguistics of the text to how language functions in a text as that which opens up a world to be appropriated for human living. Central to this hermeneutical enterprise is a reflection on the structural features of the dynamic of action that shape our select eucharistic text as a whole and which carry the reader from one side of the text (pre-understanding) to the other side of the text (self-understanding). Text mediates the pre-understanding of participation and the new self-understanding characteristic of the moment of appropriation. Its ability to bridge these two moments consists in the fact that linguistic symbols "are interpretents internally related to some action."[1] That is, the language of a text captures dimensions of human existence inasmuch as language dynamically configures human action.

In this chapter, we look to the dynamics of action and communication of our select text and ask, What are the possibilities opened by our analytic as broader dimensions of the text implicating life? Here, we are removing the brackets placed around human cultural existence in our analytic of the sense and thereby are allowing the text's ontological vehemence to appear. We consider, in the first part of the chapter, the moment of participation as a re-enactment of the Christian existence out of which and into which the text functions. In the second part of the chapter we come back to our analytic in order to show how the explanatory mode helps to put at a distance our participation in human cultural existence, opening up to us new possibilities. Our guiding question is, What is the divine and human action that is emplotted in the language of the select text? By uncovering the text's deep structure we expose its reference whereby we see how the analytic moment bridges our pre-understanding and new self-understanding. In the third part of the chapter we consider the moment of appropriation, by which we insert our Christian existence into the larger world of praxis (informed by the distanciation) as required by "reading" the text. Finally, in the fourth section on liturgy as language of faith we ask the question, How does language function in the liturgical text as language of faith?

A. Participation: Re-enactment of Christian Existence

Liturgy can never be divorced from actual human existence. Liturgy is not something "out there" we "go to," but it is an actual expression of our Christian existence. Liturgical celebration presupposes a certain competency in human living as well as a competency in Christian living, a humanization process taken up and ritualized as symbolic mediation (in our case liturgical language). In this respect liturgy's action is related to human living as an action. The structure of liturgy,

---

[1]P. RICOEUR, *Time and Narrative*, Volume 1, trans. K. McLaughlin and D. Pellauer (Chicago: University of Chicago Press, 1984), p. 58.

then, reflects the structure of human, Christian existence. While this relationship between the action of liturgy and the action of human living is important in order to ensure a starting point for interpretation, it is even more important in terms of ensuring a certain "readability" of the text. Our participation in Christian existence enables our participation in Christian liturgy because liturgy presumes a level of bonding with Christian existence by means of its originary events.

To flesh this out in terms of our methodological moment of participation, we divide this part of the chapter into two sections. The first addresses the question, What enables a reading of liturgy from within our lived Christian existence? Here we show how the nonmethodic pole of understanding is a "pre-understanding" of the objectification of the structures of our very existence. The second section addresses the question, What are the various dimensions of human experience out of which liturgy speaks? Here we show how cognizance of the pre-understanding pole of our method invites liturgists to be concerned with the whole of human living.

1. Belonging: Participation in Christian Existence

The methodological moment of participation implies that we find our selves, our existence, our way of living, already immersed in a world with an archaeology older than our own. Ricoeur has suggested that we can be aware of our participation by studying culture through its symbolic and historical mediation. For us Christians, this means that our own Christian existence is immersed in a Christian world with a recognizable tradition mediated by liturgy (as one example of symbolic mediation).

Understanding derives from the interpreter's way of existing. The task of understanding concerns our mode of existence, the signs of which are objectified in a text. It is not contradictory, then, to its inherent challenge to refigure self that liturgy first presupposes on the part of those gathered, a pre-understanding or familiarity with its celebration. This means we celebrate liturgy out of recognition of an initial shape and meaning. The pre-understood familiarity with Christian liturgy develops from our Christian belief in and experience of God's divine concern for creation and God's ongoing relationship to the Christian community.

Our moment of participation is a participation in life, in existence, which has been given a uniquely Christian realization mediated by symbols. "Symbol" here is not taken in the usual sense of standing for something else or having layers of meaning. Symbolic mediation refers to the "cultural processes that articulate experience."[2] Further, "*cultural* processes" emphasizes a public character to symbolic mediation: "symbolism is not in the mind ... but a meaning incorporated into action and decipherable from it by other actors in the social interplay."[3] "Cultural processes" also emphasizes that symbolic mediation arises in experience and is the concrete articulation of that experience. The Christian community enters into the tradition of the liturgical experiences of the Church as symbolically mediated by celebration. The written text is an objectification of our normative tradition of lived Christian existence. Rooted deeply in life's experiences, liturgy expresses the community's accumulated, structured expressions of their bonding with life.

Liturgy is truly a "telling" of Christian existence. At the same time, a liturgical text affords a critique of that Christian existence. Text, then, is a double-edged sword: it is first of all an objectification of the structures of Christian living; secondly, it provides a corrective to Christian ideology by what happens in its celebration. Both cutting edges are sharpened by the fact that liturgical texts are not episodic, but configured (structured) so that liturgical celebration is the realization of an event that can be re-enacted.[4] This is to say that there is a sedimentation element in liturgy whereby its symbols objectify

---

[2]P. RICOEUR, *Time and Narrative*, p. 57.

[3]Ibid.

[4]W.T. WHEELOCK makes a similar point though his approach and context are quite different. In his article "The Problem of Ritual Language: From Information to Situation" (*The Journal of the American Academy of Religion* 50 [1982], 49-71), he proposes that the language of ritual does not essentially convey information but it is intended to create a *situation* (59, 61, and passim). For Wheelock, "the speaking of the text *presents* the situation" (p. 60; italics his) while at the same time it presupposes the participants' understanding of "the pre-determined situation that the ritual re-enacts" (62). He contends that "ritual utterances serve both to engender a particular state of affairs, and at the same time express recognition of its reality. Text and context become manifest simultaneously" (58). If Wheelock is correct in his insight, and I believe he is, it suggests that built into the liturgical

Christian living as well as provide "rules of meaning for interpretation."[5] The liturgical assembly recognizes certain structures enabling them to "read" the liturgical text as re-enactment. Here, liturgical anamnesis is not just a "recall" of originary events. It incorporates an historical dimension that is caught up in its cycle of participatory celebrations. In liturgy, anamnesis implies a metamorphosis in terms of reshaping events as new emplotments of life. Rooted deeply in life's experiences, liturgy celebrates the community's accumulated, structured expressions of their bonding with life and reshapes those expressions as new ways of living.

Though participation precludes the Christian community from ever standing outside of the Christian milieu, interpretation invites a refiguration whereby liturgical innovation realizes fresh beginnings. While participation permits an initial reading because of familiarity with its tradition, participation also permits newness to impinge on that tradition. The reference of the text opens as a possible world entailing wholly new possibilities, wholly new ways of living to be appropriated which in turn become a new moment of participation. Because liturgical participation is Christian living from an already-being-lived appropriation, Christian living itself is always a reflection of a previous reading of liturgy. This affords us our first glimpse at the relationship between liturgy and everyday Christian living which enables us to refer to liturgy as a language of faith. Liturgy embodies the language which expresses how our deepest, conscious being stands in relationship to the Sacred. Language functions in liturgy as a symbolic mediation of the community's presupposed participatory faith relationship to the Sacred.

2. Communication: Dimensions of Human Experience

Since a reading of liturgy always begins from our participation in Christian existence, liturgy's celebration is none other than a celebration of the one life that is lived (as its objectification) and communicated through a distance embodied

---

text itself and its intention to be ritualized is an inherent methodological guess as to both the meaning and value of the liturgical celebration. Indeed, "the 'message' of the ritual is less an idea to be taught and more a reality to be repeatedly experienced" (66).

[5]P. Ricoeur, *Time and Narrative*, p. 58.

in tradition. Though we insist that we participate in a Christian tradition, many dimensions of human cultural existence influence and shape that tradition.

The communication of Christian tradition has not always lived up to its ideals. Our method challenges certain articulations of Christian existence, offering a corrective. For example, our method particularly challenges any dualistic way of living. The celebration of liturgy essentially shatters dualisms that divide our selves into body and soul, our world into secular and sacred, our experiences into human and divine, our sense of time into chronometry and eternity. Liturgists can clarify how liturgical understanding takes place within our comprehension of Christian existence and human cultural existence not as two "existences" but as one way of Christian living. It is not surprising to us that some liturgists are particularly attentive to how liturgy incorporates a wide range of human experiences. Liturgists have broadened their task to reflect on more and more dimensions of experience.[6] Important in our context is how scholars are attending to the relationship between liturgy and humanization and the place of Christianity in the world.[7] Let us pursue this more specifically.

---

[6]See L.L. Mitchell, "Liturgics, Whence and Whither?" *Anglican Theological Review* 63 (1981): 302-308. Speaking to the formation of working committees of the North American Academy of Religion, Mitchell notes that at NAAL's inauguration in 1975 there were four committees dealing with liturgical theology, liturgy of the hours, Eucharistic prayer, and ritual activity. In 1977 a working committee dealing with liturgy and social justice was formed. In 1978 the ritual group added language to the concerns of that committee and a working committee dealing with the liturgical year was formed. In 1979 the ritual group subdivided into fine arts and social sciences subsections and a working group on Christian initiation was formed. Since then, groups have been formed to deal with liturgy and spirituality, music and liturgy, the American parish, and liturgical preaching.

[7]See, for example, A. SCHMEMANN, *The World as a Sacrament* (London: Darton, Longman & Todd, 1966); A. SCHMEMANN, *For the Life of the World* (London: Darton, Longman & Todd, 1966); K.W. IRWIN, "Human Life and Christian Worship," Chapter Three in *Liturgy, Prayer and Spirituality* (New York: Paulist Press, 1984); J. POWERS, *Spirit and Sacrament: The Humanizing Experience* (New York: Seabury, 1973).

Even though liturgical studies are opening to broader dimensions of Christian living, we do not bring "perfect" selves to liturgy so that we may become a "perfect" community. Rather, the ideology of perfection is critiqued when we assert that *all* of life is brought into liturgy. Another important dimension of current liturgical research is the relationship of liturgy and life.[8] This is not to say that there is nothing wrong with the way we live or that we can do no wrong or that it does not make any difference if we do. Rather, it says that we are invited by God to enter into the liturgical celebration *as we are*. It is in the celebrating, by entering into God's world and thereby being offered other possible ways of living, that liturgy reconciles all to Godself. Significant in this regard are the countless studies undertaken on ritual as a dimension of life. Indeed, M. Collins sees a "structural congruence between rites and life."[9]

Liturgy raises fundamental questions about another dimension of life: How we are together. Now, though, within a life-encompassing liturgical perspective, our being together is not just a question of being "in church" together, but implies the liturgical assembly is coextensive with the Christian community. This statement might leave us a bit uncomfortable, since "being

---

[8]See, for example, L. BOUYER, *Life and Liturgy* (London: Sheed and Ward, 1965); K. RAHNER, "Secular Life and the Sacraments: A Copernican Revolution," *The Tablet* 6 & 13 (1971), 236-238 and 267-268; A. SCHMEMANN, *Liturgy and Life: Lectures and Essays On Christian Development Through Liturgical Experience* (New York: Department of Religious Education, Orthodox Church in America, 1974); N. PITTENGER, *Life as Eucharist* (Grand Rapids: William B. Eerdmans Publishing Company, 1973); J.H. WESTERHOFF and W.H. WILLIMON, *Liturgy and Learning through the Life Cycle* (New York: Seabury Press, 1980).

[9]"Liturgical Methodology and the Cultural Evolution of Worship in the United States," *Worship* 49 (1975), 94. Other select works dealing with liturgical rites as a dimension of life include C. GEERTZ, *The Interpretation of Cultures* (New York: Basic Books, Inc., Publishers, 1973); W.J. FREBURGER, *Liturgy: Work of the People* (Mystic, Connecticut: Twenty-third Publications, 1984); A.W. WATTS, *Myth and Ritual in Christianity* (Boston: Beacon Press, 1968); L.L. MITCHELL, *The Meaning of Ritual* (New York: Paulist Press, 1977); A.J. CHUPUNGCO, O.S.B., *Cultural Adaptation of the Liturgy* (New York: Paulist Press, 1982); R. GRAINGER, *The Language of the Rite*, Foreword by D. Martin (London: Darton, Longman & Todd, 1974).

together" as Christians leads us to ask, How well are we together? In this context we might also raise an ecumenical question, and liturgists are doing their homework in this dimension of human living together as well.[10]

When we reflect on the broad implications of liturgy being an objectification of our Christian existence, all of the human experiences we bracketed in the analytic of Chapter Five can be incorporated into our understanding of liturgy. Yet, if we never distance ourselves from Christian existence, we can never move beyond ourselves toward a new self-understanding. We now look to the possibilities for the new self-understanding our analytic suggests.

B. Through Sense toward Reference

The methodological moment of distanciation allows us to put ourselves at a "distance" from our human cultural existence and provides the opportunity for a deeper penetration into the meaning of our Christian living. Without the challenge of a fresh look at ourselves and our possibilities, the culmination of the hermeneutical process in the moment of appropriation would be impossible. For Ricoeur, written text is the paradigm of distanciation because a text (as enduring) communicates human experience in and through distance.

Our task in this part of the chapter is to look to the structure of our Christian existence as objectified by the structure of our select eucharistic text and uncovered in the explanatory moment, and let that structure suggest new possibilities for appropriation. We continue our methodological probings: How does the sense of a text already point to reference? How, then, does this show the explanatory moment as mediating understanding on both sides of the text?

The reference of a text is made apparent in a critical, reflective evaluation of the dynamic movement uncovered in analyzing its linguistic sense. We have seen how Ricoeur gives Jakobson positive marks for recognizing that meaning resides in the *total* act of communication. With respect to language's

---

[10]For just two examples, see *Baptism, Eucharist and Ministry*, Faith and Order Paper No. 111 (Geneva: World Council of Churches, 1982) and E.L. BRAND, "Response to the Berakah Award: Ecumenism and the Liturgy," *Worship* 58 (1984): 305-315.

relationship to human cultural existence, however, the differences between Ricoeur and Jakobson are crucial. (1) In terms of code, Ricoeur extends the metalingual function to the capacity of language through reflection to designate itself and its other. (2) Ricoeur rejects Jakobson's eclipse of reference in the poetic function. (3) For Ricoeur, reference is reached through language in use which relates the text to the participatory experience brought to it. Ricoeur, then, departs from Jakobson in that the explanation of the linguistic sense already pushes us toward understanding its reference as relating the "what is said" of the text to existence. We follow up on Ricoeur's venture into the world of reference through sense by coming back to the two foci of our analytic tool, action and communication.

1. Dynamic of Action

With an eye toward reference, we return to the sets of the four divisions of our select text. Recall that the four communication sets are CONTACT--MESSAGE--CONTEXT--CODE. We are interested in addressing two questions: What is the configuration of action that renders the liturgical text complete and whole rather than episodic and disjointed? What does this say about our understanding of Christian existence?

We assume a certain unity to the action. But we also know that the liturgical text has a great many disparate elements: greeting and preparing, listening to the word, celebrating Eucharist, dismissing. What draws these elements into a single action that is unified, complete and whole? How does a liturgy proceed from a beginning (as open possibilities) through the rite to an end (as a necessary or usual sequel)?[11] What principle--idea--generative process has forged a unity out of the liturgical action as it unfolds through its four divisions?

As we pointed out in Chapter Five, examination of one liturgical text does not allow us to identify its generative factor, which we would call "liturgical genre." We can suggest from our analysis a basic postulate of liturgical genre: the action of liturgy draws the community ever deeper into God's personal presence, which is to say ever deeper into the mystery of salvation. The dynamic characteristic of the eucharistic rite is such that the liturgical story unfolds as a structure not only

[11] See P. RICOEUR, *Time and Narrative*, p. 38.

mimetic of the structure of our human existence, but also mimetic of the structure of God's divine existence (in terms of God's interaction with us). Liturgical genre permits an understanding of liturgy that at once helps us to recognize the intersection of God's world and our own in the very unfolding of liturgy's structure.

In Christianity, a moment of distanciation is the liturgical celebration whereby we enter as an assembled community into God's presence, into the poetic reference opened up by the proclamation of the word, into the context of the eucharistic prayer, and, ultimately, even into living a fuller dimension of Christianity itself. But rather than coming to closure, liturgy opens up space for meaning to unfold as possibilities for a new understanding of how to live the Christian mystery. We now take a more penetrating look at the possibilities for a new way to live Christian existence by looking to the configuration of action of the four divisions.

1) Through the phatic function of the Introductory Rites people are constituted a liturgical assembly and recognize themselves as this assembly before the Lord. Essentially, Eucharist is enacted by an assembly, not by individuals. It is the assembled liturgical community which is drawn into the presence with God and each other through the phatic function of the Introductory Rites to become a "self-in-community." The possibility of community opened up by liturgy is not just any popular notion of community, but that suggested by the corrective of our analytic. In the constitution of the liturgical assembly, the worshippers come from dissimilar places to the worship space where they become a community of faith. From the very beginning of the eucharistic rite the participation in Christian living which characterizes the "I" who comes to the rite is in tension with a new self now defined by *being in a faith community.* This is the first moment in the drama of self-understanding inherent in applying Ricoeur's method of textual hermeneutics. By letting go of "I" and entering into a community of faith embracing a dialectical distinction of self-in-community from "I," we open up to ourselves the possibility of confronting how we are presently living our Christian existence with how we *might live* as first played out in the present celebration. Thus liturgy invites a hospitality of life marked by an encounter of Presence with presence (Act with act, Life with life).

2) Through the poetic function of the Liturgy of the Word the assembly is fed with God's word. The focus here is on the

word proclaimed.[12] Proclamation of the word lays before the community a *particular* word proclaiming more than information. The message is meaning-laden; that is, it has multivalent, referential import that opens up new possibilities for the community. The poesy of the word points to an indirect reference which is, ultimately, the possibility of encounter with the personal presence of Christ. The proclamation, then, is the proclamation of a *person* present who can be encountered[13] in such a way that the word is particularized for this given time and this given community. The creative word penetrates those gathered. Thus the reference of the poetic function indicates a more penetrating relationship between our human existence and the word proclaimed. The action of the Liturgy of the Word unites the community (which makes public its assent) with the proclamation and by so doing the community enters into a deeper personal presence with God.

3) Through the referential function of the Liturgy of the Eucharist the assembly by blessing, thanking, remembering, offering, and eating and drinking actually lives the mystery of the deeds of salvation in their retelling of the Christian story. Anamnetic narration affords the Christian community the possibility of reading the Christian story anew. The world of God's proffering of salvation is a possibility before the community, one that can be directly realized through the action

---

[12]Ricoeur sees proclamation as "the permanent re-interpretation of the text which is grounding the community ... " (P. RICOEUR, "The 'Sacred' Text and the Community" in *The Critical Study of Sacred Texts*, ed. W.D. O'Flaherty, Berkeley Religious Studies Series #2 [Berkeley: Graduate Theological Union, 1979], p. 274). Proclamation is fundamental to the Christian community because in receiving anew God's word, a continual constitution of the meaning of Christian texts takes place. Since the constitution of meaning is contemporaneous with the constitution of self (see P. RICOEUR, "What is a Text? Explanation and Understanding" in *Hermeneutics and the Human Sciences: Essays on Language, Action and Interpretation*, ed. and trans. J.B. Thompson [Cambridge: Cambridge University Press, 1981], p. 159), the liturgy in proclaiming the word, offers new possibilities for a new self.

[13]We recall from our analysis that the Gospel is central and the language of address accompanying it witnesses to our speaking *to* someone; the reference of the Gospel is a person, Jesus Christ, who is present to us in the proclamation of the word.

of eating and drinking. The many instances of code during this division constantly invite the community's participation in these actions. The depth of presence achieved at this point in the eucharistic action is a oneness with God symbolized by ingesting the Body and Blood of Christ, signaling a change from self-in-community to self-in-community-in-Christ. Human presence and divine presence are commingled in the action of eating and drinking, a promise of the fullness of Presence to presence.

4) Through the metalingual function of the Concluding Rite the assembly affirms its own willingness to hear the Christian story of salvation and continue living it by serving the Lord. The metalingual function here points to more than a checking on whether the language is understood. The metalingual function of the Concluding Rite characterizes language's capacity to designate itself and its other. Reading liturgy with the same code suggests the "other" that its language designates is the same for all. And what is that other? It is the presence of God into which the community has entered more and more deeply during the unfolding eucharistic action. Acclamation is a ritualization of a decision to appropriate possibilities for Christian living opened up by penetrating more deeply into the Divine Presence. In effect, acclamation describes the way a religious people who have celebrated Eucharist live. Our whole life is an act of worship, a living out of the worship event that is eucharistic action. Acclamation, then, rejects closure and opens up the unique reading of the Christian story that refigures the self-in-community in terms of a new self-understanding. The community is invited to make an affirmation that defines the "YES" of faith.

The dynamic of action unfolding in the eucharistic celebration opens up a world of possibilities circumscribed by community formation, proclamation, anamnetic narrative, and acclamation. This dynamic of action is a configured action: liturgy unfolds an ever deeper penetration into the Divine Presence which is paralleled by the liturgical assembly being refigured into a community more like Christ. How then might we understand the "experience" we call "Eucharist"? In terms of its dynamic of action, it would be the experience of letting go of "I" to become self-in-community and to become self-in-community-in-Christ to live as Christ. But this is only a partial understanding of eucharistic experience, based on the dynamic of action. We must add to this the possibilities suggested by the process of communication.

2. Process of Communication

Having reflected on the configuration of the dynamic of action, we now focus on the process of communication which unfolds in the eucharistic celebration. If we return to our analysis of the four major divisions of the eucharistic rite of Chapter Five, the meaning of the select eucharistic text is telling both by what noticeably contributes to its internal dynamic as well as by what is conspicuously absent. The four sets of the major divisions unfold as CONTACT--MESSAGE--CONTEXT--CODE. At either end of the communication spectrum the focus is on persons, God and community, through the contact set of the Introductory Rites and the code set of the Concluding Rite. Yet, we note that neither addresser nor addressee is the set of any of the divisions. Though God and community (as addresser or addressee) are conspicuously "absent" as a major set of a division, they are profoundly present in other respects. Reflection on the interlocutors leads us to another aspect of understanding the eucharistic experience.

Is not, perhaps, God absent as a set of one of the major divisions because we cannot name the "Unnameable?" Why is God not named? Maybe because God cannot be brought into history as "something." The world of the eucharistic text is not a human, historical world as we know ours to be, but it is God's world that interacts with our own. Because the "Unnameable" cannot be brought into history as "something," the reading of liturgy leads to wholly *new* possibilities offered for our appropriation. The "newness" of these possibilities derives from the "other" of God's world of salvific activity. Yet God reigns over history; it is God's world of acts and communication of Godself with which the community is confronted. Hence, the communication set of each of the divisions must be interpreted under the umbrella of God's self-communication. This is rather straightforward for message and context. The other communication factors of the first and last divisions of the rite take on an interesting new dimension.

While we said above that the contact of the Introductory Rites draws us into a self-in-community standing in God's presence, we ask, Does this not occur at God's initiative? The relinquishing of "I" to become self-in-community is not even totally our choice nor disposition, but happens by God's invitation. A similar corrective must be made for the metalingual import of the Concluding Rite. We would imagine that the affirmation is certainly our own. Yet, is not even this affirmation interpreted in terms of God's self-communication, which is to say that our understanding of the world of the eucharistic rite is not accomplished apart from God's self-communication? This is not a self-communication that comes from outside the celebration at its final affirmation, but it comes *through* the rite *toward* that metalingual response. We suggest that another aspect of the experience we call Eucharist is God's self-communication, available for our understanding. But so far we have only focused on one "absent" interlocutor. Let us look to the other interlocutor.

Is not, perhaps, the self-in-community absent as a set of one of the major divisions because to name the "nameable" would render "complete" those who are being refigured toward a different self-understanding? While the self-in-community knows one dimension of her/himself as living in Christian existence, not naming the self-in-community in liturgy's communication process breaks open Christian existence so that the Sacred may more fully enter and integrate life into Life. Because the "nameable" is not complete, we can read liturgy from the point of view of Christian living and permit fuller dimensions of God's world to shape our Christian self-understanding.

God's self-communication in the reading of liturgy is not dependent on our own recognition nor affirmation of it. In the reading we are "caught up" in the dynamic by the self-communication of the Unnameable. We mean to say that the rite can never be divorced from our affirmation of it nor from our very existence which is radically (radical = "root") transformed by it.

We believe that liturgy, by naming neither the "Unnameable" nor the "nameable," creates an inherent communicative tension between God's world and Christian living. We identify this liturgical tension as the interaction between the poetic and referential communication functions (of the Liturgy of the Word and the Liturgy of the Eucharist) with their being framed by God and self-in-community (phatic and metalingual functions of the Introductory Rites and Concluding Rite). Language functions in liturgy as a dynamic tension between the language of possibilities proffered by God's world and our own historical existence. This dynamic tension points to liturgy as language of faith, a language which speaks the community's relationship to the Sacred as an interpretation of God's language of self-revelation to the assembled faith community, available to it as a new self-understanding.

The eucharistic liturgy comes not to closure, but continues into the daily existence to which the assembled community returns. This does not happen by simply walking out the church doors. On the contrary, the eucharistic liturgy continues by a "thinking from" liturgical celebration which characterizes living from a new self-understanding. Liturgy is a language of faith to the extent that it captures the accumulated faith experiences of its participants and holds those experiences in dynamic tension with the new possibilities opened up by the celebration.

We have been directing our remarks to the celebration of liturgy as a way for our Christian existence to be challenged by new possibilities. We see in this how the moment of explanation is in a dialectical relationship to the moment of pre-understanding (participation) and offers a corrective to our present way of living. The corrective, though, operates not only in the direction of life vis-à-vis liturgy. From another perspective, the explanation-understanding dialectic can say something by way of evaluation about the *text* that is prescriptive for the liturgical celebration. We organize an evaluation of our methodological moment of explanation in terms of its structural, semantic, and analytic advantages.

Structurally, the many elements are seen to be a whole, rendering the communication and action as both dynamic and configured. Elements of the rite can be examined in relation to their immediate context: Does this element fit, structurally, with its proximate complements? How do the elements flow sequentially from one to another? This allows a structural critique of the present rite which could shape its future development.

Semantically, our method allows a critique of the words of the text with respect to how the communication takes place. For example, a liturgical text is celebrated by a community, and so the language is communitarian, plural. Many of the singular utterances contradict this communitarian dimension.

Analytically, our method can incorporate any number of possibilities. Our analytic has allowed us to see what kind of factors are involved in the communication process and the dynamic of action. Other analytics could address other aspects of liturgy, for example the metaphoric prayer language or its genetic factors. Openness to differing analytic tools permits the method to remain timely as new sets of questions open up in different historical and cultural situations. In any case, the method analyzes a text *qua* text, and this within a specific text theory.

While the results of our specific analytic are promising, we admit that the method is limited by the choice of analytic tools.

Other aspects important for a fuller explication of the meaning of the eucharistic rite cannot be addressed without going outside our chosen analytic. Thus, our method does not take into account the full dynamic of an actual celebration nor does it evaluate what is done with a text in that celebration. It brackets the text's historical development with its inherent theological and pastoral weaknesses. It brackets the thematic content of the text and the sources for the content and it does not capitalize on the richness of the text's metaphoric prayer language. What our method does do is show the generic possibilities inherent in the language of a text and promise results in several areas by allowing for different analytics.

A reading of liturgy reminds us of the source of the possibilities that are open to us: God's presence in the Christian story. In this way our living out the possibilities is not severed from the liturgical celebration which gives rise to them. At the same time, a reading of liturgy moves the self-in-community beyond the linguistic code into a world of praxis which characterizes the moment of appropriation. Appropriation refocuses on the life of the participants, but now within the broad dialectic of life circling back to liturgy and the refiguration of life resulting from celebrating. The effect of liturgy on those who celebrate is constitutive of the very act of reading the text itself.[14]

C. Appropriation: Project of Life

What project does liturgy promote? Through its moment of appropriation, "reading" a text sets the stage for a new way of living Christian life which is wholly within its continuing tradition. In the "grace of imagination"[15] (that is, the capacity to let new worlds shape our self-understanding) the world of the text is interpreted as possibilities before the self, as new ways of existing. While new possibilities are countless in terms of different readings of a text, a reflective moment clarifies them in terms of a critique of the signs of self-existence which results in appropriation, a making our own the world of the text's possibilities. In celebrating liturgy, our engagement in the action invites the appropriation of new

---

[14]See P. RICOEUR, *Time and Narrative*, p. 77.

[15]See P. RICOEUR, "The Language of Faith" in *The Philosophy of Paul Ricoeur: An Anthology of his Work*, ed. C.E. Reagan and D. Stewart (Boston: Beacon Press, 1968), p. 237.

ways of living out our Christian existence. In this part of the chapter we explore liturgical appropriation under two aspects: the self-engaging requirement of true celebration and the self-understanding which liturgy promotes.

1. Active Involvement

Certain features of liturgical celebration enable the moment of appropriation to be disengaged from being simply a component of a method of textual hermeneutics to being a dialogue with a text. There are any number of ways that the text itself indicates the moment of appropriation. Through its words, gestures, music, symbols, postures, actions, etc., the rite embraces the whole person. Active involvement in the liturgical celebration enables the liturgical text "to unfold its inherently dynamic character."[16] The linguistic symbols of liturgy engage the individual with the text in such a way that their involvement in the celebration is already an interpretation of the action embedded in the text. The dynamic flow of the text draws the assembly deeper and deeper into its world. What makes sense in the text that beckons the community to enter into it? The sense of the text is its structure. But structure is not some disembodied, objective entity "out there." The structure of the text is a dynamic of action inherent within a text which draws the "reader" into an engagement with it. What invites engagement? We venture a few examples here.

Liturgy calls for a level of engagement on the part of the assembled community that parallels the kind of "*active reading*" required to "get into" any text. Some components of the liturgy have as their primary purpose to more actively involve the assembly in the action. For example, music in liturgy often accompanies action not directly including the entire assembly: the opening hymn accompanies the entrance of the ministers into the worship space, a hymn at the Preparation accompanies the presentation of gifts, a recessional hymn accompanies the exit of the ministers. At other times music is a fuller way for the community to express their heightened emotion: during the singing of the Gloria, acclamations, litanies. As related to appropriation, then, music in liturgy is not an end in itself, but it should not be taken lightly. Those engaged in music

---

[16]W. ISER, "The Reading Process: A Phenomenological Aproach" in J.P. Tompkins, ed., *Reader-Response Criticism: From Formalism to Post-structuralism* (Baltimore: Johns Hopkins University Press, 1981), 51.

ministry and the study of the role of music in liturgy have an important task: to animate liturgical music so that the assembly comes to a more active involvement in order to make the process of appropriation more apparent.

Our analytic of Chapter Five alluded to the fact that even the taken-for-granted postures of sitting, standing, and kneeling have a direct bearing on the action that is taking place. We need to ask in various cultural settings whether the present postures are adequate? The same question needs to be plied to the various actions and symbols: Are they adequate? appropriate? What about the ritualized way we greet one another? extend a sign of peace? extend our offering of food and/or money? What about frequently only eating and not drinking? And what about the "bread" we do eat? What about the word being proclaimed out of a pamphlet rather than a visibly symbolic, richly bound book? What about the arrangement of the physical space in ordered rows where it is difficult to see faces?

Other components of the text also invite engagement. The liturgical text contains throughout numerous phatic indications that draw the assembly into the celebration. Is there not a difference between a presider who says "The Lord be with you" with hands stretched toward the assembly while looking at them and smiling and a presider who does not? Further, a careful planning of various options of the text can do wonders for introducing a "proper variety" into eucharistic celebrations and help particularize a celebration for a special feast or occasion.

We wish to draw special attention to the role of acclamations with respect to the appropriative moment. In our analysis of the select eucharistic text, we noted the importance of metalingual acclamations: acclamations not only conclude each of the major divisions, but they are found throughout the rite. We especially noted how often acclamations mark the Liturgy of the Eucharist. It is liturgy's acclamatory moments which witness to an eclipse of the cultic occasion and an impingement on ordinary life. Through affirmation of the eucharistic action we enter into a process of opening ourselves to the possibilities offered by the world of the text. But liturgy effects more than just opening self to possibilities. Liturgy's action invites a refiguration of self that is played out in life as a new self-understanding. It seems plausible to claim that the acclamations are critical moments in the text which concentrate us on turning points in the celebration.[17] At the primary points where liturgy draws out of us an acclamatory response to its dynamic of action we also recognize the foci of the world of the text: the word and bread/cup (Christ and salvific activity). The acclamations punctuate how liturgy refigures our life as Christ's life, continuing God's salvific activity. To acclaim the action of the liturgy is to refigure our world as God's world.

The way in which liturgy is appropriated depends more on the community than on the text.[18] In fact, without an assembly, liturgy does not happen.[19] Moreover, as we have seen, the *manner* of involvement is important: the way we sit and stand, speak and sing, listen and respond, gesture and remain still. These are all implied by active involvement.[20] The meaning of liturgy, then, cannot be separated from our own responses to and involvement in it: "it [text] owes its presence in our minds to our own reactions, and it is these that make us animate the meaning of the text as a reality."[21] What characterizes a liturgical celebration with life implications from a liturgy that

---

[17]Two acclamations intensify our response to the presence of Christ: the Gospel acclamation and Eucharistic acclamation (two Eucharistic acclamations ["Dying you destroyed our death ... " and "Lord, by your cross and resurrection you have set us free ... "] are second person address and most clearly underscore the presence of Christ). We would also add here the exchange between minister and communicant ("Body of Christ." "Amen."); while not an acclamation, the "Amen" is a metalingual response having the same communication function (affirmation and commitment) as an acclamation. Two acclamations strengthen our awareness of God's salvific activity: the "Holy, Holy, Holy" and the great "Amen." We would also add here the metalingual Profession of Faith.

[18]See W. ISER, *The Act of Reading: A Theory of Aesthetic Response* (Baltimore and London: Johns Hopkins University Press, 1981), p. 107.

[19]This, perhaps, makes the liturgical text unique among texts and again points to its unique genre. A liturgical text is composed only for the sake of celebration.

[20]Studies on "rubrics" are important in this regard, as the manner of involvement paves the way for appropriation.

[21]W. ISER, *The Act of Reading*, p. 128.

merely "goes through the motions"? In both cases the same ritual unfolds. What makes one rich in meaning and the other meaningless?

These questions raise a whole gamut of pastoral problems. Our analytic has shown that, by and large, the structure of our select text is configured with a dynamic of action and communication that accounts for liturgy's engagement of life.[22] Yet, we admit in many cases liturgy is anything but "dynamic." Certainly, presidential style, quality of music, aesthetics of the worship space, preparedness of other ministers, the way the community is together all enhance or diminish liturgy's staying power. But if we identify the effectiveness of liturgy only by these elements, we have, in effect, limited God's initiative by human resources. Nevertheless, we are naive, to say the least, if we assert that liturgy is essentially God's action and the human factor comes into play only at the level of attention and intention.

If we identify the effectiveness of liturgy primarily with our readiness and willingness to do God's action, in effect we relegate the concrete manifestations (the ceremony) of a given celebration to something peripheral. On the contrary, our structural analysis shows that the entire rite (both its verbal and nonverbal dimensions) contributes to its dynamism. It would seem, then, if we judge the effectiveness of liturgy (judge liturgy to be "good" or "bad") by concentrating on any one aspect, we distort liturgical reality. We suggest that what is characteristic of "good" liturgy is a delicate balance between the "what" and the "why" so that the full weight of effectiveness is derived from neither but from both.

By suggesting that a "delicate balance" characterizes "good" liturgy we set in motion a relationship among God's initiative and presence, our own motives and mode of presence in celebrating liturgy, and the unfolding of the ritual itself. The delicate balance is mutually helpful for both the personal and ritual dimensions. What good speaker does not respond enthusiastically to an attentive audience? On the other hand, well-planned, well-enacted celebration can do wonders with respect to inviting engagement. What happens when the balance is upset by deficiencies in either or both dimensions?

---

[22]Our comments under the sections "Critical Reflection" in Chapter Five show some areas of ambiguity and difficulty with the structure of the select text, but the structure as a whole manifests life-implications of the text.

Liturgy has its own built-in corrective in that it is always a *community* celebration.[23] Community, it seems, is the corrective that bridges the two dimensions of personal and ritual. If the ritual enactment is deficient, the totality of community provides an ambience larger than self to allow an encounter of Presence with presence. If our engagement is deficient, the community continues the ritual action and by so doing continually invites the individual to celebration. While the symbolic richness of liturgy is most apparent when the delicate balance between personal and ritual is preserved, nevertheless the extravagance of possible worlds is not limited by these dimensions.

The eucharistic liturgy's world surpasses the confines of the cultic occasion and becomes a part of the very life that is lived in our everyday existence. Liturgy is not something apart from our everyday living, but a vital informant of it. There is no separation of the sacred and secular. We live our lives totally in the life of the Divine Presence. The ultimate truth of liturgy consists in living out Christian understanding as a refigured existence enlarged by the very shape of the liturgical celebration. The meaning of liturgy is known in the hermeneutical process freely embraced by the participants. The self within is an agent of the world of the liturgical text.

The refiguration resulting from embracing the world of the text is indicative of the effect of the text on its reader.[24] Hence, configuration gives way to refiguration of the reader in the very act of reading. The world of possibilities that are part of the deep structure of the text are released as new possibilities for self-understanding. We are necessarily challenged to a new self-understanding by a text because "when we are present in an event, something must happen to us. ... The literary text relegates our own prevailing views into the past by itself becoming a present experience. ..."[25] The challenge of the liturgical celebration must be *received* by the participants. Self is an active agent of the world proffered by

---

[23]Our conception of community is that it is the Sacred assembly of the Lord, not a group where people necessarily "feel good" together.

[24]W. Iser puts it: "The written text contains a sequence of aspects which imply a totality" (*The Act of Reading*, p. 146).

[25]Ibid., p. 131.

the text for appropriation. The self-understanding of appropriation is the action whereby we *decide* to appropriate the world of the text into our present experience and this becomes the new constitution of our "YES" to life.

2. Self-understanding

The appropriation that culminates the hermeneutical process in Ricoeur's theory is a new self-understanding. Though one is presented with new possibilities for living the Christian ideal by the world of the liturgical text, appropriation permits a destruction of that Christian ideal *as an ideology* and yields a more originary word.[26] By reflection we make the world of the liturgical text our own, emplotting a new way of existing for ourselves, a new project of life. "Living in" a liturgical text must give way to "thinking from." When this happens, our whole life is a "thinking from" liturgy and evidences the refiguration that accompanies active engagement in the liturgical celebration. Nothing is "automatic" in a liturgical celebration, least of all its effects on the assembly.

The originary word of the world of divine and human action released as possibilities for self-appropriation by a liturgical celebration affects both community and self. A more originary word releases a historical adventure that challenges the community to become more whole. Specifically, this means a greater conformity to the Christian ideal in terms of the salvific world of the liturgy. A more originary word releases a personal adventure that challenges the self to become more whole. Specifically, this means a greater conformity to the Christian ideal in terms of the person of Christ encountered in liturgy.

To the extent that the celebration of liturgy by the worshipping community is *their* lived expression of Christian existence, the language of liturgy (its words, gestures, music, symbols, postures, actions, etc.) is the mediary between the expression of religious faith as well as the liturgical experience of new possibilities and the historical situation to be lived in a Christian context. If the celebration of liturgy does not culminate in appropriation, liturgy itself is incomplete. This has at least two important consequences for the individual and for the Christian community.

---

[26]See P. RICOEUR, "The Language of Faith" in *The Philosophy of Paul Ricoeur*, pp. 234-235.

The first, and most obvious, consequence is that if liturgy does not culminate in appropriation, the new self-understanding resulting from a deeper penetration into the world of liturgy is never internalized. Thus, the self leaving the cultic occasion is simply the same "I" who came. With no real transformation, the community (Body of Christ) is not built up. The actants in the liturgical drama are central. The interanimation of Presence with presence does more than configure the self-in-community. In the moment of appropriation, the community itself is refigured to the degree the individuals who comprise it are. Ultimately, the mark of liturgy upon human existence is measured by the refigured self of the act of appropriation.

Second, the more important consequence is that if the celebration of liturgy does not culminate in appropriation, then liturgy's language of faith is relegated to mere words spoken and actions undertaken during a cultic occasion. The only way liturgy is truly a language of faith is when its expression eclipses the cultic occasion to become a project of life. When language functions in liturgy in this way, the transformed "I" consequent upon living in the world of liturgy is a self turned toward the Unnameable, a "turning toward" that is recognizable in the way we live. Liturgy is a project of life because its truth is judged by the way we live.

In the final analysis, then, liturgy's moment of appropriation suggests that the religious dimension of life is not separate from the praxical. In fact, praxis assures the identity between our religious life and our ethical life.[27] We ask with T. Balasuriya:

> Why is it that in spite of hundreds of thousands of eucharistic celebrations, Christians continue as selfish as before? Why have the "Christian" peoples been the most cruel colonizers of human history? Why is the gap of income, wealth, knowledge, and power growing in the world today--and that in favor of the "Christian" peoples. Why is it that persons and people who proclaim eucharistic love and sharing deprive the poor people of the world of food, capital, employment, and even land? Why do they prefer cigarettes and liquor to food and drink for the one-third of humanity that goes hungry to bed each night? Why are cars, cosmetics, pet dogs, horses, and bombs preferred to human

---

[27]Cf. P. RICOEUR, *Time and Narrative*, p. 47.

> children? Why mass human sterilization in poor countries and affluence unto disease and pollution of nature among the rich?[28]

These are agonizing questions to us because we know the worship of Christians is eucharistic, yet we see so little effect at a global level (and sometimes, too, at a local level). We are left with the question, To what extent is the eucharistic liturgy "read"?

We agree with M.K. Hellwig that the "simple, central action of the Eucharist is the sharing of food--not only eating but sharing."[29] While the focus of the Liturgy of the Eucharist as ritual action is the eating and drinking, the praxical responsibility effected by appropriation demands a sharing of the fruits of that eating and drinking. That is, the oneness between self-in-community and Christ that is the deeper dimension of the eating and drinking is that which is carried over into daily living in the appropriative act as sharing the fruits of being self-in-community-in-Christ. In effect, the moment of appropriation of Christian liturgy implicates the political, economic, social, and ethical dimensions of human living. This is what is meant by our statement that "living in" a liturgical text must give way to "thinking from." The latter is not just a cognitive activity, but a way of living Christian praxis that witnesses to the unity of the religious and practical spheres of life. Many liturgists today are becoming more and more sensitive to liturgy's relationship to all aspects of Christian living, and by so doing are advancing the cause of breaking down the barrier between liturgical life and social relationships.[30] We do not live two lives, but one life: the Christian life.

---

[28]T. BALASURIYA, *The Eucharist and Human Liberation* (Maryknoll, NY: Orbis Books, 1979), xi-xii.

[29]M.K. HELLWIG, *The Eucharist and the Hunger of the World* (New York: Paulist Press Deus Book, 1976), p. 10.

[30]For select examples, see R. AVILA, *Worship and Politics* (Maryknoll: Orbis Books, 1981); F. CARNEY, ed., "Focus on Liturgy and Ethics," *Journal of Religious Ethics* 7 (1979), 139-248; B. DE CLERCQ, "Political Commitment and Liturgical Celebration," *Concilium* 9-4 (1973, trans. D. Smith), 110-116; J. GELINEAU, "Celebrating the Paschal Liberation," *Concilium* 10-2 (1974, trans. V. Green), 107-119; A. HAMMAN, *The Grace to Act Now:*

What we are saying about the praxical implications of the moment of appropriation runs far deeper than saying that liturgy motivates us to "do good." The corrective of our analytic to such a facile association of liturgical life and ethical life lies in the growth from an "I" to self-in-community to self-in-community-in-Christ. Liturgy's deeper penetration into the Divine Presence enables a new self-understanding that is more closely aligned to the person of Christ. Praxis which is the result of "thinking from" liturgy is the praxis of Christ; that is, the ministry of Christ. Our analytic, then, qualifies praxis as *Christian* praxis. In effect, the language of praxis is the language of faith.

D. Liturgy as Language of Faith

What language does liturgy speak? Our method of interpretation provides a way of speaking to our Christian

---

Liturgy and the Apostolate in the Light of the Early Christian Communities (Chicago: Franciscan Herald Press, 1966); D. HOLLENBACH, "A Prophetic Church and the Catholic Sacramental Imagination" in *The Faith that Does Justice*, J.C. Haughey, ed. (New York: Paulist Press, 1977), pp. 234-263; C.F. JEGEN, "Worship and Missio," *Jurist* 39 (1979), 88-112; C. KIESLING, "Liturgy and Consumerism," *Worship* 52 (1978), 359-368; C. KIESLING, "Liturgy and Social Justice," *Worship* 51 (1977), 351-361; E. McDONAGH, "Liturgy and Christian Living" in *Invitation and Response: Essays in Christian Moral Theology* (Dublin: Gill and MacMillan, 1972), pp. 96-108; J.H. McKENNA, "Liturgy: Toward Liberation or Oppression?" *Worship* 56 (1982), 291-308; H.-B. MEYER, "The Social Significance of the Liturgy," *Concilium* 10-2 (1974, trans. F. McDonagh), 34-50; J. MOLTMANN, "The Liberating Feast," *Concilium* 10-2 (1974, trans. F. McDonagh), 74-84; P.J. ROSSI, "Narrative, Worship, and Ethics: Empowering Images for the Shape of Christian Moral Life," *The Journal of Religious Ethics* 7 (1979), 239-248; D.E. SALIERS, "Liturgy and Ethics: Some New Beginnings," *The Journal of Religious Ethics* 7 (1979), 173-189; H. SCHMIDT, "Lines of Political Action in Contemporary Liturgy," *Concilium* 10-2 (1974, trans. H. Hoskins), 13-33; M. SEARLE (ed.), *Liturgy and Social Justice* (Collegeville: The Liturgical Press, 1980); A. VANNUCCHI, "Liturgy and Liberation," *International Review of Mission* 65 (1976), 186-195; W.H. WILLIMON, *The Service of God: How Worship and Ethics are Related* (Nashville: Abingdom Press, 1983).

existence *out of* our Christian existence. Faith is not once and for all, but it is a dynamic commitment to live out of our human cultural existence our basic orientation to the Sacred. While liturgy provides a *structure* for growth in faith, liturgy can be a *language* of faith only to the extent that it enables a refiguration of self that enables our conscious being to be more completely turned toward God. This refiguration happens within the specific parameters of the possibilities offered by the world of the text and is lived out in ordinary human existence. To speak of liturgy as a language of faith is necessarily to speak the language of ordinary living as God's language.

Our allegation that liturgy functions as a language of faith is a modest one making limited claims in terms of our chosen analytic. We admit that our application brackets certain aspects of a liturgical text which are as important as our own aspects (structure of action and communication). Our concern in applying our method to a select text is not to come up with a definitive meaning for the eucharistic liturgy, but rather to show how (1) the relationship between text and its celebration and (2) the relationship of liturgy and life must necessarily figure in *any* explication of the meaning of the eucharistic text. Most significantly, our method shows how a text arises from the author's experience (participation) and culminates in the reader's experience (appropriation). In this, we say text has something to do with life, with human cultural existence. More, we say that the liturgical text's celebration establishes an essential link between sacred language, its celebration, and the way we live. By calling liturgy a language of faith we claim that liturgy as language which refigures us through the appropriation of its world speaks of a deepening of our relationship to the Sacred. Liturgy as language of faith implies that liturgy is a way to live our conscious being's commitment to God, not only as a cultic occasion but as the primary dimension of Christian living.

Our method calls for a sensitivity to liturgical language in two ways. First, as an objectification of the structures of Christian existence, we need to respond to an ongoing concern with the living nature of language, searching for ever fresher determinations of liturgical language. We note that a qualification is in order when we assert the essential relationship between a text and its celebration. While a text is prescriptive, it is not definitive. It is necessary to constantly monitor liturgical texts, their development and promulgation. Historical text studies can certainly provide much insight into text genesis, development, and the meaning of many of the components of a rite. But we claim that these studies must then be measured over against and complemented by a method that determines *this* particular text's effect on *this* particular community.

Second, our method calls for a sensitivity to liturgical language in terms of the relationship of liturgical language and Christian living. By this we suggest that eucharistic praying must respect the text's characteristic objectification of signs of Christian existence. Without this sensitivity, eucharistic praying risks being an exercise outside the tradition of celebration, shattering the integrity of one Bread, one Body and thus fragmenting into many a Eucharist that remains one, once and for all.

In these chapters we have proposed a method of interpretation of liturgical texts that enables a "reading" of liturgy which implicates life. Certain areas could still be fruitfully explored. While our own study proposes a complementary liturgical methodology, to date no comprehensive account of liturgical methodologies in current use has been undertaken by recent liturgists. We are thinking here especially in terms of encouraging liturgical scholars to analyze and systematize what they are actually doing methodologically.

In this study we have noted that our method employs both synchronic and diachronic aspects. In terms of synchrony, we believe other analytics could be applied to the select text and that we could apply our own analytic to other liturgical rites. Both projects would add to liturgical data. Further, we discussed a liturgical genre which generates liturgical texts, but we have not examined other texts to see what else is characteristic of liturgical genre. If this task were undertaken, a helpful tool to understand the generating of new liturgical texts would be available.

We believe that especially the diachronic aspect could be plumbed further in terms of the inherent historicity of liturgy. In particular, how would the temporal structures of our Christian existence be captured by the structure of our celebration?

These and other questions are generated by our study. We cannot hope to answer them here. Let us close by saying that Ricoeur's method has given us a framework in which we could show that our central question, the relationship of liturgy and life, is addressed in terms of both the tradition of participation in life that gives rise to the liturgical text and the ongoing appropriation that continues to shape our Christian tradition. We say one more time: liturgy is a language of faith. As language of faith, liturgy embodies a mystery, which means that it can never be exhausted: it turns the nameable irrevocably toward the Unnameable. We realize in this turning toward the Unnameable an ultimate relationship between liturgy and life, Life and life.

BIBLIOGRAPHY OF CITED WORKS

ALDWINCKLE, R.F. "Worship and Prayer: Principles and Problems: Liturgy and Language," *Canadian Journal of Theology* 15 (1969): 157-165.

ANDERSON, F.R. "Liturgy in the Vernacular," *Reformed Liturgy and Music* 17 (1983): 185.

AUSTIN, J.L. *How to Do Things With Words.* The William James Lectures Delivered at Harvard University in 1955. Oxford: At the Clarendon Press, 1963.

AVERY, G. "Dvornick on National Churches," *Eastern Churches Review* 10 (1978): 17-25.

AVILA, R. *Worship and Politics.* Maryknoll: Orbis Books, 1981.

BALASURIYA, T. *The Eucharist and Human Liberation.* Maryknoll, NY: Orbis Books, 1979.

Baptism, Eucharist and Ministry. Faith and Order Paper #111. Geneva: World Council of Churches, 1982.

BAUMSTARK, A. *Comparative Liturgy.* Revised by B. Botte, O.S.B. English edition by F.L. Cross. Westminster, Maryland: Newman, 1958.

BENVENISTE, E. *Problems in General Linguistics.* Translated by M.E. Meek. Coral Gables, Florida: University of Miami Press, 1971.

BLACKLOCK, M. "Popularizing Non-sexist Liturgies," *Witness* 64 (1981): 10-11.

BOUYER, L. *Eucharist: Theology and Spirituality of the Eucharistic Prayer.* Translated by C. Underhill Quinn. Notre Dame: University of Notre Dame Press, 1968.

_________. *La vie de la liturgie: une critique constructive du mouvement liturgique.* Paris: Editions du Cerf, 1956.

_________. *Life and Liturgy.* London: Sheed and Ward, 1965.

BOS, J.W.H. "To Whom Then Will You Liken Me," *Reformed Liturgy and Music* 17 (1983): 169-171.

BIBLIOGRAPHY

BOUCHER, M. "Scriptural Readings: God-language and Nonsexist Translation," *Reformed Liturgy and Music* 17 (1983): 156-159.

BRAND, E.L. "Response to the Berakah Award: Ecumenism and the Liturgy," *Worship* 58 (1984): 305-315.

BREWER, D. "Liturgy: Need and Frustration," *Theology* 80 (1977): 173-177.

BRINKMAN, B. "Sacramental Man and Speech Acts Again," *The Heythrop Journal* 16 (1975): 416-420.

BROWN, E.S. "Whose Liturgical Language?" *Dialogue* 20 (1981): 107-111.

BRUEGGEMANN, W. *The Creative Word: Canon as a Model for Biblical Education.* Philadelphia: Fortress Press, 1982.

BUTTRICK, D.G. "On Liturgical Language," *Reformed Liturgy and Music* 15 (1981): 74-82.

BUSCH, W. "Travel Notes on the Liturgical Movement," *Oratre Fratres* 1 (1926-1927): 50-55.

CARNEY, F., ed. "Focus on Liturgy and Ethics," *Journal of Religious Ethics* 7 (1979).

CHALLANCIN, J. "Presider: Member of the Community," *Modern Liturgy* 11 (1984): 5-7.

CHAPMAN, R. "Linguistics and Liturgy," *Theology* 76 (1973): 594-599.

CHUPUNGCO, A.J., O.S.B. *Cultural Adaptation of the Liturgy.* New York: Paulist Press, 1982.

COCKERELL, D. "The Language of Initiation: A Critique of Series 3 Baptism," *The Modern Churchman* 23 (1980): 21-29.

_________. Liturgical Language, Dead and Alive," *Theology* 80 (1977): 110-116.

COLLINS, M. "Liturgical Methodology and the Cultural Evolution of Worship in the United States," *Worship* 49 (1975): 85-102.

CRICHTON, J.D., ed. *The Liturgy and the Future.* Tenburgy Wells, Worcestershire: Fowler Wright Books, 1966.

BIBLIOGRAPHY

CRYSTAL, D. "Linguistics and Liturgy," *Christian Quarterly* 2 (1969): 23-30.

CULLY, K.B. *Sacraments: A Language of Faith.* Philadelphia: Christian Education Press, 1961.

DALMAIS, I.-H. "The Expression of the Faith in Eastern Liturgies," *Concilium* 9-2 (1973, translated by F. McDonagh): 77-85.

DALY, R.J. *Christian Sacrifice: The Judaeo-Christian Background before Origin.* Studies in Christian Iniquity 18. Washington, D.C.: The Catholic University of America Press, 1978.

DAUENHAUER, B.P. "Some Aspects of Language and Time in Ritual Worship," *International Journal for the Study of Philosophy of Religion* 6 (1975): 54-62.

DAVIES, D. "Social Groups, Liturgy and Glossolalia," *The Churchman* 90 (1976): 193-205.

DE CLERCQ, B. "Political Commitment and Liturgical Celebration," *Concilium* 9-4 (1973, translated by D. Smith): 110-116.

DE MARCO, A.A. *Rome and the Vernacular.* Westminster, Maryland: Newman Press, 1961.

DE SAUSSURE, F. *Cours de linguistique générale.* Paris: Payot, 1971.

DEWART, L. *Religion, Language and Truth.* New York: Herder and Herder, 1970.

DILLISTONE, F.W. *Traditional Symbols and the Contemporary World.* London: Epworth Press, 1973.

_________, ed. *Myth and Symbol.* London: S.P.C.K., 1966.

DIX, G. *The Shape of the Liturgy.* 2nd Edition. Westminster: Dacree Press, 1945.

DONOVAN, P. *Religious Language.* New York: Hawthorn Books, 1976.

DUFORT, J.M. "Le langage de l'espérance dans la prière liturgique," *Science et Esprit* 26 (1974): 233-250.

BIBLIOGRAPHY

DUFRASNE, D. "Les chances du 'Gloire à Dieu,'" *Communautés et Liturgies* 64-1 (1982): 23-33.

DULLES, A.R. *A Church to Believe In: Discipleship and the Dynamics of Freedom.* New York: Crossroads, 1982.

ECO, U. "The Influence of Roman Jakobson on the Development of Semiotics." In *Roman Jakobson: Echoes of His Scholarship.* Edited by D. Armstrong and C.H. Van Schooneveld. Lisse: The Peter de Riddler Press, 1977.

_________. *The Role of the Reader: Explorations in the Semiotics of Texts.* Bloomington: Indiana University Press, 1979.

ELLARD, G. "Gregory and Pius, Fathers of Liturgy," *Orate Fratres* 1 (1926-1927: 12-16.

_________. *Men at Work at Worship: America Joins the Liturgical Movement.* New York: Longmans, Green, 1940.

EMMINGHAUS, J.H. *The Eucharist: Essence, Form, Celebration.* Translated by M.J. O'Connell. Collegeville: The Liturgical Press, 1978.

FINBERG, H.P.R. "The Problem of Style." In *English in the Liturgy: A Symposium.* London: Burns and Oates, 1956: pp. 109-122.

FINK, P.E. "Three Languages of Christian Sacraments," *Worship* 52 (1978): 561-575.

FITZER, J. "Liturgy, Language and Mysticism," *Worship* 47 (1973): 66-79.

FOLEY, J.B. "An Aural Basis for Oral Liturgical Prayer," *Worship* 56 (1982): 132-152.

FREBURGER, W.J. *Liturgy: Work of the People.* Mystic, Connecticut: Twenty-third Publications, 1984.

FROST, D.L. "Dying Church, or a Living World?" *Theology* 74 (1971): 499-512.

GANOCZY, A. *An Introduction to Catholic Sacramental Theology.* Translated by W. Thomas with A. Sherman. New York: Paulist Press, 1984.

GARRETT, P.D. "Problems of Liturgical Translation: A Preliminary Study." *St. Vladimir's Theological Quarterly* 22 (1978): 83-113.

________. "The Problem of Liturgical Translation: An Addendum [Φῶς ἱλαρόν]," *St. Vladimir's Theological Quarterly* 24 (1980): 37-50.

GEERTZ, C. *The Interpretation of Cultures.* New York: Basic Books, Inc., Publishers, 1973.

GELINEAU, J. "Celebrating the Paschal Liberation," *Concilium* 10-2 (1974, translated by V. Green): 107-119.

GIGNAC, A. "Prière liturgique et 'langue vivante,'" *Liturgie et vie chrétienne* 75 (1971): 22-30.

GILKEY, L. "Addressing God in Faith," *Concilium* 9-2 (1973): 62-76.

GILL, S.D. "Prayer as Person: The Performative Force in Navaho Prayer Acts," *History of Religions* 17 (1977): 143-157.

GODGETTS, M. "Sense and Sound in Liturgical Translation," *Worship* 57 (1983): 496-513.

GOTTERI, N. "Tradition and Translation," *Sobornost* 2 (1980): 41-49.

GRAINGER, R. *The Language of the Rite.* Foreword by D. Martin. London: Darton, Longman & Todd, 1974.

GRIMES, R.L. *Beginnings in Ritual Studies.* Washington, D.C.: University Press of America, 1982.

GRINDAL, G. "The Language of Worship and Hymnody: Tone," *Worship* 52 (1978): 509-516.

______. "Stopping by the Pit Stop: Liturgies Call for the Prose of Speech Rather than the Prose of Print," *Christian Century* 94 (1977): 453-457.

GUARDINI, R. "Über die systematische Methode in der Liturgiewissenschaft," *Jahrbuch für Liturgiewissenschaft* 1 (1921): 97-108.

BIBLIOGRAPHY

HAMMAN, A. *The Grace to Act Now: Liturgy and the Apostolate in the Light of the Early Christian Communities.* Chicago: Franciscan Herald Press, 1966.

HARRIES, R. "Alternative Services: The Test of Practice," *Theology* 79 (1976): 221-226.

HAUSSLING, A. "Die kritische Funktion der Liturgiewissenschaft," *Liturgie und Gessellschaft.* Edited by H.-B. Meyer. Innsbruck: Tyrolia, 1970: pp. 103-130.

HAWKES, T. *Structuralism and Semiotics.* Berkeley: University of California Press, 1977.

HELLWIG, M.K. *The Eucharist and the Hunger of the World.* New York: Paulist Press Deus Book, 1976.

HOLLENBACH, D. "A Prophetic Church and the Catholic Sacramental Imagination." In *The Faith that Does Justice.* Edited by J.C. Haughey. New York: Paulist Press, 1977.

HOLLENSTEIN, E. *Roman Jakobson's Approach to Language: Phenomenological Structuralism.* Translated by C. Schelbert and T. Schelbert. Bloomington: Indiana University Press, 1976.

HOVDA, R.W. *Strong, Loving and Wise: Presiding in Liturgy.* Foreword by G. Diekmann, O.S.B. Washington, D.C.: The Liturgical Conference, 1977.

HOWELL, C. "The Use of English in the Liturgy." In *The Liturgy and the Future.* Edited by J.D. Crichton. Tenburgy Wells, Worcestershire: Fowler Wright Books, 1966: pp. 88-104.

HUCK, G. *Liturgy with Style and Grace.* Chicago: Liturgy Training Publications, 1984.

HUGHES, H.K. *The Opening Prayers of the Sacramentary: A Structural Study of the Prayers of the Easter Cycle.* Doctoral Dissertation, University of Notre Dame, 1981.

ICEL. *Documents On the Liturgy 1963-1979: Conciliar, Papal, and Curial Texts.* Collegeville: The Liturgical Press, 1983.

________. "The Problem of Exclusive Language with Regard to Women," *Afer* 23 (1981): 312-317.

IRWIN, K.W. *Liturgy, Prayer and Spirituality.* New York: Paulist Press, 1984.

ISAMBERT, F. *Rite et efficacité symbolique: Essai d'anthropologie sociologique.* Rite et Symboles #8. Paris: Les Editions du Cerf, 1979.

ISER, W. *The Act of Reading: A Theory of Aesthetic Response.* Baltimore: Johns Hopkins University Press, 1981.

_________. "The Reading Process: A Phenomenological Approach." In *Reader-Response Criticism: From Formalism to Post-structuralism.* Edited by J.P. Tompkins. Baltimore: Johns Hopkins University Press, 1981.

ISHAK, F.M. "Celebration of the Eucharist in Appropriate Language," *Coptic Church Review* 1 (1980): 27-29.

JAKOBSON, R. "Closing Statement: Linguistics and Poetics." In *Style in Language.* Edited by T.A. Sebeok. Cambridge: The M.I.T. Press, 1960.

_________. *The Framework of Language.* Michigan Studies in the Humanities, Number 1. 1980.

_________. *Selected Writings II.* Five Volumes. s'Gravenhage: Mouton & Co., 1962-1979.

JAUSS, H.R. *Toward an Aesthetic of Reception.* Translated by T. Bahti. Introduction by P. de Man. Theory and History of Literature Volume 2. Minneapolis: University of Minnesota Press, 1982.

JEFFNER, A. *The Study of Religious Language.* London: SCM Press, 1972.

JEGEN, C.F. "Worship and Missio," *Jurist* 39 (1979): 88-112.

JONES, C., WAINWRIGHT, G., and YARNOLD, E., S.J. *The Study of the Liturgy.* New York: Oxford University Press, 1978.

JONES, P. *English in the Liturgy: Some Aesthetic and Practical Problems.* London: G. Chapman, 1966.

JUNGMANN, J. *The Mass of the Roman Rite.* Two Volumes. Translated by F.A. Brunner. New York: Benzinger Brothers, Inc., 1951, 1955.

BIBLIOGRAPHY

KAVANAGH, A. "Cultural Diversity and Liturgical Language," *Una Sancta* 24 (1967): 69-71.

________. "Confirmation: A Suggestion from Structure," *Worship* 58 (1984): 386-394.

________. *Elements of Rite: A Handbook of Liturgical Style.* New York: Pueblo Publishing Company, 1982.

KENNY, A. *Action, Emotion and Will.* London: Routeledge & K. Paul, 1963.

KERR, H.T. "Wash Your Language," *Theology Today* 30 (1973): 211-217.

KIESLING, C. "Liturgy and Consumerism," *Worship* 52 (1978): 359-368.

________. "Liturgy and Social Justice," *Worship* 51 (1977): 351-361.

KOROLEVSKY, C. *Living Languages in Catholic Worship: An Historical Inquiry.* Translated by D. Attwater. London: Longmans, Green, 1957.

KRETSCHMAR, G. "Recent Research on Christian Initiation," *Studia Liturgica* 12 (1977): 87-106.

LADIRERE, J. *Language and Belief.* Translated by G. Barden. Notre Dame: University of Notre Dame Press, 1972.

________. "The Performativity of Liturgical Language," *Concilium* 9-2 (1973, translated by J. Griffiths): 50-62.

LARDNER, G.V. "Communication Theory and Liturgical Research," *Worship* 51 (1972): 299-306.

________. "Liturgy as Communication: A Pragmatic Perspective," *Religious Education* 77 (1982, Dissertation Abstract, Temple University, 1980): 438.

LARSEN, K.J. "Language as Aural," *Worship* 54 (1980): 18-35.

________. "Some Observations about Symbols and Metaphors," *Worship* 54 (1980): 221-245.

LAWSON, E.T. "Ritual as Language," *Religion* 6 (1976): 123-139.

LO BELLO, A. "From East to West: On Certain ICEL Translations," *Communio* 8 (1981): 392-399.

________. "The Mass in Latin and in English," *Downside Review* 101-344 (1983): 194-215.

LUCIER, P. "Le statut épistémologique de la situation liturgique," *Liturgie et vie chrétienne* 82 (1972): 256-278.

LUKKEN, G. "The Unique Expression of Faith in the Liturgy," *Concilium* 9-2 (1973, translated by D. Smith): 11-21.

LYLES, J.C. "The NCC's Nonsexist Lectionary," *Christian Century* 100 (1983): 1148-1150.

________. "New Language for Liturgy," *Christian Century* 98 (1981): 1358-1359.

LYONS, J. *Semantics.* Volume 1. Two Volumes. Cambridge: Cambridge University Press, 1977.

MANIGNE, J.-P. "The Poetics of Faith in the Liturgy," *Concilium* 9-2 (1973, translated by F. McDonagh): 40-50.

MARCH, W.E. "Language About God: What Shall We Say?" *Reformed Liturgy and Music* 17 (1983): 152-155.

MARTINICH, A. "Reply to B. Brinkman, 'Sacramental Man and Speech Acts Again,'" *The Heythrop Journal* 17 (1976): 188-189.

________. "Sacraments and Speech Acts," *The Heythrop Journal* 16 (1975): 289-305.

MAXWELL, J.M. "Inclusive Language in Theology and Worship," *Austin Seminary Bulletin* 97 (1981): 37-45.

McANALLY, T. "Language and Liturgy in the COCU Context," *Mid-Stream* 21 (1982): 422-423.

McDONAGH, E. "Liturgy and Christian Living." Chapter 6 in *Invitation and Response: Essays in Christian Moral Theology.* Dublin: Gill and MacMillan, 1972: pp. 96-108.

McKENNA, J.H. "Liturgy: Toward Liberation or Oppression?" *Worship* 56 (1982): 291-308.

MEYER, H.-B. "The Social Significance of the Liturgy," *Concilium* 10-2 (1974, translated by F. McDonagh): 34-50.

_______, ed. *Liturgie und Gessellschaft.* Innsbruck: Tyrolia, 1970.

MITCHELL, L.L. *The Meaning of Ritual.* New York: Paulist Press, 1977.

_______. "Liturgics, Whence and Whither?" *Anglican Theological Review* 63 (1981): 302-308.

MOLTMANN, J. "The Liberating Feast," *Concilium* 10-2 (1974, translated by F. McDonagh): 74-84.

MURRAY, P. "The Holy Spirit and God Language," *Witness* 66 (1983): 7-9.

MVENG, E. "Christ, liturgie et culture," *Bulletin de théologie africaine* 2 (1980): 247-255.

The Mystery of Faith: A Study of the Structural Elements of the Order of the Mass. Washington, D.C.: Federation of Diocesan Liturgical Commissions, 1981.

"NCC's Bisexual Lectionary Brings More Problems," *Christianity Today* 27 (1983): 40.

OESTERLEY, W.O.E. *The Jewish Background of the Christian Liturgy.* New York: Oxford Press, 1975.

PENFIELD, J.H. "COCU Consultation on Language and Liturgy," *Journal of Ecumenical Studies* 19 (1982): 668-669.

PERELMAN, C., ed. *Dialectic/Dialectiques.* International Instutite of Philosophy. The Hague: Nijhoff, 1973.

PITTENGER, N. *Life as Eucharist.* Grand Rapids: William B. Eerdmans Publishing Company, 1973.

POWER, D. "People at Liturgy," *Concilium* 170 (1983: 9-11.

_________. "Theological Trends. Symbolism in Worship: A Survey, I," *The Way* 13 (1973): 310-324.

_________. "Theological Trends: Symbolism in Worship IV," *The Way* 15 (1975): 137-146.

_________. "Two Expressions of Faith: Worship and Theology," *Concilium* 9-2 (1973): 95-103.

_________. *Unsearchable Riches: The Symbolic Nature of the Liturgy.* New York: Pueblo Publishing Company, 1984.

POWER, R. "The Liturgy in Translation," *Orate Fratres* 1 (1926-1927): 203-207.

POWERS, J. *Spirit and Sacrament: The Humanizing Experience.* New York: Seabury, 1973.

RAHNER, K. "Secular Life and the Sacraments: A Copernican Revolution," *The Tablet* 6 & 13 (1971): 236-238 and 267-268.

RAMSHAW-SCHMIDT, G. "An Inclusive Language Lectionary," *Worship* 58 (1984): 29-37.

_________. "The Language of Eucharistic Praying," *Worship* 57 (1983): 419-437.

RASCHKE, C. "Meaning and Saying in Religion: Beyond Language Games," *Harvard Theological Review* 67 (1974): 79-116.

REAGAN, C.E., ed. *Studies in the Philosophy of Paul Ricoeur.* Athens: Ohio University Press, 1979.

_________ and STEWART, D., eds. *The Philosophy of Paul Ricoeur: An Anthology of His Work.* Boston: Beacon Press, 1978.

RIBOUL, O. *Langage et idéologie.* Paris: Presses universitaires de France, 1980.

RICHARDS, I.A. "Functions of and Factors in Language," *Journal of Literary Semantics* 1 (1972): 25-40.

RICHARDSON, C.C., ed. and trans. *Early Christian Fathers.* 4th paperback ed. New York: Macmillan Publishing Co., Inc., 1978.

RICOEUR, P. "Biblical Hermeneutics," *Semeia* 4 (1975): 29-148.

_________. *The Conflict of Interpretations: Essays in Hermeneutics.* Edited by D. Ihde. Evanston: Northwestern University Press, 1974.

_________. *Cours sur l'herméneutique.* Louvain: Institut Supérieur de Philosophie, 1971-1972. Mimeograph.

BIBLIOGRAPHY

_________. *Fallible Man*. Philosophy of the Will, Part II: Finitude and Guilt. Book I: *Fallible Man*. Translated by C. Kelbley. Chicago: Regnery, 1965.

_________. *Hermeneutics and the Human Sciences: Essays on Language, Action and Interpretation*. Edited and translated by J.B. Thompson. Cambridge: Cambridge University Press, 1981.

_________. "History and Hermeneutics," *The Journal of Philosophy* 73 (1976, translated by D. Pellauer): 683-695.

_________. *History and Truth*. Translated with an Introduction by C.A. Kelbley. Evanston: Northwestern University Press, 1965.

_________. *Interpretation Theory: Discourse and the Surplus of Meaning*. Ft. Worth: The Texas Christian University Press, 1979.

_________. "Le sentiment." In *Edmund Husserl: 1859-1959*. Recueil commémoratif Publié à l'occasion du centenaire de la naissance du philosophie. Edited by H.L. Van Breda and J. Taminiaux. Phaenomenologica 4. La Haye: Martimus Nijhoff, 1959.

_________, ed. *Main Trends in Philosophy*. New York: Holmes & Meier Publishers, Inc., 1979.

_________. "Philosophy and Religious Language," *Journal of Religion* 54 (1974): 71-85.

_________. *The Rule of Metaphor: Multi-disciplinary Studies of the Creation of Meaning in Language*. Translated by R. Czerny with K. McLaughlin and J. Costello, S.J. Toronto: University of Toronto Press, 1977.

_________. "The 'Sacred' Text and the Community." In *The Critical Study of Sacred Texts*. Edited by W.D. O'Flaherty. Berkeley Religious Studies Series #2. Berkeley: Graduate Theological Union, 1979.

_________. *Sémantique de l'action*. Louvain: Université Catholique de Louvain--Cercle de Philosophie, 1971. Polycopy.

_________. *Time and Narrative*. Volume 1. Translated by K. McLaughlin and D. Pellauer. Chicago: University of Chicago Press, 1984.

ROSSI, P.J. "Narrative, Worship, and Ethics: Empowering Images for the Shape of Christian Moral Life," *The Journal of Religious Ethics* 7 (1979): 239-248.

ROUSSEAU, O. *Histoire du mouvement liturgique: esquisse historique depuis le début du xixe siècle jusqu'au pontificat de Pie X*. Paris: Editions du Cerf, 1945.

ROUTLEY, E. "The Gender of God: A Contribution to the Conversation," *Worship* 56 (1982): 231-239.

________. "Sexist Language: A View From a Distance," *Worship* 53 (1979): 2-11.

SALIERS, D.E. "Language in the Liturgy: Where Angels Fear to Tread," *Worship* 52 (1978): 482-488.

________. "Liturgy and Ethics: Some New Beginnings," *The Journal of Religious Ethics* 7 (1979):173-189.

________. "On the 'Crisis' of Liturgical Language," *Worship* 44 (1970): 399-411.

________. *The Soul in Paraphrase: Prayer and the Religious Affections*. New York: Seabury Press, 1980.

SCHMEMANN, A. *Introduction to Liturgical Theology*. 2nd. ed. Translated by A.E. Moorhouse. New York: St. Vladimir's Seminary Press, 1975.

________. *Liturgy and Life: Lectures and Essays On Christian Development Through Liturgical Experience*. New York: Department of Religious Education, Orthodox Church in America, 1974.

________. *The World as a Sacrament*. London: Darton, Longman & Todd, 1966.

________. *For the Life of the World*. London: Darton, Longman & Todd, 1966.

SCHMIDT, G.R. "A Dream of the Rood," *Dialogue* 18 (1979): 103-107.

SCHMIDT, H. "Language and Its Function in Christian Worship," *Studia Liturgica* 8 (1970-1972): 1-25.

________. "Lines of Political Action in Contemporary Liturgy," *Concilium* 10-2 (1974, translated by H. Hoskins): 13-33.

SCHMIDT, K.L. " ἐκκλησία ." In *Theological Dictionary of the New Testament.* Volume III. Ten Volumes. Edited by G. Kittel and G. Friedrich. Translated by G.W. Bromiley. Grand Rapids: Wm B. Eerdmans Publishing Company, 1964-1976, pp. 501-536.

SCHMUDE, K.G. "Redeeming the Word: The Future of Christian Language," *Communio* 7 (1980): 157-169.

SEARLE, M., ed. *Liturgy and Social Justice.* Collegeville: The Liturgical Press, 1980.

_____. "Liturgy as Metaphor," *Worship* 55 (1981): 98-120.

SEASOLTZ, K. "Anthropology and Liturgical Theology: Searching for a Compatible Methodology," *Concilium* 112 (1979): 3-13.

SENN, F.C. *Christian Worship and its Cultural Setting.* Philadelphia: Fortress Press, 1983.

SHEPHERD, M.H. *The Reform of Liturgical Worship: Perspectives and Prospects.* New York: Oxford University Press, 1961

________, ed. *The Liturgical Renewal of the Church: Addresses by Theodore Otto Wedel [and Others].* New York: Oxford University Press, 1960.

SHEPPARD, L., ed. *The People Worship: A History of the Liturgical Movement.* New York: Hawthorn Books, Inc., 1967.

SKOUSGAARD, S. *Language and the Existence of Freedom: A Study in Paul Ricoeur's Philosophy of Will.* Washington, D.C.: University Press of America, 1979.

SPEAIGHT, R. "Liturgy and Language," *Theology* 74 (1971): 444-456.

STEVICK, D.B. "Language of Prayer," *Worship* 52 (1978): 542-560.

________. *Language in Worship: Reflections on a Crisis.* New York: Seabury Press, 1970.

_________. "Toward a Phenomenology of Praise." In *Worship Points the Way: A Celebration of the Life and Work of Massey Hamilton Shepherd, Jr.* Edited by M.C. Burson. New York: The Seabury Press, 1981: pp. 151-166.

SWATOS, W.H. "Liturgy and *Lebensform*: The Personal God as a Social Being," *Perspectives in Religious Studies* 7 (1980): 38-49.

TAFT, R. "The Structural Analysis of Liturgical Units: An Essay in Methodology," *Worship* 52 (1978): 314-329.

TALLEY, T.J. "The Literary Structure of Eucharistic Prayer," *Worship* 58 (1984): 404-419.

TEGELS, A. "The Demand for Latin in the Liturgy," *Worship* 56 (1982): 63-65.

THOMPSON, J.B. *Critical Hermeneutics: A Study in the Thought of Paul Ricoeur and Jürgen Habermas.* Cambridge: Cambridge University Press, 1981.

TILLICH, P. "The Religious Symbol." In *Myth and Symbol.* Edited by F.W. Dillistone. London: S.P.C.K., 1966.

TOPOROSKI, R. "Language of Worship," *Communio* 4 (1978): 226-260.

_________. "Language of Worship," *Worship* 52 (1978): 489-508.

TRUDINGER, L.P. "Onward Christian Peacemakers," *Frontier* 18 (1975-1976): 235-238.

TUCKER, D. "The Council of Trent, Gueranger and Pius X," *Orate Fratres* 10 (1935-1936): 538-544.

VAGAGGINI, C. *Theological Dimensions of the Liturgy: A General Treatise on the Theology of the Liturgy.* 4th ed. Translated by L.J. Doyle and W.A. Jurgens. Collegeville: The Liturgical Press, 1976.

VAN DEN HENGEL, J.W. *The Home of Meaning: The Hermeneutics of the Subject of Paul Ricoeur.* Washington, D.C.: University Press of America, 1982.

VANNUCCHI, A. "Liturgy and Liberation," *International Review of Mission* 65 (1976): 186-195.

VERGOTE, A. "Symbolic Gestures and Actions in the Liturgy" *Concilium* 7-2 (1971, translated by B. Wall): 40-52.

VOLPE, R. "La liturgie en tant que comportement social: Réflexions en vue de l'elaboration de méthodes empiriques de recherches," *Social Compass* 22 (1975): 157-174.

WAINWRIGHT, G. *Doxology: The Praise of God in Worship, Doctrine and Life: A Systematic Theology.* New York: Oxford University Press, 1980.

WARE, J.H., Jr. *Not With Words of Wisdom.* Washington, D.C.: University Press of America, 1981.

WATTS, A.W. *Myth and Ritual in Christianity.* Boston: Beacon Press, 1968.

WAUGH, L.R. *Roman Jakobson's Science of Language.* Lisse: The Peter de Ridder Press, 1976.

WEGMAN, H.A.J. *Christian Worship: A Study Guide to Liturgical History.* Translated by G.W. Lathrop. New York: Pueblo Publishing Company, 1985.

WELBERS, T. "What's in a Name?," *Modern Liturgy* 11 (1984): 4.

WESTERHOFF, J.H. and WILLIMON, W.H. *Liturgy and Learning through the Life Cycle.* New York: Seabury Press, 1980.

WESTLAKE, J.H.J. "Problems of Modern Vernacular Liturgy," *Studia Liturgica* 6 (1969): 147-157.

WHEELOCK, W.T. "The Problem of Ritual Language: From Information to Situation," *Journal of the American Academy of Religion* 50 (1982): 49-71.

_________. "The Mass and Other Ritual Texts: Computer Assisted Approach," *History of Religions* 24 (1984): 49-72.

WHITE, J.F. "Justice and the Work of Liturgical Renewal," *Christianity and Crisis* 40 (1980): 173-177.

WILLIMON, W.H. *The Service of God: How Worship and Ethics are Related.* Nashville: Abingdon Press, 1983.

WINKLER, G. "Confirmation or Chrismation? A Study in Comparative Liturgy." *Worship* 58 (1984): 2-16.

WINNINGER, P. *Langues vivantes et liturgie.* Preface by Mgr. J.-J. Weber. Paris: Editions du Cerf, 1961.

APPENDIX

SELECT EUCHARISTIC TEXT

INTRODUCTORY RITES — CONTACT

The purpose of these rites is[6] to help[2] the assembled people to become[2] a worshiping community and to prepare[2] them for listening to God's word and celebrating the eucharist. [Note: See General Instruction, No. 24.]

Addressee
Perlocutionary
Context

ENTRANCE SONG[1]

Addresser

After the people have[6] assembled, the priest and the ministers go to the altar while[6] the entrance song is being sung[1]. When the priest comes[6] to the altar, he[6] makes the customary reverence[5] with the ministers, kisses[5] the altar and (if incense is used) incenses[5] it[6]. Then, with the ministers, he goes to[6] the chair.

Context

GREETING[3]

Contact

After the entrance[6] song, the priest and the faithful remain standing[6] and make the[6] sign of the[6] cross, as the priest says:

SIGLA: 1=ADDRESSER; 2=ADDRESSEE; 3=CONTACT;
4=CODE; 5=MESSAGE; 6=CONTEXT

In the name[6] of the Father, and of the Son, and of the Holy Spirit. Context

The people answer:

Amen[4]. Code

Then the priest, facing the people[6], extends his[3] hands and greets all[3] present with one of the following greetings[3]: Contact

a. **The grace of our[1] Lord Jesus Christ and the love of God and the fellowship of the Holy Spirit be[6] with you[2] all.** Contact

The people answer:

And also with[3] you.

b. Or the priest says:

The grace and peace of God our[1] Father and the Lord Jesus Christ be with you[2].

The people answer:

Blessed be God, the Father of our[1] Lord Jesus Christ.

or:

And also[3] with you.

SIGLA: 1=ADDRESSER; 2=ADDRESSEE; 3=CONTACT; 4=CODE; 5=MESSAGE; 6=CONTEXT

c. Or the priest says:

The Lord be[3] with you.

(Instead of the greeting, The Lord be with you, a bishop says, Peace be with you.)

The people answer:

And also[3] with you.

The priest, deacon, or other suitable minister may[1] very briefly introduce[3] the Mass of the day. Contact

A. The rite of blessing and sprinkling holy water may[1] be celebrated in all churches and chapels at all Sunday Masses celebrated on Sunday or on Saturday evening.

Or

B. The penitential rite follows.

Or

C. If the Mass is preceded by some part of the liturgy of the hours, the penitential rite is omitted, and the Kyrie may[1] be omitted. (See General Instruction on the Liturgy of the Hours, nos. 94-96.)

SIGLA: 1=ADDRESSER; 2=ADDRESSEE; 3=CONTACT; 4=CODE; 5=MESSAGE; 6=CONTEXT

APPENDIX

A. RITE OF BLESSING AND SPRINKLING HOLYWATER — Addressee

When this rite is celebrated it takes the place of the penitential rite at the beginning of Mass. The Kyrie is also omitted.

After greeting the[6] people the priest remains standing at[6] his chair. A vessel containing the water to be blessed is placed before[6] him. Facing the people, he[6] invites[3] them[6] to pray, using these or similar words: — Context

> **Dear friends[2], this[6] water will be used to remind us[1] of our[1] baptism. Let[1] us[1] ask God to bless it[6] and to keep us[1] faithful to the Spirit he[6] has given us[1].** — Contact

After a brief silence[6], he[6] joins his[2] hands and continues:

> **a. God our Father[2], your[2] gift of water brings life and freshness to the earth; it[6] washes away our[1] sins and brings us[1] eternal life. We[1] ask[2] you[2] now to bless[2] + this[6] water, and** — Addressee

SIGLA: 1=ADDRESSER; 2=ADDRESSEE; 3=CONTACT; 4=CODE; 5=MESSAGE; 6=CONTEXT

to give[2] us[1] your[2] protection on this[6] day which you[2] have made[6] your[2] own. Renew[2] the living spring of your[2] life within us[1] and protect[2] us[1] in spirit and body, that we[1] may be[1] free from sin and come into your[2] presence to receive your[2] gift of salvation. — Perlocutionary

We[1] ask[2] this[6] through Christ our[1] Lord.

b. Or

Lord God Almighty[2], creator of all life, of body and soul, we[1] ask[2] you[2] to bless + this[6] water: as we[1] use it[6] in faith forgive[2] our[1] sins and save[2] us[1] from all illness and the power of evil. — Addressee, Perlocutionary

Lord[2], in your[2] mercy give[2] us[1] living water, always springing up as a fountain of salvation: free[2] us[1], body and soul, from every danger, and admit[2] us[1] to your[2] presence in purity of heart.

Grant[2] this[6] through Christ our[1] Lord.

SIGLA: 1=ADDRESSER; 2=ADDRESSEE; 3=CONTACT; 4=CODE; 5=MESSAGE; 6=CONTEXT

C. Or (during the Easter season):

Lord God almighty[2], hear[2] the prayers — Addressee Perlocutionary
of your[2] people: we[1] celebrate our[1]
creation and redemption. Hear[2] our[1]
prayers and bless[2] + this[6] water which
gives fruitfulness to the fields,
and refreshment and cleansing to
man. You[2] chose[6] water to show your[2] — Context
goodness when you[2] led[6] your[2] people to
freedom through the Red Sea and
satisfied[6] their[6] thirst in the desert
with water from the rock. Water was[6]
the symbol used[6] by the prophets to
foretell your[2] new covenant with man.
You[2] made[6] the water of baptism holy
by Christ's baptism in the Jordan:
by it[6] you[2] give us[1] a new birth and — Addressee Perlocutionary
renew us[1] in holiness. May[1] this[6]
water remind us[1] of our[1] baptism, and
let[1] us[1] share the joy of all who
have been baptized[6] at Easter.
We[1] ask[2] this[6] through Christ our[1] Lord.

SIGLA: 1=ADDRESSER; 2=ADDRESSEE; 3=CONTACT;
4=CODE; 5=MESSAGE; 6=CONTEXT

Where it is customary, salt may[1] be mixed with the holy water. The priest blesses the salt, saying:

> **Almighty God[2], we[1] ask[2] you[2] to bless + this[6] salt as once you[2] blessed[6] the salt scattered over the water by the prophet Elisha. Wherever this[6] salt and water are sprinkled, drive[2] away the power of evil, and protect[2] us[1] always by the presence of your[2] Holy Spirit.**
>
> **Grant[2] this[6] through Christ our[1] Lord.**

Addressee
Perlocutionary

Then he[6] pours the salt into the water in silence[6].

Taking the sprinkler, the priest sprinkles[3] himself[6] and his[6] ministers, then the rest of the clergy and people. He[6] may[1] move through the church for the sprinkling of the people. Meanwhile[6], an antiphon or other appropriate song is sung[1].

When[6] he[6] returns to his[6] place and the song is finished, the priest faces the people and, with joined hands[2], says:

SIGLA: 1=ADDRESSER; 2=ADDRESSEE; 3=CONTACT; 4=CODE; 5=MESSAGE; 6=CONTEXT

May[1] almighty God cleanse[1] us[1] of our[1] sins, and through the eucharist we[1] celebrate make[2] us[1] worthy to sit at his[6] table in his[6] heavenly kingdom.

Addresser
Illocutionary

The people answer: Amen[4].

Code

When it is prescribed, the Gloria is then sung[1] or said.

B. PENITENTIAL RITE

Addresser

After the introduction[6] to the day's Mass, the priest invites[3] the people to recall their[6] sins and to repent of them[6] in silence[6]. He[6] may[1] use[6] these or similar words.

Contact

a. As[6] we[1] prepare to celebrate the mystery of Christ's love, let[1] us[1] acknowledge[1] our[1] failures and ask[1] the Lord for pardon and strength.

Addresser
Illocutionary

b. Coming together as[6] God's family, with confidence let[1] us[1] ask[1] the Father's forgiveness, for he[6] is full of gentleness and compassion.

c. My brothers and sisters[2], [Foot-note: at the discretion of the

Addressee

SIGLA: 1=ADDRESSER; 2=ADDRESSEE; 3=CONTACT; 4=CODE; 5=MESSAGE; 6=CONTEXT

priest, other words which seem more suitable under the circumstances, such as friends, dearly beloved, brethren, may be used. This also applied to parallel instances in the liturgy.] **to prepare ourselves[1] to celebrate the sacred mysteries, let[1] us[1] call[1] to mind our[1] sins.**

Addresser
Illocutionary

A pause for silent reflection[6] follows.

Context

After the silence[6], one of the following three forms is chosen:

a. All say: **I[1] confess[1] to almighty God, and to you, my brothers and sisters[2], that I[1] have sinned[6] through my[1] own fault**

Addresser
Illocutionary
Addressee

They[6] strike their[6] breast:

in my[1] thoughts and in my[1] words, in what I[1] have done[6], and in what I[1] have failed[6] to do; and I[1] ask[2] blessed Mary, ever virgin, all the angels and saints, and you, my brothers and sisters[2], to pray[2] for me[1] to the Lord our[1] God.

Addressee

SIGLA: 1=ADDRESSER; 2=ADDRESSEE; 3=CONTACT; 4=CODE; 5=MESSAGE; 6=CONTEXT

The priest says the absolution:

May[1] almighty God have mercy[1] on us,[1] forgive[1] us[1] our[1] sins, and bring[1] us[1] to everlasting life.

Addresser Illocutionary

The people answer: **Amen[4].**

Code

b. The priest says:

Lord,[2] we[1] have sinned[6] against you:[2]

Addressee Perlocutionary

The people answer: **Lord,[2] have mercy[1].**

Priest: **Lord,[2] show[2] us[1] your[2] mercy and love.**

People: **And grant[2] us[1] your[2] salvation.**

The priest says the absolution:

May[1] almighty God have mercy[1] on us,[1] forgive[1] us[1] our[1] sins, and bring[1] us[1] to everlasting life.

Addresser Illocutionary

The people answer: **Amen[4].**

Code

c. The priest (or other suitable minister) makes the following or other invocations:

Priest: **You[2] were sent[6] to heal the contrite: Lord,[2] have mercy[1].**

Addressee Perlocutionary

The people answer: **Lord,[2] have mercy[1].**

Priest: **You[2] came[6] to call sinners: Christ,[2] have mercy[1].**

People: **Christ,[2] have mercy[1].**

SIGLA: 1=ADDRESSER; 2=ADDRESSEE; 3=CONTACT; 4=CODE; 5=MESSAGE; 6=CONTEXT

Priest: You[2] plead for us[1] at the right hand of the Father: Lord[2], have mercy[1].

People: Lord[2], have mercy[1].

The priest says the absolution:

May[1] almighty God have mercy[1] on us[1], forgive[1] us[1] our[1] sins, and bring[1] us[1] to everlasting life. — Addresser Illocutionary

The people answer: Amen[4]. — Code

[Seven more choices for Option C with parallel structure to the one given here in the text follow; they are omitted for the sake of brevity.]

KYRIE — Addressee

The invocations[2], Lord[2], have mercy[1], follow, unless they have already been used in one of the forms of the act of penance.

V. Lord[2], have mercy[1]. R. Lord[2], have mercy[1]. — Addressee Illocutionary

V. Christ[2], have mercy[1]. R. Christ[2], have mercy[1].

V. Lord[2], have mercy[1]. R. Lord[2], have mercy[1].

GLORIA — Addresser

This[6] hymn is said or sung[1] on Sundays outside

SIGLA: 1=ADDRESSER; 2=ADDRESSEE; 3=CONTACT; 4=CODE; 5=MESSAGE; 6=CONTEXT

Advent and Lent, on solemnities and feasts, and in solemn local celebrations.

[Note: See General Instruction, No. 31.]

Glory to[1] God in the highest, and	Addresser Illocutionary
peace[1] to his[6] people on earth.	
Lord God, heavenly[2] King, almighty	Addressee
God and[2] Father, we[1] worship[1] you,[2] we[1]	Addresser Addressee
give[1] you[2] thanks,[1] we[1] praise[1] you[2] for	Perlocutionary
your[2] glory. Lord Jesus[2] Christ, only	
Son of the Father, Lord God,[2]	
Lamb of God,[2] you[2] take away the sin	
of the world: have mercy[1] on us;[1] you[2]	
are seated[6] at the right hand of the	
Father: receive[2] our[1] prayer. For you[2]	Addressee
alone are the Holy[1] One, you[2] alone	Addresser
are the[1] Lord, you[2] alone are the[1]	
Most High,[1] Jesus Christ,[2] with[6] the	
Holy Spirit,[6] in the glory of God[6] the	
Father.[6] Amen.[4]	

OPENING PRAYER	Addresser

Afterwards[6] the priest, with hands joined,[2] sings[1] or says:

SIGLA: 1=ADDRESSER; 2=ADDRESSEE; 3=CONTACT; 4=CODE; 5=MESSAGE; 6=CONTEXT

Let us[3] pray.	Contact
Priest and people pray silently[6] for a while.	
Then the priest extends his[1] hands and sings[1] or says the opening prayer, at the end of which the people respond:	Addresser
Amen[4].	Code
LITURGY OF THE WORD	**MESSAGE**
FIRST READING[5]	Message
The reader goes to the[6] lectern for the first reading. All sit and listen. To indicate[6]	
the end, the reader[6] adds: This is the[3] Word of the[3] Lord. All respond: Thanks be[3] to God.	Contact
RESPONSORIAL[4] PSALM	Code
The cantor sings[1] or recites the psalm, and the people respond.	Addresser
SECOND READING[5]	Message
When there is a second[6] reading, it[6] is read at the[6] lectern as before. To indicate[6]	
the end, the reader[6] adds: This is the[3] Word of the[3] Lord. All respond: Thanks be[3] to God.	Contact

SIGLA: 1=ADDRESSER; 2=ADDRESSEE; 3=CONTACT; 4=CODE; 5=MESSAGE; 6=CONTEXT

ALLELUIA OR GOSPEL ACCLAMATION[4]	Code
The alleluia or other chant[1] follows. It[6] may[1] be omitted if not sung[1].	
[Note: General Instruction, No. 39.]	
GOSPEL[5]	Message
Meanwhile[6], if incense[5] is used, the priest puts some in the censer. Then[6] the deacon who is to proclaim[1] the gospel bows[5] to the priest and in a low voice[6] asks[1] his[6] blessing:	
Father[2], give[2] me[1] your[2] blessing.	Addressee Perlocutionary
The priest says in a low voice[6]:	
The Lord be in your[2] heart and on your[2] lips that you[2] may[1] worthily proclaim[1] his[6] gospel. In the name[6] of the Father, and of the Son, + and of the Holy Spirit.	Context
The deacon answers: **Amen[4]**.	Code
If there is no deacon, the priest bows[5] before the altar and says quietly[6]:	
Almighty God[2], cleanse[1] my[1] heart and my[1] lips that I[1] may[1] worthily proclaim[1] your[2] gospel.	

SIGLA: 1=ADDRESSER; 2=ADDRESSEE; 3=CONTACT; 4=CODE; 5=MESSAGE; 6=CONTEXT

Then[6] the deacon (or the priest) goes to the[6] lectern. He[6] may be accompanied[1] by ministers with[5] incense and candles. He[6] sings[1] or says:

The Lord be with[3] you. — Contact

The people answer: **And also with[3] you.** — Contact

The deacon (or priest) sings[1] or says:

A reading from[3] the holy gospel according[3] to N.

He[6] makes the sign of the[6] cross on the book, and then on his forehead, lips[6] and breast.

The people respond:

Glory[1] to you,[2] Lord. — Addresser Addressee

Then[6], if incense[5] is used, the deacon (or priest) incenses the[5] book, and proclaims[1] the gospel.

At the end of the gospel, the deacon (or priest) adds:

This is the gospel[3] of the Lord. — Contact

All respond:

Praise[1] to you, Lord Jesus[2] Christ. — Addresser Addressee

Then[6] he[6] kisses the[5] book, saying quietly[6]:

SIGLA: 1=ADDRESSER; 2=ADDRESSEE; 3=CONTACT; 4=CODE; 5=MESSAGE; 6=CONTEXT

May[1] the word[s][5] of the gospel wipe away[1] our[1] sins.

HOMILY[5] — Message

A homily[5] shall be[2] given on all Sundays and holy days of obligation; it is recommended for other days.

PROFESSION[4] OF FAITH — Code

After the[6] homily, the profession of[4] faith is said on Sundays and solemnities; it[6] may[1] also be said[1] in solemn local celebrations.

[Note: See General Instruction, No. 44.]

We[1] believe[4] in[6] one God, the Father, the Almighty, maker of heaven and earth, of all that is seen and unseen. — Addresser / Code / Context

We[1] believe[4] in[6] one Lord, Jesus Christ, the only Son of God, eternally begotten of the Father, God from God, Light from Light, true God from true God, begotten, not made, one in Being with the Father.

Through[6] him[6] all things were made[6]. — Context

SIGLA: 1=ADDRESSER; 2=ADDRESSEE; 3=CONTACT; 4=CODE; 5=MESSAGE; 6=CONTEXT

For us[1] men and for our[1] salvation he[6] came down[6] from heaven:

All bow[5] during these two lines:

by the power[6] of the Holy Spirit he[6] was born[6] of the Virgin Mary, and became[6] man.

For our[1] sake he[6] was crucified[6] under Pontius Pilate; he[6] suffered, died,[6] and was buried[6]. On the third day he[6] rose[6] again in fulfillment of the Scriptures; he[6] ascended[6] into heaven and is seated[6] at the right hand of the Father. He[6] will come again in glory to judge the living and the dead, and his[6] kingdom will have no end.

We[1] believe[4] in[6] the Holy Spirit, the Addresser
Lord, the giver of life, who Code
proceeds from the Father and the Context
Son. With the Father and the Son he[6] is worshiped and glorified. He[6] has spoken[6] through the Prophets. We[1] Context
believe[4] in[6] one holy catholic and

SIGLA: 1=ADDRESSER; 2=ADDRESSEE; 3=CONTACT; 4=CODE; 5=MESSAGE; 6=CONTEXT

apostolic Church. We[1] acknowledge[1] one baptism for the forgiveness of sins. We[1] look for the resurrection of the dead, and the life of the world to come. Amen[4].

Addresser

Code

GENERAL INTERCESSIONS

Addresser/
Addressee

Then follow[6] the general intercessions (prayer of the faithful). The priest presides at the prayer. With a brief introduction, he[6] invites[3] the people to pray; after the intentions he[6] says the concluding prayer. It is desirable that the intentions be announced[3] by the deacon, cantor, or other person.

[Note: See General Instruction, No. 47.]

LITURGY OF THE EUCHARIST — **CONTEXT**

PREPARATION OF THE ALTAR AND THE GIFTS — Addresser

After the liturgy of the word[6], the offertory song[1] is begun. Meanwhile[6] the ministers place the corporal, the purificator[3], the chalice, and the missal[3] on the altar.

Addresser

Contact

SIGLA: 1=ADDRESSER; 2=ADDRESSEE; 3=CONTACT; 4=CODE; 5=MESSAGE; 6=CONTEXT

Sufficient hosts (and wine) for the communion of the faithful are to be prepared. It is most important [3]that the faithful should receive the body [3]of the Lord in hosts consecrated at the [3]same Mass and should share the cup when [3]it is permitted. Communion is thus a clearer sign of sharing in the sacrifice which is actually taking place.

[Note: General Instruction, No. 56h.]

It is desirable that the [3]participation of the [3]faithful be expressed by members of the congregation bringing up the bread and wine for the celebration of the eucharist or other gifts for the needs of the Church and the poor. — Contact

The priest, standing [6]at the altar, takes the paten with the bread and, holding it slightly [6]raised above the altar, says [6]quietly:

> **[1]Blessed are you, Lord, [2]God of all [2]creation. Through [2]your goodness [1]we have [6]this bread to offer, which earth [6]has given and human hands** — Addresser Illocutionary

SIGLA: 1=ADDRESSER; 2=ADDRESSEE; 3=CONTACT; 4=CODE; 5=MESSAGE; 6=CONTEXT

have made[6]. It[6] will become for us[1] the bread of life.

Then he[6] places the paten with the bread on the corporal.

If no offertory song is sung[1], the priest may say[1] the preceding words in an audible[6] voice; then the[6] people may[1] respond:

Blessed be God[1] for ever. Addresser

The deacon (or the priest) pours wine and a little water into the chalice, saying quietly[6]:

By[6] the mystery of this[6] water and wine may[1] we[1] come[1] to share in the divinity of Christ, who humbled[6] himself[6] to share in our[1] humanity. Addresser Illocutionary

Then the[6] priest takes the chalice and, holding it[6] slightly[6] raised above the altar, says quietly[6]:

Blessed[1] are you, Lord[2], God of all creation[2]. Through[6] your[2] goodness we[1] have this[6] wine to offer, fruit of the vine and work of human hands. It[6] will become our[1] spiritual drink. Addresser Illocutionary

SIGLA: 1=ADDRESSER; 2=ADDRESSEE; 3=CONTACT; 4=CODE; 5=MESSAGE; 6=CONTEXT

Then he[6] places the chalice on the corporal.

If no offertory song is sung[1], the priest may say[1] the preceding words in an audible [6]voice; then the[6] people may [1]respond:

> **Blessed be God[1] for ever.**

Addresser

The priest bows[5] and says quietly[6]:

> **Lord[2] God, we[1] ask[2] you[2] to receive us[1] and be pleased[2] with the sacrifice we[1] offer[1] you[2] with humble and contrite hearts.**

Addressee
Perlocutionary

He[6] may[1] now[6] incense[5] the offerings and the altar. Afterwards[6] the deacon or a minister incenses[5] the priest and people.

Next[6] the priest stands at the side of the altar and washes his[6] hands, saying quietly[6]:

> **Lord[2], wash away[2] my[1] iniquity; cleanse[2] me[1] from my[1] sin.**

Addressee
Perlocutionary

Standing at the center[6] of the altar, facing the[3] people, he[6] extends[3] and then[6] joins[2] his[6] hands, saying:

> **Pray, brethren[2], that our[1] sacrifice maybe acceptable[1] to God, the almighty Father.**

Addresser

SIGLA: 1=ADDRESSER; 2=ADDRESSEE; 3=CONTACT; 4=CODE; 5=MESSAGE; 6=CONTEXT

The people respond:

May[1] the Lord accept[1] the sacrifice at Addresser
your[2] hands for the praise and glory
of his[6] name, for our[1] good, and the
good of all his[6] Church.

PRAYER OVER THE GIFTS Addresser

With hands[1] extended, the priest sings[1] or says
the prayer over the gifts, at the end of
which the people respond: Amen[4]. Code

EUCHARISTIC PRAYER Context

The priest begins the eucharistic prayer.
With hands[3] extended he[6] sings[1] or says:

The Lord be[3] with you. Contact

The people answer:

And also with[3] you.

He lifts up his[6] hands and continues:

Lift[6] up your[2] hearts. Context

The people:

We[1] lift[6] them[6] up to the[6] Lord.

With hands[3] extended, he[6] continues: Contact

Let us give thanks to the[1] Lord our Addresser
God[1].

SIGLA: 1=ADDRESSER; 2=ADDRESSEE; 3=CONTACT;
4=CODE; 5=MESSAGE; 6=CONTEXT

The people:

It is right to give him[1] thanks and praise[1].

The priest continues the preface with hands extended[1].

Father[2], it[6] is[1] our[1] duty[1] and our[1] salvation[1], always and everywhere to give[1] you[2] thanks[1] through your[2] beloved Son, Jesus Christ.

Addresser
Illocutionary

He[6] is the Word[1] through[6] whom you[2] made[6] the universe, the Savior you[2] sent[6] to redeem us[1]. By[6] the power of the Holy Spirit he[6] took[6] flesh and was born[6] of the Virgin Mary.
For our[1] sake he[6] opened[6] his[6] arms on the cross; he[6] put an end to death and revealed[6] the resurrection. In this[6] he[6] fulfilled[6] your[2] will and won for you[2] a holy people.

Context

And so we[1] join the angels and the saints in proclaiming[1] your[2] glory as we[1] say:

Addresser

SIGLA: 1=ADDRESSER; 2=ADDRESSEE; 3=CONTACT;
4=CODE; 5=MESSAGE; 6=CONTEXT

ACCLAMATION[4] — Code

At the[6] end of the preface, he[6] joins his[2] hands and, together with the[6] people, concludes it[6] by singing[1] or saying aloud[6]:

Holy, holy,[1] holy, Lord, God of[2] power and might[2], heaven and earth are full[6] of your[2] glory. — Code

Hosanna in the[1] highest.

Blessed[1] is he[6] who comes in the[6] name of the Lord.

Hosanna in the[1] highest.

In all Masses the priest may say[1] the eucharistic prayer in an audible voice[6]. In sung[1] Masses he[6] may sing[1] those parts of the eucharistic prayer which may be[1] sung in concelebrated Mass.

The priest, with hands[1] extended, says: — Addresser

Lord[2], you[2] are holy[6] indeed, the fountain of all holiness. — Addressee, Context

He[6] joins his[2] hands and holding[6] them outstretched over the[6] offerings says:

Let[2] your[2] Spirit come[2] upon these[6] gifts to make them[6] holy, so that — Addressee, Perlocutionary

SIGLA: 1=ADDRESSER; 2=ADDRESSEE; 3=CONTACT; 4=CODE; 5=MESSAGE; 6=CONTEXT

they[6] may[1] become for us[1] Context Addresser

He[6] joins his[2] hands and, making the[6] sign of the[6] cross once over both bread and chalice, says:

the body + and blood of our[1] Lord, Jesus Christ.

He[6] joins his[2] hands.

The words of the Lord in the following formulas should be[2] spoken clearly and distinctly, as their meaning demands.

Before he[6] was given[6] up to death, a death he[6] freely accepted[6], Context

He[6] takes the bread and, raising it[6] a little[6] above the altar, continues:

he[6] took[6] bread and gave[6] you[2] thanks. He[6] broke[6] the bread, gave[6] it[6] to his[6] disciples, and said[6]:

He[6] bows[5] slightly.

Take[2] this[6], all of you[2], and eat[2] it[6]: this[6] is[6] my[1] body which will be given up for you[2].

He[6] shows[3] the consecrated host to the people, places it[6] on the paten, and genuflects[5]

SIGLA: 1=ADDRESSER; 2=ADDRESSEE; 3=CONTACT; 4=CODE; 5=MESSAGE; 6=CONTEXT

in adoration[5].

Then he continues[6]:

When[6] supper was ended[6], he[6] took[6] the cup. Context

He[6] takes the chalice and, raising it[6] a little above the[6] altar, continues:

Again he[6] gave[6] you[2] thanks and praise, gave[6] the cup to his[6] disciples, and said[6]:

He[6] bows[5] slightly.

Take[2] this[6], all of you[2], and drink[2] from it[6]: this[6] is[6] the cup of my[1] blood, the blood of the new and everlasting covenant. It[6] will be shed for you[2] and for all men so that sins may be[1] forgiven. Do[2] this[6] in memory of me[1].

He[6] shows[3] the chalice to the people, places it[6] on the corporal and genuflects in[5] adoration.

Then[6] he[6] sings[1] or says:

Let us proclaim[3] the mystery of faith[3]: Contact

SIGLA: 1=ADDRESSER; 2=ADDRESSEE; 3=CONTACT; 4=CODE; 5=MESSAGE; 6=CONTEXT

And the people take up the acclamation[4] in these or similar words:

a. **Christ has died[6], Christ is risen, Christ will come again.**

Code

b. **Dying you[2] destroyed[6] our[1] death, rising you[2] restored[6] our[1] life. Lord Jesus[2], come[2] in glory.**

c. **When[6] we[1] eat this[6] bread and drink this[6] cup, we[1] proclaim[1] your[2] death, Lord Jesus[2], until you[2] come in glory.**

d. **Lord[2], by[6] your[2] cross and resurrection you[2] have set[6] us[1] free. You[2] are the Savior[1] of the world.**

Then[6], with hands extended[1], the priest says:

Context
Addresser
Illocutionary

In[6] memory of his[6] death and resurrection, we[1] offer[1] you, Father[2], this[6] life-giving bread, this[6] saving cup. We[1] thank[1] you[2] for your[2] counting us[1] worthy to stand in your[2] presence and serve you[2]. May[1] all of us[1] who share in the body and blood of Christ be brought together[1] in unity[6] by the Holy Spirit.

Addressee

SIGLA: 1=ADDRESSER; 2=ADDRESSEE; 3=CONTACT; 4=CODE; 5=MESSAGE; 6=CONTEXT

Lord[2], remember[2] your[2] Church throughout the world; make[2] us[1] grow in love, together with N. our[1] Pope, N. our[1] bishop, and all the clergy. Addressee Perlocutionary

In Masses for the dead the following may be added[1]:

Remember[2] N., whom you[2] have called[6] from this[6] life. In baptism he (she)[6] died[6] with Christ. May[1] he (she)[6] also share[1] his[6] resurrection. Context

Remember[2] our[1] brothers and sisters who have gone[6] to their[6] rest in the hope of rising again; bring[2] them[6] and all the departed into the light of your[2] presence. Have mercy[1] on us[1] all; make[2] us[1] worthy to share eternal life with Mary, the virgin Mother of God, with the apostles, and with all the saints who have done[6] your[2] will throughout the ages. May[1] we[1] praise[1] you[2] in union with them[6], and give[1] you[2] glory. Context

SIGLA: 1=ADDRESSER; 2=ADDRESSEE; 3=CONTACT;
4=CODE; 5=MESSAGE; 6=CONTEXT

He[6] joins his[2] hands.

through[6] your[2] Son, Jesus Christ.

He[6] takes the chalice and the paten with the host and, lifting them[6] up, sings[1] or says:

Through him, with[6] him, in him, in the unity of the Holy[6] Spirit, all glory and honor is yours[2], almighty Father[2], for ever and ever. — Context / Addressee

The people respond: Amen[4]. — Code

COMMUNION RITE — Addresser

LORD'S PRAYER — Addresser

The priest sets down[6] the chalice and paten and with hands[2] joined, sings[1] or says one of the following:

a. **Let[1] us[1] pray[1] with confidence to the Father in the words our[1] Savior gave[6] us[1].** — Contact

b. **Jesus taught[6] us[1] to call God our[1] Father, and so we[1] have the courage to say:**

SIGLA: 1=ADDRESSER; 2=ADDRESSEE; 3=CONTACT; 4=CODE; 5=MESSAGE; 6=CONTEXT

c. **Let[1] us[1] ask[1] our[1] Father to forgive our[1] sins and to bring us[1] to forgive those[6] who sin against us[1].**

d. **Let[1] us[1] pray[1] for the coming of the kingdom as Jesus taught[6] us[1].**

He[6] extends his[1] hands and he[6] continues, with the people:

Our Father[2], who art in[1] heaven, Addresser
hallowed be[1] thy[2] name; thy[2] kingdom Addressee
come[1]; thy[2] will be done[1] on earth as
it is in heaven. Give[2] us[1] this[6] day
our[1] daily bread; and forgive[2] us[1] our[1] Perlocutionary
trespasses as we[1] forgive those[6] who
trespass against us[1]; and lead[2] us[1] not
into temptation, but deliver[2] us[1] from
evil.

With hands[1] extended, the priest continues alone:

Deliver[2] us[1], Lord[2], from every evil, Addresser
and grant[2] us[1] peace in our[1] day. In Perlocutionary
your[2] mercy keep[2] us[1] free from sin and
protect[2] us[1] from all anxiety as we[1]

SIGLA: 1=ADDRESSER; 2=ADDRESSEE; 3=CONTACT; 4=CODE; 5=MESSAGE; 6=CONTEXT

wait in joyful hope for the coming

of our[1] Savior, Jesus Christ.

He[6] joins his[2] hands.

DOXOLOGY Code

The people end the prayer with the

acclamation[4]:

For the kingdom, the power[4] and the Code

glory are yours, now[4] and for ever.

SIGN OF PEACE Addresser

Then the priest, with hands[1] extended, says

aloud[6]:

Lord Jesus Christ[2], you[2] said[6] to your[2] Addressee

apostles: I[1] leave you[2] peace, my[1] Addresser

peace I[1] give you[2]. Look[2] not on our[1] Perlocutionary

sins, but on the faith of your[2]

Church, and grant[2] us[1] the peace and

unity of your[2] kingdom

He[6] joins his[2] hands.

where[6] you[2] live for ever and ever.

The people answer: **Amen[4].** Code

The priest, extending[3] and joining his[2] hands,

adds:

SIGLA: 1=ADDRESSER; 2=ADDRESSEE; 3=CONTACT; 4=CODE; 5=MESSAGE; 6=CONTEXT

The peace of the Lord[3] be with you always[3]. — Contact

The people answer: **And also with[3] you.** — Contact

Then[6] the deacon (or the priest) may add[1]:

Let[1] us[1] offer[1] each other the sign of peace.

All make an appropriate sign of peace, according to local custom.

The priest gives the sign of peace to the deacon or minister.

BREAKING OF THE BREAD — Addresser

Then[6] the following is sung[1] or said:

Lamb of[2] God, you[2] take away the sins — Addressee
of the world: have mercy[1] on us[1]. — Addresser

This[6] may be repeated[1] until the breaking of the bread is finished, but the last phrase is always:

Lamb of[2] God, you[2] take away the sins of the world: grant[2] us[1] peace.

Meanwhile[6], he[6] takes the host and breaks it[6] over the paten. He[6] places a small piece in the chalice, saying quietly[6]:

SIGLA: 1=ADDRESSER; 2=ADDRESSEE; 3=CONTACT; 4=CODE; 5=MESSAGE; 6=CONTEXT

May[1] this[6] mingling of the body and blood of our[1] Lord Jesus Christ bring[1] eternal life to us[1] who receive it.[6] — Addresser

PRIVATE PREPARATION OF THE PRIEST — Addressee

Then[6] the priest joins his[2] hands and says quietly[6]:

Lord, Jesus[2] Christ, Son of the living God, by the will of the Father and the work of the Holy Spirit your[2] death brought[6] life to the world. By your[2] holy body and blood free[2] me[1] from all my[1] sins, and from every evil. Keep[2] me[1] faithful to your[2] teaching, and never let[1] me[1] be parted from you[2]. — Addressee

Or:

Lord, Jesus[2] Christ, with faith in your[2] love and mercy I[1] eat your[2] body and drink your[2] blood. Let[1] it[6] not bring[1] me[1] condemnation, but health in mind and body.

SIGLA: 1=ADDRESSER; 2=ADDRESSEE; 3=CONTACT; 4=CODE; 5=MESSAGE; 6=CONTEXT

COMMUNION Addresser

The priest genuflects[5]. Taking the host, he[6] raises[6] it[6] slightly[6] over the paten and, facing the people[3], says aloud[6]: Contact

a. **This[6] is the Lamb of God who takes away the sins of the world.** Context

Happy are[1] those[6] who are called to his[6] supper. Addresser

b. **These[6] are God's[1] gifts to his[6] holy people: receive[2] them[6] with thanksgiving.**

He[6] adds, once only, with the people:

Lord[2], I[1] am not worthy[6] to receive you[2], but only say[2] the word and I[1] shall be healed[6]. Addressee / Addresser

Facing the altar[6], the priest says quietly[6]:

May[1] the body of Christ bring[1] me[1] to everlasting life. Addresser Illocutionary

He[6] reverently[5] consumes the body of Christ. Then[6] he[6] takes the chalice and says quietly[6]:

May[1] the blood of Christ bring[1] me[1] to everlasting life.

He[6] reverently[5] drinks the blood of Christ.

SIGLA: 1=ADDRESSER; 2=ADDRESSEE; 3=CONTACT; 4=CODE; 5=MESSAGE; 6=CONTEXT

After[6] this[6] he[6] takes the paten or other vessel and goes to the[6] communicants. He[6] takes a host for each one, raises it[6] a little, and shows[3] it[6], saying:

The body of[3] Christ. — Contact

The communicant answers: **Amen,**[4] — Code

and receives communion.

When[6] a deacon gives communion, he[6] does the same.

The sign of communion is more complete when given under both kinds, since the sign of the eucharistic meal appears more clearly. The intention of Christ that the new and eternal covenant be ratified in his[6] blood is better expressed, as is the relation of the eucharistic banquet to the heavenly banquet.

[Note: General Instruction, No. 240.]

If any are receiving in both kinds, the rite described elsewhere is followed. When he[6] presents the chalice, the priest or deacon says:

The blood of[3] Christ. — Contact

SIGLA: 1=ADDRESSER; 2=ADDRESSEE; 3=CONTACT; 4=CODE; 5=MESSAGE; 6=CONTEXT

The communicant answers: **Amen**[4], — Code

and drinks it[6].

The deacon and other ministers may receive[1] from the chalice at a Mass with singing[1].

[Note: General Instruction, No. 242.]

COMMUNION SONG[1] — Addresser

While the priest receives[6] the body of Christ[6], the communion song[1] is begun.

The vessels are cleansed by the priest or deacon after the communion[6] or after Mass, if possible at the side table.

[Note: General Instruction, No. 238.]

Meanwhile[6] he[6] says quietly[6]:

> **Lord**[2], **may**[1] **I**[1] **receive**[1] **these**[6] **gifts in purity of heart. May**[1] **they**[6] **bring**[1] **me**[1] **healing and strength, now and for ever.** — Addresser Illocutionary

PERIOD OF SILENCE OR SONG[1] **OF PRAISE** — Addresser

Then[6] the priest may[1] return to the[6] chair. A period of[6] silence may[1] now be observed[1], or a psalm or song of praise[1] may be sung.

SIGLA: 1=ADDRESSER; 2=ADDRESSEE; 3=CONTACT; 4=CODE; 5=MESSAGE; 6=CONTEXT

PRAYER AFTER COMMUNION	Addresser
Then,[6] standing at the chair[6] or at the altar, the priest sings[1] or says:	
Let us[3] pray.	Contact
Priest and people pray in silence[6] for a while, unless a period of silence has already been observed. Then[6] the priest extends his[1] hands and sings[1] or says the prayer after communion, at the end of which the people respond:	
Amen[4].	Code

CONCLUDING RITE	**CODE**
If there are any brief announcements[3], they[6] are made at this[6] time.	
GREETING	Contact
Facing the[3] people, the priest extends his[3] hands[3] and sings[1] or says:	
The Lord be[3] with you.	Contact
The people answer: **And also with[3] you**.	Contact

SIGLA: 1=ADDRESSER; 2=ADDRESSEE; 3=CONTACT; 4=CODE; 5=MESSAGE; 6=CONTEXT

APPENDIX

BLESSING	Addressee
A. Simple form	
The priest blesses the people with these[6] words:	
May[1] almighty God bless[1] you[2], the Father, the Son, + and the Holy Spirit.	Addresser Illocutionary Addressee
The people answer: **Amen[4]**.	Code
On certain days or occasions another more solemn form of blessing or prayer over the people may be[1] used as the rubrics direct.	
B. Solemn blessing	
Text of all the solemn blessings are given on pages 549-558.	
Deacon: **Bow[2] your[2] heads and pray[2] for God's blessing.**	Addressee Illocutionary
The priest always concludes the solemn blessing by adding:	
May[1] almighty God bless[1] you[2] the Father, and the Son, + and the Holy Spirit.	Illocutionary
The people answer: **Amen[4]**.	Code

SIGLA: 1=ADDRESSER; 2=ADDRESSEE; 3=CONTACT; 4=CODE; 5=MESSAGE; 6=CONTEXT

C. Prayer over the people

Text of all prayers over the people are given on pages 561-564.

After the prayer over [6] the people, the priest always adds:

May [1] almighty God bless [1] you [2], the Father, and the Son, + and the Holy Spirit. — Illocutionary Addressee

The people answer: **Amen** [1]. — Code

DISMISSAL — Code

The dismissal sends each member of the congregation to do good works, [4] praising and blessing [4] the Lord.

[Note: See General Instruction, No. 57.]

The deacon (or the priest), with hands [2] joined, sings [1] or says:

a. **Go [2] in the peace of Christ.** — Addressee Illocutionary

b. **The Mass is ended, go [2] in peace.**

c. **Go [2] in peace to love and serve the Lord.**

The people answer: **Thanks be [4] to God**. — Code

The priest kisses [5] the altar as at [6] the

SIGLA: 1=ADDRESSER; 2=ADDRESSEE; 3=CONTACT; 4=CODE; 5=MESSAGE; 6=CONTEXT

beginning[6]. Then[6] he[6] makes the customary reverence[5] with the ministers and leaves.

If any liturgical service follows immediately, the rite of dismissal is omitted.

INDEX

INDEX

INDEX

INDEX

About the Author: Joyce Ann Zimmerman, C.PP.S., is professor of liturgy at Saint Paul University, Ottawa, Ontario, Canada.